Inflation, Financial Markets, and Economic Development: The Experience of Mexico

CONTEMPORARY STUDIES IN ECONOMIC AND FINANCIAL ANALYSIS VOL. 16

Editors: Professor Edward I. Altman and Ingo Walter, Associate Dean
Graduate School of Business Administration, New York University

CONTEMPORARY STUDIES IN ECONOMIC AND FINANCIAL ANALYSIS

An International Series of Monographs

To my parents

Inflation,
Financial Markets,
and Economic Development:
The Experience of Mexico

by JOHN K. THOMPSON
Mellon Bank, N.A.

Foreword by RAÚL MARTÍNEZ OSTOS

JAI PRESS INC.

Greenwich, Connecticut

Library of Congress Cataloging in Publication Data

Thompson, John K
  Inflation, financial markets, and economic development.

  (Contemporary studies in economic and financial analysis; v. 16)
  Bibliography: p.
  Includes index.
  1. Mexico—Economic policy. 2. Mexico—Economic
conditions—1918–   3. Inflation (Finance)—Mexico.
4. Finance—Mexico. I. Title. II. Series.
HC135.T48   330.9′72′082   77-7787
ISBN 0-89232-084-2

CONTENTS

ACKNOWLEDGMENTS

This study, originally my doctoral dissertation at New York University, encompassed three and a half years' preparation from start to finish. It involved research and writing in two countries, and the assistance of many institutions and individuals. Therefore, it is inevitable that I will forget to thank some who have made significant contributions. Nevertheless, I shall try to mention by name those persons whose assistance was most valuable. In keeping with their function of helping a graduate student progress from diffuse notions about an ill-defined topic to an acceptable finished piece of research, my advisers at New York University, Professors Gately, Ness and Katz assisted first by helping me formulate a concrete research proposal, and later by providing constructive criticism of successive drafts of the dissertation.

A significant portion of the research for this work was carried out in Mexico. I would like to express my gratitude for the assistance of many capable and cooperative Mexicans. I want to specifically thank the Bank of Mexico for allowing me access to their research facilities, and providing me office space in their Research Department. In particular, Sergio Ghigliazza and Gilberto Escobedo of the Research Department of the Bank of Mexico assisted me in advancing my research and discussing at length many of the ideas that form the basis for the dissertation. Interviews with Mexican economists and policy-makers were invaluable in the preparation of the work. Raúl Martínez Ostos, Antonio Carillo Flores, and Rafael Galván provided candid discussions based on their direct experience of the periods of inflation, devaluation, and stabilization. My interviews with Carlos Bazdresch, Rafael Izquierdo, Leopoldo Solís, David Ibarra, and Alfredo Navarrete were indispensible in formulating and refining many of the concepts elaborated in the dissertation. I would like to express my special thanks to my good friend, the late Luis Yáñez-Pérez of CEMLA who aided me both by discussing the substantive material of the study and by steering me to many of the key decision makers of the devaluation period. E. Walter Robichek of the International Monetary Fund also contributed valuable insights into the decision-making process of that period.

Several friends of mine generously contributed their own time to the preparation of this work. Lawrence Cavanagh helped in the preparation of statistical data. Patricia Reynolds assisted in the early proofreading. Thomas Draper provided editorial assistance. James F. Kelly read the manuscript in careful detail and provided many thoughtful comments. Andrew Popper, A, Christopher Widness and Elena Décima Zamecnik proofread later versions of the manuscript. Wanda Marrero, Carol Padelski, Conchita Labrada, James Gladden, Diane Dawson and Sabine St. Germain typed successive drafts. Finally, I would like to thank my wife, Daniele, for her patience and encouragement throughout the entire project.

As the above list suggests, I am indebted to many people for the realization of this work. Any and all shortcomings are my own.

John Thompson

LIST OF TABLES

LIST OF CHARTS

LIST OF ABBREVIATIONS

AID	U.S. Agency for International Development
CEMLA	Center for Latin American Monetary Studies
CTM	Confederación de Trabajadores Mexicanos (Mexican Trade Union Federation)
ECLA	United Nations, Economic Commission for Latin America Also known by Spanish Initials (CEPAL)
Eximbank	Export-Import Bank of the United States
IDB	Interamerican Development Bank (Also IADB; Spanish initials—BID)
IBRD	International Bank for Reconstruction and Development (World Bank)
IMF	International Monetary Fund (also called "the Fund")
Nafin	Nacional Financiera, S. A. (Official Mexican Development Bank)
OECD	Organization for Economic Cooperation and Development
PRI	Party of the Institutional Revolution (Official Mexican Political Party)
UNCTAD	United Nations, Commission on Trade and Development

FOREWORD

This work by John Thompson constitutes one of the more objective analyses of the Mexican economic experience during the last 40 years and represents an important contribution to the literature on Mexican economic development. It examines the origins, functioning, and consequences of the policies that, both under inflation and price stability, permitted Mexico to attain a high rate of growth for long periods of time.

After stating the purposes and plan of the work and analyzing the different challenges and difficulties of economic development, an overview of the postwar situation of Latin America is given. Mexican development strategy, particularly that of freedom of foreign exchange transactions, is contrasted to the prevailing use of exchange controls and multiple exchange rate practices in South America.

The work then examines the stages of inflationary development from 1935 to 1940, from 1940 to 1946, and then from 1947 to 1954. After discussing the transition from inflation to stability, this work turns to the period from 1954 until the early 1970s when a high and sustained rate of growth was attained with price stability, freedom of exchange transactions and a fixed exchange rate. In discussing the transition to stability, the author uses the concepts of political economy to analyse the factors that led to the adoption of this new strategy of development. He outlines the policy debate between the structuralists and monetarists and concludes that the Mexican success in achieving a high rate of growth with stability in an open economy for almost two decades does not support the major arguments of the structuralists.

In the final part of the work an explanation is given of the problems that led to the resurgence of inflation after 1972. Policymakers at the highest levels (many of whom belonged, or acted as if they belonged, to the structuralist school of thought) began to question the capacity of the country to solve the country's persistent problems within the framework of development that had existed since 1954. This loss of faith in the system of stable development led to a relapse into inflationary policies that culminated in the devaluation of the peso on September 1, 1976.

The concluding chapter comments on the options Mexico now has for its future growth, pointing out the advantage represented by its experience of stable growth from 1954 to 1971 including the intensive use of major international financial markets. It is argued that a pattern of stable development is adequate to confront the present challenges of development and to also achieve better allocation of resources, increased employment, and export-led instead of import-substituting growth.

In commenting on a study made about events which one has lived or being involved with, directly or indirectly, one is often tempted to interject one's own interpretation of those events or the environment in which they originated as well as to their relative relevance. I, however, have chosen to resist that temptation since my own interpretations of those circumstances do not alter the purpose and conclusions of such a study. I have adopted this attitude toward Mr. Thompson's work, which has achieved its purpose of giving an objective explanation with a strictly detached attitude of the strategy for the financing of the Mexican economic development. Some aspects of the Mexican experiences have been adroitly used by Mr. Thompson to clarify various controversial issues in economic growth. In particular, the discussion of the role that exchange policy played in Mexico in the process of economic development for two long periods, both under inflation and price stability, should be of special interest not only to Mexican policymakers but also to those of other developing countries.

Raúl Martínez Ostos
Mexico D. F.

Introduction

On September 1, 1976, the Mexican government reluctantly decided to abandon the exchange rate of 12.5 pesos per dollar, at which the peso had been fixed for more than twenty-two years, whereupon the peso began to depreciate rapidly, with the price of dollar-denominated imports rising more than 100 percent within a few months. The decision to float followed a resurgence of inflation in the early 1970s that put an end to twenty years of stability. It also followed an erosion of the commitment to price and exchange rate stability that underlay Mexico's earlier successes. Not merely did the country appear to have difficulty remaining on the path of stable development that had apparently served it well for two decades, but also many of the best minds in public service and in private life seemed to have lost their faith in the system of stable finance. The very foundations of economic development in Mexico, which as recently as the early 1970s had seemed unshakable, were now in doubt.

It is impossible at this time to predict with certainty what Mexico's future pattern of economic development will be like now that the fixed exchange rate has become a thing of the past. The outlines of the new system will emerge only slowly through economic change and the political process. In the meantime, however, fundamental questions about the importance of financial policy in Mexican economic development remain unanswered. Mexico has used two systems of achieving high rates of growth. From the mid-1930s to the mid-1950s, growth took place with inflation; thereafter growth occurred with stability. There is a need for an assessment of the roles that price, exchange-rate policy, stability and external borrowing have played in Mexican development. More generally it is desirable to develop an idea of how the Mexican economy arrived at its present historical position. This inquiry will show what forces led to each kind of growth, how growth was achieved in each period, and the reasons that ultimately led to the abandonment of each pattern of development.

In the remaining sections of this chapter, the historical and economic questions that are examined throughout the work will be defined with greater precision, and the existing literature on these topics will be reviewed. Those whose main interest is the substantive material of the book may turn immediately to the next chapter.

Unresolved Issues Concerning the Role of Price Stability in the Economic Development of Mexico

Despite the basic differences of opinion over the influence of price stability and the exchange-rate system on Mexican economic development, many of the essential facts about the origins, functioning and implications of the financing of Mexican economic development are unknown. Virtually all historical studies of the Mexican financial system mention that the country passed through a stage of growth accompanied by inflation and currency depreciation beginning in the 1930s. Real growth had averaged nearly 7 percent yearly under inflation, but the authorities nevertheless felt obliged to make a determined effort to introduce price stability in the mid-1950s. After the mid-1950s, growth was characterized by price and exchange-rate stability.[1] Yet, nowhere is it explained why this profound change of policy occurred. In order to explain the change of policy this study will apply the concepts of political economy to the decision to introduce price stability. Specifically, it will be argued that Mexico was obliged to develop a new system of noninflationary finance because the inflationary finance of development had unacceptable regressive effects on the distribution of income and proved to be a source of political instability. In a broader sense, the Mexican experience suggests that inflationary policies can only be used under narrowly circumscribed circumstances and only for limited periods of time.

In order to approach the problem of decision making one must draw on the literature of economic analysis rooted in economic history and political economy, a literature that is both extensive and sophisticated. Manero gives a straightforward account of Mexican money and banking and financial policy through 1955. Hansen relates the objectives of economic development to growth of a political elite following the Mexican revolution.[2] Vernon, both as author and editor, provides an analysis of decision making in Mexico, giving special consideration to the way in which decision making in the public sector is related to the political process.[3] Glade and Anderson analyze the economic and financial development process in terms of the Mexican revolution and the need to develop political stability.[4]

In addition to the strictly historical question of why Mexico changed its policy to one of stability, there is the question of how development was achieved first under inflation and later under conditions of stability. The inflationary period in Mexican economic development has been intensively studied and a clear consensus regarding the sources of economic growth under inflation has emerged. In 1958, Siegal made the first attempt to describe the effects of inflation and devaluation on the finance of economic development, principally the function of permitting the authorities to bid resources away from the private sector as well as the effects of inflation in retarding the growth of the financial system.[5] Solís (1968) interpreted the economic growth of the inflationary period as related to a considerable transfer of real income and resources away from traditional patterns of consumption to sectors of the economy that undertook high levels of investment.[6] Similarly, Sturmthal saw Mexican economic growth as the result of forced savings in the form of retained earnings.[7] In this early period, development conformed to a model of economic growth through high profits and low wages made possible by an elastic labor supply. This study will extend the analysis Siegal and Solís established into the period of stability. In particular, this study holds that the development of strong financial markets with high yields on fixed-interest securities and a climate of confidence in the continuance of stable economic policies proved to be an alternative source of savings for financing economic development.

The change from inflation to stability coincided with a change from a de facto exchange-rate system of periodic devaluation to a policy of a fixed exchange rate. However, no one has specified how exchange-rate policy and foreign economic policy in general fit into the whole of the Mexican economic system. Solís and Ghigliazza (1963) and Bazdresch each consider the way in which international considerations act as a restraint on domestic monetary policy, primarily because of the close relationship between monetary expansion and international flows of capital.[8] Navarrete, Gleason Galicia and Solano discuss the use of international credits in the financing of economic development.[9] While these are important aspects of Mexican international economic policy, the whole of Mexican international economic policy is distinctive. It includes other elements such as the fixed exchange rate without controls, a specific structure of the balance of payments, and a close relationship with both public and private international financial institutions. This study seeks to specify the role that exchange-rate policy has played in the process of economic development in succeeding periods.

Beyond the questions specifically related to Mexican economic development that this inquiry seeks to answer, Mexico is a case study in the use of financial policies in economic development, and especially of the importance of stability in the development process. While price stability and growth are often competing objectives in the short run, the long-run relationship is less obvious. This study will look at inflationary and stable growth as different possible long-run development strategies with different costs and benefits.[10] Specifically, it will be argued that inflationary growth and stable growth differ most markedly in the means by which development is financed. It has often been argued that since few developing couries have sophisticated financial markets, the use of conventional financial policies are of limited relevance for the less developed countries. However, using several less developed countries as example Ronald I. McKinnon argues that by undermining the development of the financial market, inflation retards the process of economic development.[11] He then goes on to suggest that introduction of price stability and of high yields on financial assets can act as a stimulus to savings and as a viable strategy for economic development.

Clearly, it would be wrong to postulate a simple relationship between price stability and growth, for Mexico achieved high rates of growth both with inflation and with stable prices. This inquiry will make some generalizations about conditions that are necessary for either inflationary or stable policies to operate efficiently. Mexico is an interesting case in point, for its expience with rapid economic growth spans a period of forty years. The Mexican experience can be especially meaningful when compared to that of other countries that have used different systems to achieve high growth rates. For example, Ness considers the Brazilian experience with financial reform since 1964.[12] In contrast to the experience of Mexico, the Brazilian authorities were able to devise ways of improving the efficiency of the financial system despite continued inflation and currency depreciation. Therefore, an additional case study, involving a system of price stability, gives a fuller picture of the range of options available to the less developed countries.

Most less developed countries have used exchange-rate practices such as exchange controls and multiple exchange rates. Mexico, by contrast, has adhered to a regime of free convertibility. However, until uncertainties arose over the exchange rate, the country had a minimum outflow of domestic capital and indeed made extensive use of foreign capital. Moreover, Mexico developed a distinctive pattern of international economic relations as part of its economic development effort. Thus, the Mexican experience with a conventional exchange-rate scheme without exchange controls is of interest in evaluating the general effectiveness of exchange-rate policy tools in less developed countries.

The Literature on the Mexican Financial System

Although there are still some gaps in the literature on the Mexican financial system as it existed under the regime of price stability, and for the most part still exists today, the existing literature is impressive both for its size and depth. In an effort to systematize and analyze what was known about the topic, Brothers and Solís provide an excellent description and study of the development and functioning of the Mexican money and banking system and give a prolonged and deep analysis of the role of monetary policy in the stabilization of the Mexican economy.[13] This work gives a complete picture of the range of financial institutions, the functions of each, and the role each played in mobilizing funds to attain a high rate of growth under stable conditions. In a related article, Solís and Ghigliazza [1963] construct a model of the conduct of monetary policy showing the relative consideration that the authorities give to domestic monetary growth and external balance under conditions of stability. The process of formulating monetary policy was extended to a wider range of variables including international variables in an article by Bazdresch [Política Monetaria]. This work and the works of Brothers and Solís [1966] and Solís and Ghigliazza all agree that domestic monetary policy is closely related to flows of funds between Mexico and the financial markets of developed countries. This hypothesis was given strong empirical support in a recent dissertation by Ernesto Hernández Catá.[14] Furthermore, John Koehler has developed a convincing model of the decision-making process in the formulation of monetary policy and concludes that the variables that the authorities consider most seriously, given the small amount of information available, are the growth of money supply and the performance of international reserves.[15]

The responsiveness of economic performance to policy action has also been a topic of study. Gilberto Escobedo has developed a model of the Mexican economy and concludes that monetary policy has been the most effective tool of macroeconomic control.[16] Similarly, two essentially monetarist models of the Mexican economy have been developed by Griffiths and Nassef, in which a high correlation is shown to exist between the growth of money supply and a whole range of economic variables.[17]

The question of development finance has also been studied in depth, most notably by Alfredo Navarrete, whose work over two decades combines a solid theoretical analysis with years of practical experience in the public financial sector. The exhaustive study by Falkowski discussing the operations of Nacional Financiera is a major contribution insofar as it outlines the many varied roles that the official development bank has played in Mexico and critically assesses the role of development banking in general.[18]

It will later be shown that under stability economic development was increasingly financed through the market in fixed-interest securities. In this connection, Robert Lee Bennett constructed a flow of funds model showing the changes in the pattern of domestic finance that resulted from the introduction of price stability with emphasis on the increasing role of financial intermediation.[19] Raymond Goldsmith found a rising demand for financial assets that occurred in the same period.[20] Both of these works suggest that the demand for financial assets and the ability of the financial system to mobilize funds is related to the real yields on financial assets, and this in turn is related to price stability and expectations.

As the foregoing suggests, the Mexican financial system has been studied extensively in the literature. Yet, important questions remain unanswered. The change in policy that occurred in the 1950s has not been adequately explained. This is a major failing, since the decision to adopt stability was a critical turning point in Mexican economic history. True, Manero mentions that a debate between former Finance Ministers took place in the 1950s, but his analysis does not fit this policy debate into the wider framework of Mexican deveopment. Moreover, his study was finished before the policy change was completed and hence his interpretation was necessarily incomplete.

Nor does the existing literature give an overall picture of the international economic policy of Mexico, although some authors consider international aspects of domestic monetary policy: Hernández Catá related monetary and interest-rate behavior to international flows of capital: Navarrete [1968], Gleason Galicia, and Solano give a satisfactory picture of the international finance of economic development. While these are all important elements of Mexican international economic policy, Mexican policy as a whole is distinctive. It includes other elements such as the fixed exchange rate without capital controls, a specific structure of the balance of payments and a close relationship with both public and private international financial institutions.

The Plan of This Study

The study approaches the question of Mexican economic development from two angles. In the first place, Mexico shares the problems of all less-developed countries; its objective is to raise per capita income while changing the structure of society in a way in which the majority of citizens can achieve higher standards of living. At the same time, the Mexican experience is unique, reflecting the particular historical circumstances the country has encountered. Therefore, this work will approach the topic partly from the conceptual standpoint of the economics of domestic and external balance, while also showing how the Mexican historical experience affected the ultimate evolution of the economy.

Theoretical economics is simply a means of giving abstract expression and conceptual rigor to problems that occur in thereal world, in other words a systematic way of learning from past experience. To be meaningful, an abstract idea should ultimately explain concrete events. By the same token, to treat individual events without a conceptual framework leaves one surprised by each occurrence as it comes along; if we were to do so, we would likewise not benefit from the past. Accordingly, this study will try to steer a midcourse between historical inquiry and economic analysis.

NOTES

1. For example, see: Antonio Manero, *La Revolución Bancaria en México* (Mexico: Talleres Gráficos de la Nación, 1957), pp. 303–357; and Leopoldo Solís, "The Financial System in the Economic Development of Mexico," *Weltwirtschaftliches Archiv,* Band 101 (1968), pp. 36–48.

2. Roger D. Hansen, *The Politics of Mexican Development* (Baltimore: John Hopkins University Press, 1971).

3. Raymond Vernon, *The Dilemma of Mexico's Development* (Cambridge: Harvard University Press, 1963), and Raymond Vernon (ed.), *Public Policy and Private Enterprise in Mexico* (Cambridge, Mass.: Harvard University Press, 1964).

4. William P. Glade and Charles W. Anderson, *The Political Economy of Mexico* (Madison: University of Wisconsin Press, 1963).

5. Barry N. Siegal, *Inflación y Desarrollo: La Experiencia de México* (Mexico: CEMLA, 1958).

6. Leopoldo Solís M., "Inflación, Estabilidad y Desarrollo: El Caso de México," in *El Trimestre Económico,* Vol. XXXV (July–September 1968), pp. 483–516.

7. Adolf Sturmthal, "Economic Development, Income Distribution and Capital Formation in Mexico," in *Journal of Political Economy,* Vol. LXIII (June 1955), pp. 181–197.

8. Leopoldo Solís and Sergio Ghigliazza, "Estabilidad Económica y Política Monetaria," in *El Trimestre Económico,* Vol. XXX (April–June 1963), pp. 256–265; Carols Bazdresch, "La Política Monetaria Mexicana (Una Primera Aproximación)," in *La Economía Mexicana,* Leopoldo Solís (ed.), Vol. II, *Política y Desarrollo* (Mexico: Fondo de Cultura Económica, 973), pp. 138–156.

9. Navarrete's most comprehensive work on the topic, *Finanzas y Desarrollo Económico* (Meico: Libros SELA, 1968), summarizes and updates many of his earlier works in that field. Navarrete also discusses the role of the external sector in the finance of economic development in "Mexico's Balance of Payments and External Financing" in *Weltwirtschaftliches Archiv,* Band 101 (1968), pp. 70–86. External long-term borrowing has played a critical role in the financing of the public sector in Mexico. In addition to the works of Navarrete, two studies stand out for their importance in increasing familiarity with the Mexican use of international credits in economic development. In a long article published in 1955, Rubén Gleason Galicia spelled out the function of foreign borrowing in the investment programs of the public sector, and fully discussed the Mexican uses of

foreign credit: "Papel de los Créditos del Exterior en el Financiamiento del Desarrollo Económico" in *Investigación Económica,* Vol. XV (fourth quarter, 1955), pp. 497–558. Ten years later, Martha S. Solano Moctezuma gave an updated version of the same theme: "Financiamiento Externo del Sector Público de México" (Thesis: Escuela Nacional de Economía, Universidad Nacional Autónoma de México, 1965). Because of the basic changes that had taken place in Mexican external financing, Solano's work, which is both a history of Mexican long-term borrowing since World War II and a description of Mexican use of external credit, stands as an original work in its field.

10. The issue is best stated in Harry G. Johnson's essay, "Is Inflation the Inevitable Price of Rapid Development or a Retarding Factor in Economic Growth," in *Essays in Monetary Economics* (London: Allen and Unwin, 1967), pp. 281–292.

11. *Money and Capital in Economic Development* (Washington: The Brookings Institution, 1973).

12. Walter L. Ness, Jr., "Financial Markets Innovation as a Development Strategy: Initial Results from the Brazilian Experience" in *Economic Development and Cultural Change,* Vol. XXII (April 1974), pp. 453–472.

13. Dwight L. Brothers and Leopoldo Solís, *Mexican Financial Development* (Austin: University of Texas Press, 1966).

14. "International Movements of Private Financial Capital: An Econometric Analysis of the Mexican Case" (unpublished Ph.D. dissertation, Economics Department, Yale University, 1974).

15. "Information and Policy Making: Mexico" (unpublished Ph.D. dissertation, Economics Department, Yale University, 1967).

16. "The Response of the Mexican Economy to Policy Actions" in *Federal Reserve Bank of St. Louis Review,* Vol. LV (June 1973), pp. 15–23; and "Formulating a Model of the Mexican Economy" in *Federal Reserve Bank of St. Louis Review.* Vol. LV (July, 1973), pp. 8–19; and "Los Indicadores para Medir el Resultado de la Política Monetaria en México," in *Comercio Exterior,* Vol. XXIII (October 1973), pp. 1007–1025.

17. B. Griffiths, *Mexican Monetary Policy and Economic Development* (New York: Praeger, 1972); El Sayed Nassef, *Monetary Policy in Developing Countries: The Mexican Case* (Rotterdam: Rotterdam University Press, 1972).

18. Daniel Carl Falkowski, "Nacional Financiera, S.A., de México: A Study of a Development Bank" (unpublished Ph.D. dissertation, Department of Economics, New York University, 1972).

19. *The Financial Sector and Economic Development: The Mexican Case* (Baltimore: Johns Hopkins University Press, 1965).

20. Raymond N. Goldsmith, *The Financial Development of Mexico* (Paris: OECD Development Centre, 1966).

Chapter I

Economic Development, Inflation and External Balance: The Postwar Situation of Latin America

This inquiry deals with the Mexican response to a set of challenges associated with economic development that simultaneously faced all Latin American countries. Therefore, it is worthwhile at the outset to place Mexico's experience in a wider theoretical and historical framework. In this chapter, the nature of the problem of mobilizing resources for economic development, and the effects of inflation and the balance of payments on the development process will be specified. Then, the historical context of the Mexican experience will be discussed, including: the origins of inflation in Latin America, the impact of inflation on development, and the postwar international environment. The chapter will conclude with a discussion of the range of policies Latin American countries have used in dealing with the problem of development, inflation, and external balance.

STABILITY AND ECONOMIC DEVELOPMENT

This study examines the characteristics of economic growth under inflationary and stable conditions. It is not concerned with the short-term "trade-off" between growth and inflation, but instead considers equilibrium and disequilibrium growth as alternative policies with different costs and benefits.[1] While it is true that, at any given time, policy must emphasize either growth or stabilization at the expense of the other, it is somewhat naive to project this short-term phenomenon into a long-run "trade-off." As will be seen in later chapters, Mexico achieved nearly identical rates of growth both under inflationary and stable conditions. Furthermore, in Table I-1, which compares the relative performance of the Latin American countries, no clear relationship between stability and

Table I - 1

Inflation and Growth in Latin America, 1948 – 1965
(annual average increase in percent)

Countries with high inflation	Consumer prices	Real gross domestic product
Argentina	28	1.9
Bolivia	39	1.8
Brazil	31	5.0
Chile	38	3.7
Paraguay	27	2.4
Uruguay	19	2.2
Countries with moderate inflation		
Colombia	9.8	4.4
Mexico	6.3	6.1
Peru	9.8	5.0
Countries with low inflation		
Costa Rica	3.0	5.1
Dominican Republic	0.9	3.1
Ecuador	2.2	5.1
El Salvador	3.6	4.3
Guatemala	1.5	4.5
Haiti	1.3	0.9
Honduras	1.5	3.8
Nicaragua	-0.3	6.6
Panama	-0.2	5.7
Venezuela	1.9	6.7

Sources: ECLA, *Economic Development of Latin America in the Postwar Period,* p. 18; and IMF, *International Financial Statistics.*

growth is discernible; indeed, the stable countries appear to have done better in terms of growth than the inflationary countries. This is not to deny that either inflation or stable prices will affect the process of development, or that there may be an "optimal" rate of price increase, but merely to assert that there is no simple relationship between the two.

While there is no necessary link between stability and real growth, the pattern of growth is apt to be quite different under stability than under inflation, in part due to the way in which inflation affects the savings/investment process. Inflation leads to continual changes in relative yields on alternative assets. It also leads to transfers of resources between sectors. Changes in relative prices 1) affect the distribution of resources between consumption on the one hand and the savings and investment on the other; and 2) shift resources between the internal and external sectors, a process that will also be influenced by variations in the exchange rate. Stable conditions, on the other hand, are likely to encourage the growth of savings through conventional channels, but changes in the distribution of income and shifts of resources between sectors are likely to come more slowly. The behavior of the price level and the exchange rate will obviously affect economic development through its effect on expectations and the relative profitability of alternative investments, and thereby influence decisions to save and invest.

The savings/investment process is central to the process of growth. A simple Harrod-Domar growth model stipulates that the rate of growth in any given period is determined by the level of investment and the marginal capital output ratio.[2] The potential long-term rate of growth is determined by the marginal capital output ratio and marginal propensity to save. The warranted rate of long-term growth is equal to the relationship:

$$G_w = \frac{s}{C_r}$$

Where:

$$G_w = \frac{dY}{dt}$$

$$s = \frac{dS}{dY}$$

$$C_r = \frac{dY}{dI}$$

All of these values are expressed in real terms. Assuming that the marginal propensity to save is constant, the rate of growth can be increased only by lowering the capital output ratio, that is, by using more efficient techniques to increase the yield of investment. This option will be available only if more efficient means of production already exist, but are not being employed. On the other hand, if the capital output ratio is assumed constant, growth can be increased by raising the marginal propensity to save. In practice, a society desiring to modernize would wish to devote a greater share of resources to savings and investment while also introducing more efficient means of production. The problem of financing economic development consists in finding means to increase savings equivalent to increased investment and in transferring funds from savers to investors.[3]

Having thus defined the growth process, it is now possible to relate growth to conditions of equilibrium and disequilibrium by using a simplified national income model:

$Y = C + I = C + S$	Assumptions
Where Y = national income	$I = I_0$
C = consumption	$C = f(Y)$
I = investment	$S = g(Y)$
S = savings	Equilibrium Condition: $\bar{S} = \bar{I}$
t = time	

It is specified that investment is exogenous, that is, determined by the autonomous decisions of private investors and government, but that savings and consumption are functions of the level of income, and that savings is that part of income that is not consumed; I is an exogenous variable and S is endogenous. Since the equilibrium condition is that savings equal investment, total real investment can be no more than the amount warranted by the level of savings. Since the investment term is independent but the savings term is a function of the level of income, it follows that growth is determined by investment but constrained by savings. Therefore, in order to increase growth one must increase savings.

A development policy that accepts the stability of the price level as a constraint on government action can increase savings by offering inducements to save by voluntarily postponing consumption. In principle, this can be accomplished by promoting high yields on savings, for example through policies that encourage high interest rates or high rates of return on direct investment. It would, therefore, be desirable to encourage increased savings by sectors of the economy that have potential excess savings and also to develop institutions to transfer these savings to excess investment sectors of the economy. In such circumstances, it would be appropriate to foster confidence in domestic financial institutions by creating expectations that yields on savings and investment are likely to remain stable in order to persuade net savings units in the economy to transfer funds to net investing units elsewhere in the economy.

ECONOMIC GROWTH UNDER INFLATIONARY CONDITIONS

Although inflation is likely to discourage savings through assets that will lose value with an increase in the price level, inflation may make it possible to increase savings in other forms. Furthermore, assuming that it is not feasible to raise voluntary savings under equilibrium conditions, inflationary finance may be the only practical means of increasing savings. The rate of domestic investment may be raised above the level of domestic savings and, in the resulting increase in the price level, there may occur a fall in real consumption and an ensuing process of forced savings under which real savings and real investment are brought into balance at an increased price level. The success of such a process requires that all prices not rise equally as a result of the general increase in the price occurs favoring those sectors of the economy that are more likely to save and invest as opposed to those that are likely to consume.[4] For example, as the price level increases, prices of industrial goods might rise while real wages of industrial workers decline, causing an increase in the profits of industrialists and indirectly an increase in savings through retained earnings. Similarly, if government spending or an expansion of credit generates inflation, a rise in savings will occur if recipients of credit or government spending are in high savings sectors of the economy while the rise in prices is spread throughout the economy.

Harry Johnson argues that a moderate degree of inflation might even be beneficial to development insofar as it facilitates the transfer of resources from traditional to modern sectors.[5] It is often mentioned that in economic development, the agricultural sector must at least maintain its output while transferring both excess workers and savings to the industrial sector. In sum, provided that the inflationary mechanism results in an increase in savings and a transfer of real resources to higher investment sectors of the economy, it can act as a spur to economic development. Such a policy can easily fail for several reasons. Traditional high-income sectors of the economy, such as landlords or moneylenders, may have high average propensities to save, but may support the use of inefficient techniques and undesirable social structures. The effectiveness of such a redistribution in producing savings requires that the ability of high savings groups to increase relative prices and income be greater than the ability of consuming groups to defend income shares. However, if the high-consumption sectors of society prove capable of defending or increasing income shares after inflation, the result will be a decrease in savings, and therefore growth, through inflation.

THE ROLE OF THE EXTERNAL SECTOR IN ECONOMIC DEVELOPMENT

The general equilibrium model summarized above does not take into account the important effects that the rest of the world can have on domestic economic development. The balance of payments can play a critical role in increasing savings and investment. In order to show the influence of the external sector on economic development, the earlier model can be extended to include trade and capital movements.[6] In the model shown below, S = domestic savings, I = domestic investment, X = exports of goods and services, M = imports of goods and services, and F = net inflow of foreign capital. The net inflow of foreign capital is equal to and opposite in sign to net foreign investment. A positive net capital inflow is equivalent to a negative foreign investment; foreigners have increased their claims on nationals, and external debt has increased. Using these terms, one can stipulate the following basic identities:

$$(1)\ Y = C + I + (X - M)$$
$$(2)\ Y = C + S$$
$$(3)\ I = S + F$$

Identity (1) is a simple national income model including the foreign trade sector; identity (2) defines national income as divided into consumption and savings; and identity (3) states that domestic investment equals domestic savings plus the net inflow of foreign capital (i.e., the savings of the rest of the world).

By substitution inside these identities, one can immediately derive some obvious but significant relations:

$$I - S = X - M = F$$

These identities state that the difference between domestic savings and domestic investment is equal to the current account deficit which in turn is equal to the capital flow. A country attempting to increase its rate of growth by increasing investment beyond the capacity of domestic savings creates a potential inflationary "gap" between savings and investment which is equal to the current account deficit. Similarly, net foreign investment is equal to the current account balance, while foreign capital inflow is equal and opposite in sign to the current account balance. An inflow of foreign capital has the same effect as an increase in domestic savings; foreign capital represents the savings of the rest of the world. If a flow of genuine foreign resources does not finance the additional investment, a situation of excess demand exists in which the price level rises to the point that nominal savings equals nominal investment, while real consumption falls until equilibrium is achieved. On the external side, the imbalance will be reflected in a depreciation of the exchange rate under floating exchange rates, or a loss of reserves under a fixed-rate system. (Under fixed exchange rates, a country may temporarily maintain a disequilibrium policy by running down its reserves, i.e., its past savings. In the long run, however, the level of domestic investment is still constrained by the availability of savings.)

The model implies that internal and external imbalance are essentially two aspects of the same problem and that investment in excess of domestic savings produces a balance-of-payments deficit on current account.[7] In effect, exports are the equivalent of savings, which allow for a higher level of real investment, while imports are the equivalent of consumption, which reduces the amount of resources available for investment.

The model opens up the possibility of raising the rate of net domestic savings and growth by encouraging a high rate of growth of exports (export-led growth) or by taking measures to curtail the growth of imports (import-substituting growth).[8] Exports are, by definition, a form of savings which increase the potential rate of growth. Furthermore, the goods that a country exports are those goods which the country produces with greatest efficiency, and hence export-promotion is likely to raise the overall level of efficiency by shifting resources into more efficient sectors. The development of exports may occur painlessly if external conditions or a discovery of natural resources give rise to an export boom. Otherwise, a shift of resources to the export sector involves a transfer of real income to those sectors of the economy that are likely to undertake new investment and a loss of income to those sectors that are likely to consume.

The equations indicate that an increase in domestic investment spending not balanced by an equal rise in domestic savings requires an offsetting capital flow. The equations illustrate how, with increased foreign capital, a country can finance a larger amount of domestic investment than would be possible from purely domestic savings and, thereby, increase its rate of growth while simultaneously financing a wider current account deficit. Therefore, it is clear that increased capital inflows, whether in the form of direct investment, loans, grants, or portfolio placements, increase the potential rate of growth by allowing the country to invest more than domestic savings, since $I = S + (X - M) = S + F$.

Extending the earlier analysis of a closed economy a few steps further, one can see that economic development can be encouraged by depreciation of the exchange rate, a process which is analagous to the domestic process of forced savings. By changing relative prices and income between the domestic economy and the rest of the world, existing resources are redirected from domestic consumption to the export sector.

EXCHANGE-RATE POLICY AND INTERNATIONAL ECONOMIC POLICY IN ECONOMIC DEVELOPMENT

It is clear from the foregoing analysis that the external sector has a powerful influence on the process of economic development. Accordingly, policies that affect the pattern of international payments are critical elements in the process of financing economic development. Exchange-rate policy, which is a main concern of the inquiry, is closely linked to a set of other policy instruments including demand management policy, trade policy, and relations with international financial institutions which, as a whole, constitute international economic policy.[9]

International economic policy aims at producing the most favorable balance-of-payments situation possible, given the conditions that exist in the domestic economy and in the rest of the world. Thus, international economic policy contains implicit or explicit assumptions about the pattern of trade and capital movements that would take place in the absence of defined policy and seeks to improve upon that pattern through the use of policy instruments. It involves the formulation of policies in the light of a set of problems and objectives as perceived by the authorities.

The task of mobilizing external resources has been a difficult one for the developing countries.[10] Following the initial postwar reconstruction period, the industrial countries generally have not had to subordinate objectives of domestic growth to balance-of-payments considerations. Most developing countries, by contrast, have had to struggle with persistent tendencies toward deficits in their balance of payments and have had to subordinate the goal of domestic growth to the balance of payments. Indeed, most developing lands find that they have seemingly chronic problems in obtaining sufficient foreign exchange from trade and capital inflows to support desirable development programs. Therefore, developing countries have used available forums such as the United Nations Economic Commission for Latin America (ECLA), the United Nations Conference on Trade and Development (UNCTAD), and more recently the Committee of Twenty, to voice their concern with this problem and lobby for mechanisms such as foreign aid, long-term loans, commodity support agreements, and a link between development aid and SDRs to increase their foreign exchange holdings. Moreover, most developing countries have resorted to sizable trade barriers and extensively used exchange controls in order to conserve scarce foreign exchange.

AN OVERVIEW OF THE POSTWAR INTERNATIONAL SITUATION OF LATIN AMERICA

Problems of Economic Development: Inflation, Income Distribution and External Balance

In recent decades, most Latin American countries have become increasingly committed to economic development as a national objective.

But unlike the currently industrialized countries where growth occurred in response to increased productivity or expanding trade, development in Latin America arose from a political wish to emulate the living standards of Europe and North America, and hence there was a built-in gap between expectations and the slower advances in real income. Indeed, on the political side, economic development presents an enormous paradox. The motivation in undertaking development is to raise the level of consumption of a country where most people already live at rather poor levels. Yet, as was made clear by the national income equations, in order to set the growth process in motion, what is required is to devote more resources to savings and investment and hence less to consumption. Consequently, the policy-maker will be drawn in two opposing directions. The desire to promote growth should lead to policies to foster investment, but the desire to raise the living standards of the population will lead to policies designed at least to maintain existing levels of consumption. Moreover, to the degree that the economic and political system allows, groups in society will try to defend existing levels of consumption. Thus, there may be an inherent tendency to invest in excess of domestic savings.

The problems of inflation and income distribution associated with attempts to industrialize occurred in an international environment in which the Latin American countries played only a marginal role in international payments. As Chart I-I indicates, the export performance of the region compares very poorly with that of the industrial countries. In the postwar period, the region accounted for increasingly smaller shares of world trade and capital movements. This undoubtedly reflected the policies of the countries in the region as well as the uneven growth of external demand. In any event, after expanding rapidly in the immediate postwar years, the growth of Latin American exports slowed abruptly in the mid-1950s and remained sluggish, before expanding somewhat in the early 1960s.

In part owing to the unfavorable influence of external demand on Latin American exports and domestic growth, many Latin American countries began to accept the argument that the terms of trade of countries exporting primary commodities are bound to decline. According to this argument, prices of manufactured goods tend to rise in accordance with costs and growing demand in all areas of the world, whereas de-

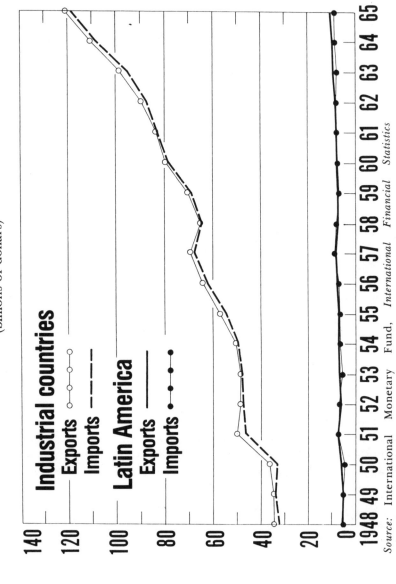

Chart 1-1. Trade of Industrial Countries and
Latin America, 1948–1965
(billions of dollars)

Industrial countries
Exports ○○○○
Imports – – – –

Latin America
Exports ————
Imports •—•—•

140
120
100
80
60
40
20
0

1948 49 50 51 52 53 54 55 56 57 58 59 60 61 62 63 64 65

Source: International Monetary Fund, *International Financial Statistics*

20

mand for raw materials rises only in line with income and population and is further weakened by the development of synthetic substitutes. Raúl Prebisch, the best-known proponent of this view, divided the countries of the world into the industrial "center" countries and the "peripheral" countries which produce raw materials.[11] The center can transmit growth to the periphery through higher demand for raw materials, which results in higher exports from the periphery. However, if the peripheral country independently increases its imports from the center, this will not perceptibly raise the purchase of primary products by the center. Thus, the center plays the leading or dynamic role in world trade, while the periphery plays a passive role. The center can determine its own rate of growth. Its demand for primary products influences the rate of growth of the peripheral countries, while the latter have no influence upon the rate of growth of the center. As a result, the peripheral countries are left with the options of allowing their rate of growth to be determined by business cycles in the center or accepting the inevitability of balance-of-payments disequilibrium and formulating policies accordingly. In addition to this unequal trading relationship between developed and developing countries, the proponents of this position also argue that the terms of trade deteriorate because:

> It is a universal characteristic of economic development that as per capita income rises above a certain minimum, the demand for primary products grows less intensely than that for industrial goods and services. Given the same rate of growth of per capita income, the demand for industrial imports in the periphery tends to grow more rapidly than demand for primary imports in the industrial center. If the population in the periphery increases more rapidly than the industrial center, the disparity in the rate of growth is aggravated. Furthermore, if the income of the peripheral country rises more rapidly than that of the center, the disparity becomes more marked . . . If a peripheral country . . . wishes to develop economically and to reduce or at least maintain the difference between them, there will be a persistent tendency toward disequilibrium.[12]

As a result of the supposedly structural inability of developing countries to earn sufficient foreign exchange to grow at an acceptable rate, those who believe that there is an inherent tendency for the terms of trade of less developed countries to deteriorate argue that policies must be formulated in the light of this inevitable disequilibrium. Countries producing raw material should pursue a policy of industrialization through import substitution, i.e., limit imports from the developed countries to those products which cannot be produced at home in order to conserve scarce foreign exchange and lessen dependency on the demand of the industrial countries.[13]

Inward-Looking Development Strategies

Given the prevailing pessimism about the possibility of expanding growth through exports—a pessimism grounded in the experience of the region and also strongly supported by ECLA and UNCTAD—and given the belief that industrialization was a superior pattern of growth, most Latin American countries evolved development strategies based on import-substituting industrialization rather than on the development of the export sector. Import substitution involved the creation of a protected manufacturing sector oriented toward the domestic market. The external sector was treated as a constraint rather than a source of growth. The direct savings in imports of import-substituting industries rather than their costs in terms of higher domestic prices and reduced exports were emphasized.[14] There were, to be sure, exceptions to this rule. Peru, Ecuador, and the Central American countries established growth patterns based on exports of petroleum, bananas, fishmeal, cotton and coffee.[15] Nevertheless, most of the other Latin American countries, with upwards of 80 percent of the region's population, pursued import-substitution as a development strategy.

The balance-of-payments strategy that accompanied an import-substitution program was aimed at assuring imports of capital goods needed to sustain import-substituting industries. It was assumed that exports were determined by world demand. As a result, export receipts in foreign exchange were usually allocated according to an officially determined set of priorities. Since the current account deficit increases in response to a rise in domestic activity, it is usually an objective of policy to run the largest possible current account deficit that could be financed over time. As a result, it became important to obtain external capital flows.[16] Direct investment was, in many cases, an important source of capital inflows. Those countries that had exportable natural resources, especially mineral products, could count on inflows of outside capital to finance such investment. In addition, widespread import-substitution

policies gave rise to sizable inflows of funds for industrialization, especially with the tariff protection that the host government could guarantee as part of overall import-substituting program. However, the
small size of the domestic market and uncertainties about the economic
and political outlook limited inflows for direct investment.[17]

Despite an obvious need for foreign capital, few Latin American countries were able to attract significant flows of private external funds into
their domestic financial markets. Indeed, in many cases, there was a persistent tendency for nationals of Latin American countries to place their
savings in the financial markets of the industrial countries, largely as a
result of the general failure to develop dynamic financial markets in
their own countries. Part of the problem was the fragmented nature of
financial markets; that is, the wide discrepancies between yields in the
markets. With a protected monopoly position, returns on direct investment may be high for those who have large sums of money to invest and
the proper connections. Yet, if efficient financial markets do not exist,
there may be no other outlets for investment in the economy.[18]

In those countries where inflation was significant, the inflationary
process tended to further impede the development of efficient financial
markets since yields on financial assets tended to be negative in real
terms. As a result, wealth-holders preferred such assets as real estate,
inventories, or foreign exchange to hedge against inflation.[19] Under
these circumstances, holders of wealth saw their options for investment
sharply curtailed. Those who have large holdings of wealth and the
proper connections can obtain high yields by investing in the firms
where they have contacts. Failing this, Latin Americans have been forced
to invest their savings in physical goods and foreign exchange, which
provide some safety and return. Needless to say, such a situation does
little to encourage the savings of middle- and lower middle-income
groups.

When the exchange risk is brought into the picture, the disincentives
to productive financial development are even more apparent. If the
country has a history of currency devaluation, the incentive to place
funds abroad, which may already exist because of political uncertainty
and the lack of alternative outlets for investment, is heightened by a
direct incentive to seek high real yields in the financial markets of advanced countries. At the same time, there is no incentive for outsiders to
place funds in the domestic financial market. Moreover, high nominal

yields may lead to shifting of funds in and out of the country in response to the perceived possibility of exchange-rate adjustment.

In view of the need to increase capital receipts and the limited possibility to expand private inflows, individual nations have made strenuous efforts to obtain funds from U.S. government agencies such as AID and Eximbank, and international lending bodies such as the IBRD. The Latin American nations pressed strongly for an Inter-American Development Bank, which was founded in 1960.

Latin America and the International Financial System

The precarious state that characterized the external finances of many Latin American countries often led to near-depletion of reserves and periodic foreign exchange crises. Consequently, these countries often found themselves dependent on international financial organizations and private creditors in the industrial countries. As reserves reached low levels, individual countries were forced to borrow from the IMF to meet short-term liquidity needs. The IMF usually prescribed a remedy that involved devaluation and attempts to introduce domestic price stability through conventional monetary and fiscal restraint.

The IMF-sponsored stabilization programs in Latin America often coincided with attempts to renegotiate foreign debt and obtain new long-term credit. Negotiations were undertaken with groups of external creditors, including the U.S. government agencies, international organizations and private commercial banks. In effect, credits from these institutions were usually available only when the debtor countries were able to come to an agreement with the IMF. By the same token, the IBRD and other organizations which specialized in long-term lending made the adoption of acceptable domestic economic policies precondition for access to long-term financing. Thus, an interlocking network of external creditors arose which effectively controlled the flow of public funds to Latin American countries, (as well as a considerable volume of private funds) and indirectly had considerable influence over their domestic policies.[20]

International Economic Policy and Income Distribution

Exchange-rate policy, though basically an economic phenomenon, also has important political overtones. When a less-developed country chooses between a "growth through trade" or an import-substitution strategy, it is, aside from the objective consideration of the possibilities of trade expansion, making an essentially political decision. The decision to adopt one of these courses may be in response to a detached evaluation of economic reality. Just as likely, the decisions are influenced by pressures from competing domestic interest groups and may reflect the relative persuasive powers of the IMF and ECLA. The exchange-rate regime is also political in as much as it exists inside the international financial system which is a system wherein individual states and international organizations exercise considerable discretionary power.[22] It was a fact of life for the Latin American countries that during the period under consideration in this study, the international financial system was dominated by the industrial countries, and, in the earlier part of the period mostly by the United States. The industrial countries also dominate the IMF, the IBRD, and other organizations with significant financial resources. By contrast, the influence of developing countries was predominant in organizations like ECLA and UNCTAD which provided platforms for airing complaints but had few financial resources.[23]

Owing to its ability to quickly influence relative prices, exchange-rate policy directly affects the distribution of resources between the export sector and other sectors that are competing for shares of national income. Therefore, the exchange rate has often become a field of conflict. An overvalued exchange rate is an implicit tax on exports and a subsidy to imports and consumption. Maintaining an overvalued exchange rate may be a means of covertly taxing income away from traditional exporting interest in order to subsidize the import-substituting sectors of the economy in circumstances where it might be impossible to accomplish the same objective through the legislative process. The preference of Latin American governments for import substitution rather than export-led growth tended to make the authorities hesitant to make needed exchange-rate changes.

The powerful effect of devaluation on domestic consumption and on industry that depends on imported inputs further explains the reluctance of the authorities to devaluate. In a context of price stability, export and import-competing interests alike favor exchange-rate depreciation, while the sectors that consume imports, for example wage earners and import-substituting industries, favor a steady exchange rate. In Latin American countries where significant inflation exists, the situation is slightly different. Kindleberger describes a situation which, as will be seen, bears some resemblance to the Mexican case:

> Export interests get squeezed by a steady exchange rate as costs rise while prices abroad are stable; they therefore plug for depreciation. Where the cost of living depends on the prices of imported goods, however, depreciation hurts labor in the domestic sector of the economy by raising the local-currency cost of imported goods. The result is a political seesaw contest between inflation, which pushes domestic prices up, and devaluation which restores the profitability of the export and import competing sector, but puts the squeeze on labor. The system is sometimes called structural inflation. One hundred percent of the population wants to consume 120 percent, say, of national income, which means that with a fixed exchange rate, there is steady inflation and a spillover into import surplus, until with depreciation, the burden is dumped on people with fixed incomes and those whose consumption is heavily weighted by imports.[24]

Exchange-rate depreciation also tends to be resisted by domestic consumers for it shifts resources into the export sector. Thus, exchange depreciation tends to erode the incomes of working class sectors of the population by decreasing domestic supplies and increasing prices of food products and other exportable goods and thereby forcing food prices up to the level implied by the change in parity, again shifting income away from the working class and toward the export sector.[25]

LATIN AMERICAN EXCHANGE-RATE POLICY

As the foregoing discussion indicates, the exchange-rate policies of the Latin American countries were influenced by domestic and international factors that were at odds with those of the industrial countries. The Bretton Woods system envisaged domestic price stability, equilibrium in international payments, free trade and stable exchange rates without exchange controls. In the postwar years, income expanded at historically high rates, integration progressed swiftly in Europe, and most industrial nations moved toward reasonable price stability. In addition, large sums of capital flowed between industrial countries. By the late 1950s, the industrial countries achieved balance-of-payments equilibrium as evidenced by widespread exchange-rate stability and a high degree of convertibility. Meanwhile, the experience of the Latin

American countries led them in an entirely different direction. The external situation was marked by the slow growth of trade, the predominance of inward-looking import-substituting policies and often by chronic inflation and balance-of-payments disequilibrium. In the resulting context of foreign exchange scarcity, many countries adopted exchange-rate policies that diverged sharply from those of the industrial countries.

Latin America and the Bretton Woods System

Although Latin American countries experimented with virtually every conceivable exchange-rate system, a number of countries in the area consistently adhered to the Bretton Woods system. The countries of Central America and the Caribbean have maintained stable exchange rates with the U.S. dollar at least since World War II and have made either no use or only limited use of exchange controls and multiple rates. Similarly, Mexico has between 1954 and 1976 made a stable exchange rate with the U.S. dollar, free from exchange controls, a keystone of domestic and external policy.[26]

The authorities of the countries that followed the Bretton Woods system accepted the stability of the exchange rate without exchange controls or multiple exchange practices as a desirable objective of overall demand-management policy. In effect, this means that, in order to avoid balance-of-payments disequilibrium, the authorities could not allow a rate of price increase very much in excess of the prevailing world rate for any significant length of time.[27] As was argued earlier in this chapter, there is no indication of a "trade-off" between growth and inflation, and hence following the Bretton Woods system did not involve sacrificing real growth. The commitment to price stability did, however, profoundly affect the pattern of growth, for it effectively precluded a pattern of inflationary government expenditure, and it ruled out the use of multiple exchange rates to transfer income between sectors. Such an exchange-rate regime implicitly assumes that the market mechanism is a more efficient and, perhaps less socially divisive, means of allocating resources than direct allocation through inflation. Other things being equal, a regime of price stability permits fuller development of the financial system. There need not be any strictly economic incentive to place funds abroad in search of safety or higher real yields. Accordingly, it leaves open the possibility of using financial policies as a means of achieving a balanced package of domestic and international aims.

There were other reasons that led these countries to remain within the Bretton Woods system. With the exception of Mexico, these countries lived under relatively conservative regimes, where only minimal social pressures arose that led to deficit spending and other inflationary policies. In Mexico, on the other hand, the decision to adopt the Bretton Woods system was a profound political choice that tested the strength of the political system.

Exchange Controls and Multiple Exchange Rates

In contrast to the equilibrium exchange-rate system of Bretton Woods, most Latin American countries have resorted to disequilibrium systems in which there was excess demand for foreign exchange. A few countries in Central America and all in South America have used systems of exchange controls and multiple exchange rates to ration foreign exchange. The assumption underlying multiple exchange-rate practices and exchange controls is there is a disequilibrium between supply of, and demand for, foreign exchange that cannot be corrected at a socially acceptable price by a change in the exchange rate. Given this imbalance, the objective of exchange controls and multiple exchange rates is to allocate scarce foreign exchange in accord with a set of officially determined priorities. Multiple exchange rates and exchange controls function in much the same way a system of taxes and subsidies, i.e., by making foreign exchange more expensive to those activities that the authorities wish to tax and cheaper to those they wish to subsidize.[28] At the same time, unlike taxes, such practices sidestep the legislative process and give the government greater freedom to maneuver. Some specific goals of exchange controls and multiple exchange rates, are: (a) to hold down the prices of essential imports, (b) to keep the demand for less essential and luxury imports from reducing official exchange reserves without the use of quota restrictions, (c) to provide revenue for the state, which often engages in foreign exchange transactions as a monopoly, (d) to protect local industry and foster industrialization, and (e) to permit invisible payments and capital exports, but at penalty rates.[29]

The Latin American countries adopted exchange controls following the collapse of demand for raw materials that occurred during the Depression in the 1930s. After 1950, as demand for exports failed to regain its earlier vigor and import-substitution proceeded apace, these practices then become integral parts of national policy.[30]

A multiple exchange-rate practice is a system wherein there is more than one rate at which domestic currency can be exchanged for foreign currency, according to the character of the transaction. Multiple exchange rates discriminate among categories in foreign exchange which is made available for transactions to be subsidized at the cheapest rate and transactions to be taxed at a more expensive rate. Some of the most common types of multiple exchange rates are:[31] (a) *commodity export rates,* under which a single export product which is a significant fraction of total exports is exchanged at an unfavorable rate, thus limiting the profitability of traditional exports without reducing the competitiveness of other exports; (b) *differential import rates,* which discriminate among imports from the most to the least necessary (in general such regulations favor essential goods while luxury items are most heavily penalized); and (c) under *financial rates,* trade transactions take place at one rate, and financial transactions at another. In cases where the authorities expect sizable capital outflows, financial rates allow the authorities to avoid supporting speculative transactions and thereby assure that the latter are undertaken at penalty rates.

As the foregoing discussion suggests, the large variety of multiple exchange-rate schemes allows the use of exchange-rate policies in a wide variety of ways depending on the particular situation of the country. An added dimension is given to the policymakers when one considers that not all rates have to be supported by official intervention. For example, commercial rates might be supported by the monetary authorities, while the financial rate floats freely.

The importance of the exchange-control mechanism varied between countries. Where growth was accompanied by price stability and external equilibrium, exchange controls and multiple exchange rates functioned as a supplement to a relatively balanced overall policy. Thus, in Venezuela, the petroleum exchange rate was mainly an additional means of levying taxes upon foreign oil companies by making dollars more expensive for oil exporters, while in other countries special exchange rates were used to tax companies exporting other natural resources.[32] The countries of Central America and Colombia used special coffee exchange rates to limit the profits of coffee exporters.[33]

In those countries where inflation was a problem, and where there was a marked tendency toward depreciation of the exchange rate, exchange controls were an indispensable policy instrument. In those circumstances, the purpose of controls was to suppress a severe external imbalance in which strong excess demand for foreign exchange existed. In an inflationary environment, the currency became increasingly overvalued and therefore the ability to manipulate exchange controls was a critical policy tool. Controls were tightened and thus partial devaluation could be accomplished by shifting different classes of imports to lower exchange rates, or by ceasing to support less essential categories of transactions. After a large devaluation, the controls could be relaxed.

The problem of administering controls can be critical. In the case of a single export, such as coffee or petroleum, transactions might be relatively easy to identify. However, as the exchange controls become more complex, the problem of classification becomes crucial and hence the discretionary power of the administrators grows. Particularly in a period of rapid change and poor information, administrators may make grave mistakes in allocation and are also vulnerable to outside pressures.

The controls may work at cross purposes. If an improvement in the country's balance of trade is the dominant consideration, only those exports with a very low elasticity of supply (i.e., those for which the country is a nonatomistic supplier) would be subject to penalty buying rates, since a broader application of such rates would presumably reduce exchange earnings significantly by keeping the average buying rate of exchange low. The objective of preventing foreign exchange loss by making foreign exchange more expensive for imports of consumer goods would, however, conflict with the objective of domestic price stability. Similarly, the objective of price stability can conflict with that of protecting domestic industry. In addition, conflicts can also arise between export-promotion and domestic price-stabilization objectives.[34]

INFLATION AND THE AJUSTMENT MECHANISM

In countries where price increases significantly exceed the world average, exchange-rate adjustments must eventually be made. In the case of Latin American countries experiencing inflation, the authorities have had to adapt the outlines of the Bretton Woods system, which assumed price and exchange-rate stability and convertible currencies, to the realities of their respective countries which were quite different.

Step Devaluation

The Bretton Woods requirement of fixed exchange rates and a combination of domestic and exchange-rate policy adjustments aiming at equilibrium was plainly unworkable in those Latin American nations where inflation exceeded the prevailing world level. The combination of fixed exchange rates and persistent inflation produced a situation in which the currency tended toward a state of constant overvaluation as the level of domestic costs and prices diverged persistently from the world level and the tendency toward capital flight became pronounced. In Mexico, which had no exchange controls, the response in the form of devaluation was relatively rapid. In other countries, exchange controls and multiple exchange-rate practices were essential to conserve existing international reserves and defend overvalued exchange rates. Under conditions of virtually limitless demand for foreign exchange, management of the exchange rate increasingly became a problem of rationing limited foreign exchange holdings in accord with an established set of priorities. Eventually, the currency must be devalued by large amounts to compensate for the difference between domestic and foreign price increases. Indeed, devaluation was often in excess of the amount implied by the purchasing power parity theorem in order to anticipate future inflation.

This system, of course, had many drawbacks. The abrupt changes in relative prices have detrimental effects on economic activity. Private decision makers expend a great deal of effort adjusting to the constantly changing relations between internal and external costs and also must try to anticipate official policy reactions. Inventories may be stockpiled when foreign exchange is available and cheap, and depleted as exchange controls are tightened. Moreover, speculation on short-term policy moves usually yields higher effective rates of return than productive investment. Furthermore, there is a clear incentive for capital flight as it becomes evident that large exchange-rate adjustments will have to be made.

Crawling Peg

Because of the distortions caused by the system of step devaluation, many countries experiencing serious inflation turned to a system of small exchange-rate adjustments taken at frequent intervals. This innovation was begun by Chile in 1962 and Brazil since 1968, and has also been used by Colombia, Argentina, and Uruguay.[35] Under this system, the distortions of inflation are minimized, the relations between foreign and domestic costs and prices are maintained, and the incentives for speculation removed. In the most publicized case, Brazil uses the crawling peg in tandem with a domestic system of indexing wages and financial instruments to the cost-of-living index, so that real values are preserved after allowing for price increases and exchange-rate depreciation. Abrupt changes in relationships between internal and external prices are minimized by small devaluations at frequent intervals. The goal of the mechanism is to make individual adjustments predictable and negligible in their impact, thereby eliminating the need to anticipate policy actions and reducing the possible gains from speculation. Thus much of the severe shock implied by overvaluation followed by step devaluation is eliminated. International reserves can be maintained at an appropriate level, and the cycle of tightening exchange controls, reserve losses, and devaluation and subsequent liberalization can thus be broken. Similarly, abrupt shifts in domestic policy taken for balance-of-payments reasons can be avoided. In effect, the crawling peg provides a means of achieving equilibrium on external accounts while still maintaining a disequilibrium domestic policy.

SUMMARY AND CONCLUSION

As has been argued in this chapter, the Latin American countries have generally pursued the objective of economic development, a process that requires the mobilization of considerable internal and external resources, and also involves considerable efforts to change existing patterns of consumption, investment and savings as well as efforts to achieve a favorable balance-of-payments pattern through international economic policy. The results have been uneven in terms of development. The Central American countries have had growth and stability, but their success has been challenged on the grounds that changes in social structure have not occurred. Many countries of South America, notably Argentina, Uruguay, and Chile have had poor growth rates, high inflation, external imbalance, and have been mired in internal political conflicts that have hampered economic progress.

There have, however, been striking examples of prolonged economic development and the successful use of international economic policy. Since 1968, Brazil has used innovations in domestic and international financial policy to achieve extremely high rates of growth. Additionally, Mexico since the 1930s has maintained a high rate of growth, along with ongoing investment in basic infrastructure, for a period that now exceeds forty years. In support of these objectives, the country used two opposing systems of domestic and international finance. From the mid-1930s until the mid-1950s, development was based upon inflationary domestic finance and depreciation of the currency. From the mid-1950s until early 1970s, growth proceeded with price stability, a stable exchange rate, and an intensive development of financial markets. The question that will be considered in the remainder of this work is the means the Mexicans used to increase savings and finance economic growth in each successive period and the reason that each successive system eventually collapsed.

NOTES

1. The issue of the role of inflation in promoting development is considered in Harry G. Johnson, "Is Inflation the Inevitable Price of Rapid Development or a Retarding Factor in Economic Growth?" in *Essays in Monetary Economics* (London: Allen and Unwin, 1967), pp. 281–292. Also see: Milton Friedman, *Money and Economic Development* (New York: Praeger, 1973), especially pp. 43 ff.

2. R. F. Harrod, "An Essay in Dynamic Theory" in *Economic Journal*, Vol. XLIX (March 1939), pp. 14–37, and "Domar and Dynamic Economics" in *Economic Journal*, Vol. LXIX (September 1959), pp. 451–464; Evsey D. Domar, "Expansion and Employment" in *American Economic Review*, Vol. XXXVII (March 1947), pp. 34–55. Although the study uses a Harrod-Domar model for expository purposes the main alternative, a neoclassical growth model recognizes similar problems. For example, see J. E. Meade, *A Neo-Classical Theory of Economic Growth* (London: Allen and Unwin, 1962), especially chapters 2–4.

3. John G. Gurley and Edward S. Shaw, *Money in a Theory of Finance* (Washington: The Brookings Institution, 1960), pp. 112–153. For an elaboration of the Gurley-Shaw model with emphasis on the possibilities for inflationary

and non-inflationary growth, see Deena R. Khatkhate, "Analytic Basis of the Workings of Monetary Policy in Developing Countries," in *IMF Staff Papers,* Vol. XIX (November 1973), pp. 533–559. In addition to its consequences for redistribution between investment and consumption, inflation also has significant consequences for the distribution of resources between the public and private sectors. The state can easily appropriate resources from the private sector, due to its ability to issue unlimited amounts of money in exchange for the real goods produced in the private sector. See: D. E. W. Laidler and J. M. W. Parkin, "Inflation—A Survey," *Economic Journal* Vol. LXXXV (December 1975), pp. 786–794.

4. Khatkhate, *op. cit.,* pp. 540–546. The theoretical literature on forced savings through inflation includes: W. Arthur Lewis, "Economic Development with Unlimited Supplies of Labor" in *Manchester School of Economic and Social Studies,* Vol. XXII (May 1954), pp. 139–191; Martin Bronfenbrenner and F. D. Holzmann, "Survey of Inflation Theory," in *American Economic Review,* Vol. LIII (February 1966), especially pp. 609–614; Nicholas Kaldor "Economic Growth and the Problem of Inflation," parts I and II in *Economica,* Vol. XXVI (August 1959), and (September 1959), pp. 212–226 and 287–298; N. Kaldor, "Alternative Theories of Distribution," in *Review of Economic Studies,* Vol. XIII (1955–56), pp. 94–100; Geoffrey Maynard, *Economic Development and the Price Level* (London: Macmillian, 1962), especially chapter II, pp. 11–42.

5. Johnson, *op. cit.,* pp. 283–284. For a theoretical discussion of the problem of transfer of resources between sectors in a developing economy see: John C. H. Fei and Gustav Ranis, *Development of the Labor Surplus Economy: Theory and Policy,* Homewood, Ill.: Richard D. Irwin, 1964), especially chapters I and II, pp. 1–58.

6. For a discussion of the problem of external balance, see: Gerald N. Meier, *The International Economics of Development* (New York: Harper and Row, 1968), pp. 66–75; and Alfred Maizels, *Exports and Economic Growth of Developing Countries* (Cambridge, England: Cambridge University Press, 1968), pp. 50–54. The model used in the text borrows from both Maizels and Meier.

7. Although this study assumes a single gap model of external balance, the "two-gap model," which treats the deficit on current account and insufficient domestic savings as two separate problems has gained acceptance in recent years. The models are summarized in Maizels, *op. cit.,* pp. 50–72, and Meier, *op. cit.,* pp. 88–90. More detailed descriptions and estimates for individual countries are given in: H. B. Chenery and M. Bruno, "Development Alternatives in an Open Economy: The Case of Israel," in *Economic Journal,* Vol. LXXII (March 1962), pp. 79–103; H. B. Chenery and A. MacEwan, "Optimal Patterns of Growth and Aid: The Case of Pakistan," in I. Adelman and E. Thorbecke (eds.), *The Theory and Design of Economic Development* (Baltimore: Johns Hopkins Press, 1966); H. B. Chenery and A. M. Strout, "Foreign Assistance and Economic Development," in

American Economic Review, Vol. LVI (September 1966), pp. 679–733; R. I., McKinnon, "Foreign Exchange Constraints in Economic Development and Efficient Aid Allocation," in *Economic Journal,* Vol. LXXVII (June 1964), pp. 388–409; G. Ranis and J. C. Fei, "Foreign Assistance and Economic Development: Comment," *American Economic Review,* Vol. LVIII (September 1968), pp. 897–912, and "Reply" by H. B. Chenery and A. M. Strout, pp. 912–916; I. Adelman, and H. B. Chenery, "Foreign Aid and Economic Development: The Case of Greece," *Review of Economics and Statistics,* Vol. XLVII (February 1966), pp. 1–19; UNCTAD, *Trade Prospects and Capital Needs of Developing Countries,* (TD/34/Rev. 1) (New York: 1968); and J. Vanek, *Estimating Foreign Resource Needs for Economic Development* (New York: McGraw Hill, 1967).

8. For a theoretical discussion of export-led growth, see: Robert M. Stern, *The Balance of Payments* (Chicago: Aldine, 1973), pp. 376–381. For a discussion of alternative growth strategies, see: Douglas S. Paauw, *Development Strategies in Open Dualistic Economies* (Washington: National Planning Association, 1970).

9. For a discussion of the foreign exchange market and exchange-rate policy, see: Gottfried Haberler, *Theory of International Trade* (London: William Hodge and Co., 1950), pp. 13–22; Charles P. Kindleberger, *International Economics* (Homewood, Ill.: Richard D. Irwin, 1973), pp. 283–301; Stern, *op. cit.,* pp. 18–70; and J. E. Meade, *The Theory of International Economic Policy,* Vol. I, *The Balance of Payments* (London: Oxford University Press 1963), especially chapters III and IV, pp. 99–231.

10. See: UNCTAD, *The International Monetary Situation: Impact on World Trade and Development,* (TD/140/Rev. 1) (New York, 1972), pp. 33–38; W. M. Corden, "International Monetary Reform and The Developing Countries: A Mainly Theoretical Paper" in *Monetary Problems of the International Economy,* Robert A. Mundell and Alexander K. Swoboda (eds.), (Chicago: University of Chicago Press, 1969), pp. 283–304.

11. The early statement of this view can be found in ECLA, *Economic Survey of Latin America,* 1949, pp. 3–22. A later elaboration with policy prescriptions can be found in Raul Prebisch, "Economic Development or Monetary Stability: The False Dilemma," in ECLA, *Economic Bulletin for LatinAmerica,* Vol. VI (March 1961), pp. 1–25.

12. ECLA, *International Cooperation in Latin American Development Policy,* p.61.

13. The terms of trade argument has been subjected to telling criticism in the literature and at best must be considered unproven. Even using ECLA data, one is hard-pressed to find support for a secular decline in the terms of trade. The pattern that emerges from the ECLA calculations shows the terms of trade rising in the late 1930s to rather high levels in the early 1950s, falling until the early 1960s, and then recovering slightly. See: ECLA, *The Economic Development of Latin America in the Post War Period* (E/CN.12/659/Rev. 1) (New York, 1964), p.

314 and pp. 122–147: and Meier, *op. cit.*, pp. 41–65. Admittedly, the 1930s was a period of depression in the industrial countries and one should expect some improvement in the terms of trade thereafter, regardless of the secular trend in terms of trade. Nevertheless, a distinct trend is still elusive. (As will be seen in Chapter IV, the trade of Mexico behaved in roughly the same manner.) However, to deny the secular tendency toward deterioration in the terms of trade is not to deny that the terms of trade may have been a difficult problem in specific periods. Indeed, it will be argued that in the 1950s the terms of trade posed a difficult problem for Mexico and Latin America in general. For a sympathetic view of the terms of trade argument, see: Ragnar Nurkse, *Problems of Capital Formation in Underdeveloped Countries and Patterns of Trade and Development* (New York: Oxford University Press, 1967), pp. 20–31. For a conflicting view, see: Irving B. Kravis, "Trade as a Handmaiden of Growth: Similarities Between the Nineteenth and Twentieth Centuries," in *Economic Journal*, Vol. LXXXIII (March 1974), pp. 203–209; and M. June Flanders, "Prebisch on Protectionism: An Evaluation" in *Economic Journal*, Vol. LXXIV (June 1964), pp. 305–326.

14. Albert O. Hirschman, "The Political Economy of Import-Substituting Industrialization in Latin America" in *Quarterly Journal of Economics*, Vol. LXXXIII (February 1968), pp. 1–8; and Dudley Seers, "A Theory of Inflation and Growth in Underdeveloped Economies Based on the Experience of Latin America" in *Oxford Economic Papers* (New Series), Vol. XIV (June 1962), pp. 173–195.

15. Hirschmann, *op. cit.*, p. 3; and Seers, *loc. cit.*

16. Spokesmen for less developed countries have stressed the importance of the "capacity to import" as a constraint on the growth of their economies. The United Nations Economic Commission for Latin America (ECLA) formalized the term "capacity to import," meaning the capacity of a country to purchase imports with earnings on current account plus capital inflows. It is assumed that a specific level of imports is needed in order to reach a targeted growth rate. The capacity to import is estimated by projecting exports and capital flows. If foreign exchange receipts are not sufficient to cover import requirements, either the growth target must be reduced or additional external support must be found. Such thinking is very close to the "two-gap" model mentioned earlier. See: ECLA, *External Financing in Latin America* (E/CN. 12/649/Rev. 1, 1965), (New York, 1950), p. 170, *Economic Survey of Latin America*, 1959, pp. 65–66, and *Economic Survey of Latin America, 1958* (E/CN. 12/498/Rev. 1) (New York, 1959), pp. 40–41.

17. For a discussion of direct investment flows, see: ECLA, *External Financing in Latin America*, pp. 138–148.

18. For the best discussion of the fragmented economy, including financial markets, see: Ronald I. McKinnon, *Money and Capital in Economic Development* (Washington: The Brookings Institution, 1973), pp. 5–18.

19. For a discussion of the phenomenon of financial repression through inflation, see: *ibid,* pp. 68–82. McKinnon also gives case studies of financial decline due to inflation, *ibid.* pp. 100–102. Also see: Walter L. Ness Jr., "Some Effects of Inflation on Financing Investment in Argentina and Brazil," in *Financial Development and Economic Growth: The Economic Consequences of Underdeveloped Capital Markets,* Arnold W. Sametz (ed.), (New York: New York University Press, 1972), pp. 223–254.

20. David Felix, "Monetarists, Structuralists and Import-Substituting Industrialization: A Critical Appraisal," in *Inflation and Growth in Latin America,* Werner Baer and Isaac Kerstenetzky (eds.), (Homewood, Ill.: Richard D. Irwin, Inc., 1964), pp. 370–382; Wolfgang Konig, "International Financial Institutions and Latin American Development," in *Latin America in the International Economy,* Victor L. Urquidi and Rosemary Thorp (eds.), (New York: John Wiley and Sons, 1973), pp. 116–126 and 157–163; and Alexandre Kafka, "Some Aspects of Latin America's Financial Relations with the International Monetary Fund," in *Socio-Economic Change in Latin America,* Alberto Martínez Piedras (ed.), (Washington: Catholic University of America Press, 1970), pp. 87–103.

21. Harry G. Johnson, *Economic Policies toward Less Developed Countries* (Washington: The Brookings Institution, 1969), pp. 44–66.

22. Harry Johnson points out there are two basic approaches to the study of the international economic system. The political economy approach sees the workings of the system as a series of conflicts of national interests and as an exercise of power by states. The economic-scientific approach views the system as a general equilibrium system. See: "Political Economy Aspects of International Monetary Reform," in *Journal of International Economics,* Vol. II (September 1972), pp. 401–416. A full appreciation of the workings of the international economic system requires some elements of both. While there are objective rules of economic behavior, which the individual state can ignore only at its own peril, the system allows considerable discretion in policy making and leaves the choice of objectives to individual states. Also see: Kindleberger, *Money and Power,* pp. 9–14.

23. In terms of their evaluation of the economic problems of Latin America and the resulting policy remedies prescribed, ECLA and the IMF are often placed at the extreme poles. The IMF supports the "monetarist" view that economic development can best take place in an atmosphere of stability where markets are allowed to operate efficiently. As a result, it advocates conservative demand-management policies and a minimum of control. ECLA on the other hand, is the fountainhead of "structuralist" thought. (The monetarist-structualist debate will be discussed at length in Chapter V.) This organization believes that market imperfections are serious enough to warrant official efforts to obtain a different pattern of development. Usually, ECLA is more willing to interpret

inflation and balance of payments disequilibrium in terms of structural imbalance, and is likely to advocate controls. See: Stephen D. Krasner, "The International Monetary Fund and the Third World," in *International Organization,* Vol. XXII (Summer 1968), pp. 670–688.

24. Charles P. Kindleberger, *Money and Power: The Economics of International Politics and the Politics of International Economics* (New York: Basic Books, 1970), p. 203.

25. For an excellent analysis of the impact of exchange-rate policy on income distribution see: Carlos F. Díaz-Alejandro, *Exchange-Rate Devaluation in a Semi-Industrialized Country: The Experience of Argentina, 1955–61* (Cambridge, Mass.: MIT Press, 1965), pp. 149–180; and G. Maynard and W. Van Rijckegham, "Argentina 1967–70: A Stabilization Effort that Failed," in *Banca Nazionale Del Lavoro Quarterly Review,* No. 103 (December 1972), pp. 396–412. For a discussion of the allocative, distributive and balance of payments problems associated with a high rate of inflation, see: Raouf Kahlil, *Inflation and Economic Growth in Brazil, 1946–63* (Oxford, England: Clarendon Press, 1973).

26. Raymond F. Mikesell, *Foreign Exchange in the Postwar World* (New York: The Twentieth Century Fund, 1954), pp. 305–307; and Francis H. Schott, *The Evolution of Latin American Exchange-Rate Policies Since World War II* (Princeton, N.J.: Princeton University Press, 1952), (Essays in International Finance, No. 32), pp. 1–5.

27. W. M. Scammell, *International Monetary Policy* (2nd. edition), (New York: St. Martin's Press, 1967), pp. 53–75 and 154–171.

28. Mikesell, *op. cit.,* pp. 59–80; Jorge Marshall, "Exchange Controls and Economic Development," in *Economic Development for Latin America: Proceedings of a Conference Held by the International Economic Association,* Howard S. Ellis and Harvey C. Wallich (eds.), (London: Macmillan, 1961), pp. 430–469; E. M. Bernstein, "Some Economic Aspects of Multiple Exchange Rates," in *IMF Staff Papers,* Vol. I (September 1950), pp. 235–237; Jorge Marshall, "Efectos Económicos de Ciertas Prácticas de Cambio Múltiple," in *El Trimestre Económico,* Vol. XX (July— September 1953), pp. 384–394; and Margaret C. de Vries, "Multiple Exchange Rates: Expectations and Experience," in *IMF Staff Papers,* Vol. XV (July 1965), pp. 282–313.

29. Mikesell *op. cit.,* p. 315; also see: Schott, *op. cit.,* pp. 7–8.

30. Mado R. Ambach, "Multiple Exchange Rates: An Instrument for Improving Foreign Trade Balance with Special Reference to the Latin American Countries" (unpublished Ph.D. dissertation, Economics Department, Yale University, 1952); and Eugene R. Schlesinger, *Multiple Exchange Rates and Economic Development* (Princeton, N.J.: Department of Economics, Princeton University, 1952), (Studies in International Finance, No. 2), pp 1–5.

31. Schott, *op. cit.*, pp. 14–21, and Mikesell, *op. cit.*, pp. 322–332.

32. John R. Woodley, "The Use of Special Exchange Rates for Transactions with Foreign Companies," in *IMF Staff Papers*, Vol. III (October 1953), pp. 254–270.

33. Mikesell, *op. cit.*, p. 314.

34. Schott, *op. cit.*, pp. 12–13.

35. Konig, *op. cit.*, pp. 153–156; Juergen B. Donges, *Brazil's Trotting Peg: A New Approach to Greater Exchange Flexibility in Less Developed Countries* (Washington: American Enterprise Institute for Policy Research, 1971); Walter L. Ness Jr., "Financial Markets as a Development Strategy: Initial Results from the Brazilian Experience," in *Economic Development and Cultural Change*, Vol. XXII (April 1974), pp. 453–472; Alexandre Kafka, "Indexing for Inflation in Brazil," in *Essays in Indexation and Inflation* (Washington: American Enterprise Association for Policy Research, 1974), pp. 87–98; and William G. Tyler, "Exchange Rate Flexibility under Conditions of Inflation: A Case Study of the Recent Brazilian Experience," in *Leading Issues in International Economic Policy*, C. Fred Bergsten and William G. Tyler (eds.), (Lexington, Mass: D. C. Heath and Company, 1973), pp. 16–50.

Chapter II

The Origin of Inflationary Development

HISTORICAL BACKGROUND

Modernization of the Mexican economy before 1900 began with the formation of export-oriented enclaves that mainly engaged in mining, petroleum, and agriculture to satisfy the rising demand for raw materials, first of Europe and later of the United States. Similarly, the rudimentary domestic banking system and the network of roads, ports, and railroads were developed to support export activities.[1] Export activity brought progress to some areas of economy, but the country remained backward and the lot of the vast majority of the population was not changed. Since the export of raw materials was associated with the Spanish conquest and the industrialization of the United States without corresponding progress in Mexico, Mexicans believed that foreigners had profited more than nationals from economic growth.

In the years 1910–1920, Mexico experienced revolution and civil war, in which perhaps one million lives were lost. The revolution and its aftermath represented conflicts between opposing Mexican elites. At the same time, these upheavals were violent reactions by traditional liberals and less-favored groups in Mexican society against an oppressive regime that ruled with the support of the traditional elite of wealthy landowners, the army, and the church, as well as powerful foreign interests. On another level, the revolution can be interpreted as a reaction of an indigenous people against centuries of Western domination.[2]

It would be a gross understatement to say that the revolution had unfavorable consequences for the economy. The agricultural base was destroyed by land seizures and abandonment by owners. There were massive losses of output, destruction of capital equipment and a virtual halt to new investment. Rural violence, falling agricultural output and land seizures led to sharp losses in the value of land and fixed capital assets. Most commercial banks failed. Mexico had no central bank and currency had been issued by large commercial banks. Emission of paper currency accelerated sharply as monetary discipline evaporated. Monetary expansion accelerated further as rival warning factions issued their own currencies. Consequently, there was a total loss of public confidence in paper money and the financial system.[3] By the end of the revolution, a large flight had occurred from domestic money into real goods and foreign exchange.

Despite the destruction it unleashed, the revolution may have advanced the modernization of the country on balance, for in many ways put forth during the 1910–1920 period called for redistribution of land, equalization of income and opportunity, political liberalization, and greater control of the domestic economy by nationals. The very fact that the old social system had been destroyed allowed the country to discard those parts of the old order which retarded development. With the displacement of the traditional elite came a more modern elite of politicians, administrators, and businessmen.[4] Furthermore, the revolution established an ideology of economic progress and social advancement that became a point of reference for successive governments.

In the years after 1920, the country began to create new economic and political institutions.[5] The Bank of Mexico was established in 1925 as the central bank with the powers to issue currency and monitor the banking system. More basically, the task of the central bank was to create a financial system where none existed, and to regain the public's confidence in paper money.[6] On the political side, the destruction of the old power structure left a vaccum at the center in which former revolutionary generals and powerful local politicians competed, often violently, for power. At the end of the 1920s, however, President Calles established a strong presidency, supported by a dominant political party that was able to defend its authority against all challengers.[7]

In summary, the period 1910–1930 was one of violent conflict, political instability and little, if any, economic progress. The beginnings of a workable political and economic system began to emerge by the late 1920s. The worldwide Depression of 1929 presented a formidable challenge to economic policy-making for the administration of President Lazaro Cardenas, who took office in 1934.

THE CÁRDENAS PERIOD, 1934—1940

Economic and Social Change

With the advent of President Cárdenas, the country embarked on a period of economic and social development. The government believed that the policies the post-revolutionary governments had pursued up to that time were inadequate, and in the midst of the Depression began to try to intensify the pursuit of economic modernization and social justice. Economically, the Cárdenas administration saw the problem as one of extending modernization beyond the small export enclaves to geographic and demographic sectors that had previously been untouched. Socially, the administration sought to promote greater equality of income and opportunity. In order to broaden the base of future economic growth, sizable infrastructure projects were undertaken in agriculture, railways, roads, irrigation, dams, and similar projects designed to unify the country into a single market and raise levels of output.[8] Official policy favored disadvantaged groups in society. A massive land redistribution program was carried out and the government fostered the development of trade unions. Strongly nationalistic, the government imposed heavy taxes on companies that exported minerals and, after a dispute between foreign-owned petroleum companies and their workers, foreign petroleum holdings[9] were nationalized in 1938.

Inflationary Finance

Despite its ambitious social and economic goals, the government had inherited a situation in which economic activity had been dealt a sharp blow by the fall in demand for Mexican exports accompanying the world pression. Domestic investment was still sluggish following the revolutionary upheaval and the collapse of the financial system. The tax structure was rudimentary and administration was poor. Foreign support for economic development which would have been minimal in any case virtually dried up owing to the distrust of Mexico in the rest of the world that resulted from the revolution, the default on external debts, and the unorthodox policies of Cárdenas including the petroleum expropriation. As a result, the government had little choice but to resort to inflationary means to finance its development program.

The federal government accelerated expenditures sharply and created a variety of development banks to channel credit to targeted sectors. Aside from the establishment of the central bank, the development banks were the most important financial innovations in Mexico before 1940. The best known and the largest of these, the Nacional Financiera, specialized in identifying "bottleneck" sectors of the economy and directing resources to those sectors in formulating projects. Other official banks were set up to direct credit to specific areas of the economy such as agriculture, public works and road building, most of which could not obtain credit on commercial terms.[10]

Along with their financial functions, the development banks had political functions. The capitalistic development of the economy and the financial system were objectives of the revolution and were means of achieving a more advanced economy and higher standards of living. Like government expenditure policy, the development banks also served another political aim, namely, to centralize power in the office of the president and thus eliminate the remnants of political conflicts that still lingered after the strife of the 1920s. Recalcitrant local chieftains could be rewarded with government projects and credit, while businessmen could be brought to support the government through the implicit threat of the withdrawal of funds as a sanction. As a result, government expenditure policy and government credit policy became deeply enmeshed in the domestic political process.

Owing to the lack of private initiative in undertaking new investments, the program involved a direct allocation of resources by the government to priority activities. This expansionary policy encouraged the growth of domestic industry as the demand for goods such as cement, steel, and other equipment grew and as consumer income rose. Thus, the modern industrial growth of Mexico also had its origins in the government spending program of the 1930s.[11]

TABLE II – 1.

Indicators of Financial Development and Inflation, 1934 – 40
(millions of pesos, unless otherwise indicated)

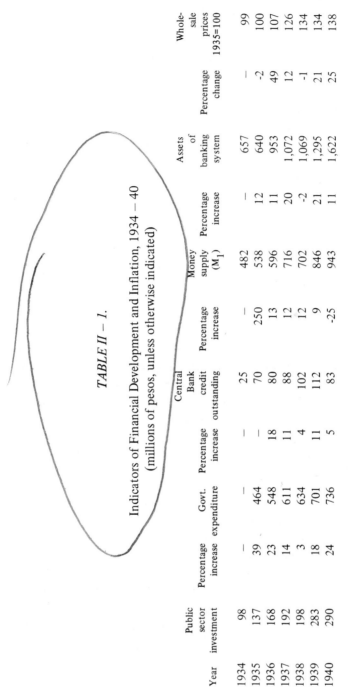

Year	Public sector investment	Percentage increase	Govt. expenditure	Percentage increase	Central Bank credit outstanding	Percentage increase	Money supply (M₁)	Percentage increase	Assets of banking system	Percentage change	Whole-sale prices 1935=100
1934	98	–	–	–	25	–	482	–	657	–	99
1935	137	39	464	–	70	250	538	12	640	-2	100
1936	168	23	548	18	80	13	596	11	953	49	107
1937	192	14	611	11	88	12	716	20	1,072	12	126
1938	198	3	634	4	102	12	702	-2	1,069	-1	134
1939	283	18	701	11	112	9	846	21	1,295	21	134
1940	290	24	736	5	83	-25	943	11	1,622	25	138

Sources: Bank of Mexico, *Annual Reports.* Roberto Santillan Lopez and Aniceto Rosas Figueroa, *Teoria General de las Finanzas Publicas y el Caso de Mexico* (Mexico, D.F., Escuela Nacional Autonoma de Mexico, 1962), appendices.

As Table II-1 indicates, the expansion of the Cárdenas epoch was financed with a large increase in credit from both the official and private banks. The central bank increased its holdings of the debt of the federal government and its rediscounts to the development banks. Likewise, little control was exercised over the expansion of credit by the private banks. As a result, the money supply expanded rapidly. Inflationary pressures arose as a result of this policy, with wholesale prices rising at a yearly average rate of 6.8 percent in the Cárdenas years, a rate that appears higher when it is remembered that price level was falling in most countries. At the same time, price pressures were moderated by deflationary conditions in the rest of the world, by a backlog of spare capacity in some sectors, and by a rising demand for domestic money encouraged by the monetization of the economy and the greater public confidence in central bank notes.[12]

Peso Depreciation

During the entire period, the exchange rate was technically fixed, and the Bank of Mexico supported the rate as much as possible. However, since reserves were extremely small, each time that sizable downward pressure on the rate developed, the central bank stepped aside and allowed the rate to depreciate. (See Table II-2 on page 44.)

Owing to the lack of confidence in the peso, there was a more or less constant tendency toward capital flight in the decade. The devaluation of the peso with respect to gold in 1932 produced a first speculative assault on the currency. The exchange rate remained relatively stable until 1938, when sizable capital outflows began in response to the petroleum and railroad expropriation.[13] In March 1938, the Bank of Mexico withdrew from the exchange market and allowed the exchange rate to depreciate. Although a new parity of 4.85 pesos per dollar was announced later in the year, the rate continued to float freely.[14] The peso underwent a persistent depreciation with respect to the U.S. dollar in the 1930s. The exchange rate absorbed a great deal of the effect of the government's inflationary policies. President Cárdenas himself admitted as much, but in view of the government's objective of persevering with its development program, it was a price that the authorities were willing to pay.[15]

Table II – 2.

Exchange Rate for the Mexican Peso, 1930 - 1940
(Average for year, pesos per U.S. dollar)

1930	2.26
1931	2.65
1932	3.17
1933	3.53
1934	3.60
1935	3.58
1936	3.60
1937	3.60
1938	4.50
1939	5.18
1940	5.40

Source: Bank of Mexico, *Annual Report* (various issues).

WORLD WAR II

Domestic Policy and Performance

President Manuel Avila Camacho, who replaced Cárdenas, was noticeably more conservative than his predecessor. There was a marked lessening of the commitment to programs of social reform, less emphasis on land distribution and less support for the trade unions. Nevertheless, public works spending and inflationary finance continued to be distinguishing features of government policy. However, the policy was given a new twist after 1940 as the problems of the country changed.[16]

The two major sources of growth during World War II were large current account surpluses and the constant rise in domestic investment financed by forced savings through inflation. The war proved to be a powerful stimulus to industrialization and growth as world demand for primary commodities as well as basic manufactured goods expanded sharply. In order to devote the maximum possible resources to the war effort, the United States imposed quotas on exports, thereby effectively preventing Mexico from importing as much as its reserve holdings would allow. As a result, Mexican industry began a spontaneous process of import substitution. The iron and steel, cement, and pulp and paper industries expanded sharply.[17] In addition, shortages in belligerent countries gave rise to a quick growth of exports of some manufactured goods. Textiles were the main sector to increase exports, but important gains were also registered in chemicals, food, drink, and tobacco.[18] Thus, in response to wartime conditions, Mexican economic growth continued, but the pattern was somewhat different.

The techniques of inflationary finance developed under Cárdenas continued to support the government's program of public works spending and to encourage increases in the rate of private investment (see Table II-3).

The money supply expanded quickly, reflecting increasing official foreign exchange holdings and an easy domestic monetary policy. Furthermore, the suppressed demand for money, which had undoubtedly dampened inflationary pressures during the Cárdenas regime, was probably largely met by 1940.[19] Since the Avila Camacho administration was interested in promoting investment, the inflationary process was allowed to take on another function. By reducing real wages, the policy in effect fostered a high rate of capital formation and thus gave an additional impetus to growth. Similarly, current government spending as a proportion of total spending was reduced while capital expenditure accelerated.[20]

Table II – 3.

Indicators of Growth, 1934 - 1946
(average annual rates in percent)

	Real GNP	Real public investment	Real private investment	Wholesale prices
1934 - 1940	4.6	11.0	n.a.	6.2
1941 - 1946	6.2	8.6	5.3	14.4

Source: Nacional Financiera, S.A., *Statistics on the Mexican Economy,* (Mexico, D F. 1966).

The Balance of Payments

Due to drastic changes in world economic conditions, the external situation was one of persistent surplus during World War II in contrast to the tendency toward deficit in the Depression period. Mexican exports expanded rapidly in response to booming world demand, while imports, somewhat restricted by the U.S. quotas on exports, were held to lower levels.[21] Therefore, as Table II-4 shows, the country enjoyed a considerable current account surplus during World War II.

On capital account as well, the situation prevailing in the Depression period was completely reversed. With the outbreak of war in Europe in 1939, Mexico began to receive reflows of Mexican flight capital as well as new capital flows from Europeans. These flows increased in importance in 1940. After falling to almost 6 pesos per U.S. dollar in early 1940, the peso came under upward pressure in the exchange market. In that year the Bank of Mexico, now in possession of some international reserves, stabilized the exchange rate at the official parity of 4.85 per dollar and, in the process, accumulated sizable international reserves.[22]

In 1942, the authorities took advantage of their comfortable reserve position to begin renegotiation of the country's foreign debt, which had been in default for nearly twenty years. In November 1942, Mexico negotiated an agreement with an International Bankers Committee under which Mexican debts would be repaid according to an agreed schedule. Mexico also agreed to compensate U.S. and British oil and railroad interests that had been expropriated in 1938. As a result of these accords, Mexico's financial standing improved, allowing the country again to borrow in international markets, beginning with a loan from the Eximbank in 1942.[23]

At the end of World War II, Mexico was fairly advanced along the path of inflationary growth. However, it should be pointed out that the process of inflationary growth occurred not because of any innovation in economic thinking, but as a political response to the conditions of the world Depression. Indeed, Mexico's experimentation with inflationary finance was looked upon with disfavor in the rest of the world. Nevertheless, the country had found a way of mobilizing domestic resources and achieving relatively high rates of growth. At the same time, the momentum of domestic inflation made it difficult to stop once it had begun.

Table II - 4

International Statistics, 1939 - 1946
(millions of dollars)

	1939	1940	1941	1942	1943	1944	1945	1946
Exports (goods and services)	216	213	243	272	410	432	401	570
Imports (goods and services)	-180	-185	-269	-250	-308	-405	-499	-744
Current account balance	36	28	- 23	22	102	27	2	-174
Change in official reserves	5	- 26	- 2	40	140	20	109	-100
Level of net official reserves[e]	23	49	47	87	227	247	356	256
Exchange rate (average for years, pesos per U.S. dollar)	5.148	5.404	4.857	4.854	4.851	4.854	4.853	4.855

Source: Bank of Mexico, *Annual Report* (various issues).
[e] estimated.

NOTES

1. For discussions of the pre-revolutionary economy of Mexico see: Clark W. Reynolds, *The Mexican Economy* (New Haven: Yale University Press, 1970), pp. 15–26; and Leopoldo Solís, "Hacia un Análisis General a Largo Plazo del Desarrollo Económico de México," in *Demografía y Economía,* Vol. I (1969), pp. 40–91. For a discussion of banking and the financial system: Virgil M. Bett, *Central Banking in Mexico: Monetary Policy and Financial Crises, 1864–1949* (Ann Arbor: University of Michigan Press, 1957), Chapter I, pp. 1–8; Antonio Manero, *La Revolución Bancaria en México 1865–1955* (Mexico: Talleres Gráficos de la Nación, 1957), pp. 21–33; and Dwight S. Brothers and Leopoldo Solís M., Mexican Financial Development (Austin: University of Texas Press, 1966), pp. 3–9.

2. Frank R. Brandenburg, *The Making of Modern Mexico* (Englewood Cliffs, N.J.: Prentice-Hall, 1964), pp. 19–45; Javier Rondero, "Características del Nacionalismo," in *México: Cincuenta Años de Revolución,* Vol. III, *La Política* (Mexico: Fondo de Cultura Económica, 1961), pp. 293–305; and Emilio Portes Gil, "Sentido y Destino de la Revolución Mexicana," *ibid.,* pp. 479–585.

3. Edwin W. Kemerer, *Inflation and Revolution: Mexico's Experience of 1912– 1917* (Princeton, N.J.: Princeton University Press, 1940).

4. For a study of the development of capitalist attitudes in Mexico, see: Flavia Derossi, *The Mexican Entrepreneur* (Paris: OECD Development Centre, 1971), especially pp. 13–32.

5. Brandenburg, *op. cit.,* pp. 47–78.

6. Bett, *op. cit.,* pp. 23–33.

7. Brandenburg, *op. cit.,* pp. 81–90.

8. Reynolds, *op. cit.,* pp. 32–36, Brandenburg, *op. cit.,* pp. 75–100; Roger D. Hansen, *The Politics of Mexican Development* (Baltimore: Johns Hopkins University Press, 1970), and Fernando Rosenzweig Hernández, "El Proceso Político y el Desarrollo Económico de México," in *El Trimestre Económico,* Vol. XXIX (October–December 1962), pp. 513–530.

9. Brandenburg, *op. cit.,* pp. 98–100; and Ernesto Lobato López, "El Petróleo en la Economía," in *Mexico: Cincuenta Años de Revolución,* Vol. I, *La Economía,* pp. 313–336.

10. Brothers and Solis, *op. cit.,* pp. 12–21; Charles W. Anderson, "Bankers as Revolutionaries," in *The Political Economy of Mexico,* William P. Glade and Charles W. Anderson (eds.), (Madison: University of Wisconsin Press, 1963), pp. 117– 129. Anderson has a description of the individual banks in his Appendix, pp. 186–191. For a more detailed description see: Octaviano Campos Salas, "Las Instituciones Nacionales de Crédito," in *México: Cincuenta Años de Revolución,* Vol. I, *La Economía,* pp. 415–444.

11. Sanford Mosk, *Industrial Revolution in Mexico* (Berkeley: University of California Press, 1950), pp. 53–60.

12. Brothers and Solís, *op. cit.*, p. 15.

13. *Ibid*, pp. 111–116.

14. Bank of Mexico, *Annual Report*, 1939, pp. 17–20.

15. Bett, *op. cit.*, p. 116.

16. Brandenburg, *op. cit.*, pp. 79–100.

17. Timothy King, *Mexico: Industrialization and Trade Policies Since 1940* (Published for OECD Development Centre; London: Oxford University Press, 1970), pp. 22–24.

18. *Ibid*, p. 25.

19. Brothers and Solís, *op. cit.*, pp. 74–75.

20. Ifigenia M. de Navarrete, *La Distribución del Ingreso y el Desarrollo Económico de México* (Mexico: Escuela Nacional de Economía, 1960), pp. 45–66.

21. Bank of Mexico, *Annual Report*, 1943, pp. 17–20.

22. Bank of Mexico, *Annual Report*, 1941, p. 19.

23. Bank of Mexico, *Annual Report*, 1943, pp. 35–37.

Chapter III

Decision Making in Mexico

THE PRESIDENT AND THE POLITICAL SYSTEM

A full understanding of the economic decision-making process requires some familiarity with the political system. In Mexico, decision-making power is heavily concentrated in the executive branch which, in fact but not in law, dominates the legislature and the courts. State and local governments are under the effective dominance of the central government. There exists a single official political party, the PRI (Institutional Revolutionary Party), that so overshadows all others as to make the system a virtual one-party regime. Within the executive branch, ultimate power lies in the hands of the president, who is elected for a six-year term and is not eligible for re-election. All presidents have come from the official party, and new presidents are traditionally chosen from among the cabinet ministers of the outgoing administration.

Surrounding the president at the highest level of power is a classic power elite. Brandenburg calls this informal group of insiders, which includes powerful political, military, labor and business figures, the "revolutionary family."[1] It influences the selection of a new president and exercises an advisory function with regard to policy-making.[2]

Once installed in power, the president sets the tone and direction of policy for his term.[3] Though the president is the final arbiter of all issues, he does not by any means rule by whim. The long and difficult quest for political stability between 1910 and 1930, in which Mexico suffered from factionalism and unrestrained struggles for power, deeply affected the way that the country's leaders deal with potential opposition. They identify political stability with their ability to gain the support of all significant organized groups, while generally rejecting the use of force. When new groups demonstrate their broad appeal, the reaction of the authorities usually is to try to convince their leaders to support the government, persuading partly by using the power of the state to grant favorable treatment. In addition, an elaborate procedure of consultations has evolved under which the president, key officials, and the entire ruling group practice widespread consultation before introducing any change in policy.[4] Opinions about possible policy measures are solicited and channeled back to the president through the bureaucracy, the PRI, and the informal network of contacts of the elite, which include both the public and private sectors. The decision-making process tries not merely to gain as much consensus as possible for policy decisions but to formulate policy in such a way that all interests are satisfied. Once decisions are made, the party and the elite are used to mobilize opinion in support of policy. Since the Mexican system places a premium on consensus, the authorities try to confine criticism to private circles, where issues are quietly settled behind closed doors and opposition is generally kept from the public.[5] As a rule, those who wish to influence decisions seriously do not place themselves in open opposition to the official policy.[6]

Although significant shifts of policy have occurred, Mexican presidents all justify their actions in terms of the "revolutionary" ideology, which claims to be the outcome of the 1910–1920 revolution as well as earlier progressive developments in Mexican history. It includes democracy, social justice, economic progress and stability, nationalism, and political liberalism.[7] The function of this ideology is mainly symbolic. Successive presidents have given so many varying interpretations to the original ideology, that it can be used to support nearly any policy. The ideal of equalization of income has been largely neglected as the country sought high rates of growth and hence tolerated sizable concentrations of wealth in order to foster capital formation. Likewise, despite the professions of economic nationalism, foreign capital has played a crucial role in Mexico's economic development. One observer went so far as to allege that the most solid achievement of Mexico's revolutionary ideology has been to create a public relations smokescreen for regressive policies:

> Mexico manages to maintain the image, at home and abroad, of a progres-
> sive and even semi-socialist country; while preserving, in part as a result of
> very low rates of effective direct taxation of incomes and profits, tolerance
> of monopolistic positions in business and a pronounced inequality of per-
> sonal incomes, an environment very favorable to profitable private enter-
> prise, particularly for indigenous capital.[8]

This is the most cynical interpretation of Mexican policy. It would probably be closer to a balanced picture of reality to say that since the time of
Cárdenas the authorities have, more often than not, placed economic
growth and modernization higher on their list of priorities than egalitarian redistribution of income.[9]

Or looking at it another way, one could say that the Mexican government usually favored investment over consumption, which almost always
results in a less equitable distribution of income. Especially from the van-
tage point of the present, it is easy to be harsh in criticizing Mexican
policy-makers of earlier decades. The policies they adopted are certainly
open to criticism on grounds of social equity, and venality may at times
have been a hindrance to effective decision making in the public interest.
Nevertheless, it is wrong to oversimplify the issue. It is a basic misreading
of the situation to suggest that the Mexican authorities deliberately chose
a regressive path of economic development when a more equitable pattern was plainly available. Mexican policy-makers were groping, amidst
incomplete information and a poorly defined conceptual framework, for
policies that would produce acceptable results. By a process of experimentation, they were able to arrive at policies that led to high rates
of growth. Pressures to adopt a more egalitarian policy might have been
seen as potentially undermining the country's accomplishments in
promoting industrialization, undertaking investment in infrastructure,
and achieving high rates of capital formation. Even on a conceptual
plane, there was, and is, no clear-cut alternative means of achieving
growth with social equity; if there were, most countries would probably
adopt it immediately.

Beyond this, it is important to spell out the economic and political
criteria by which one is judging policy-makers. Alongside the economic
problems of evolving a workable pattern of economic development is the
political problem of maintaining social order and political stability, while
promoting social change and broader political participation. Moreover,

in countries that, at least in principle, adhere to democratic values (of which Mexico is one) there is the additional objective of adhering to democratic forms, or at very least of respecting individual freedoms, of tolerating a plurality of institutions, and of not resorting to force to implement decisions. When it is recalled that most developing countries have had little experience with democratic practices, it becomes clear that the demands placed on the policy-maker are enormous. Thus, it should hardly be surprising that virtually no government of any developing country has been able to meet all of these conditions.

As had already been argued in an earlier chapter, the allocation of resources between investment and consumption is an ongoing dilemma for developing countries. Moreover, it is a dilemma for which few countries have found really satisfying solutions. Few governments that refrain from the use of force have been strong enough to exact the necessary sacrifices from their populations to increase the level of investment. South American countries, notably Argentina, Uruguay, Brazil (before 1966), and Chile (before 1973) stand out in this regard. Owing to their inability to decide squarely in favor of investment, they have failed to channel enough resources to development and have therefore had poor records of growth and, it should be added, rather intractable political problems arising from social discontent. Nor is this dilemma peculiar to market economies. Indeed, Communist countries have deliberately reduced levels of mass consumption in trying to promote rapid growth and industrialization.

While Mexico's performance is undoubtedly open to criticism on the grounds that little has been done to redistribute income, it is equally true that sizable numbers of Mexicans have advanced into the middle classes as a result of economic growth.[10] Furthermore, while the Mexican power structure seems to effectively exclude the majority from decision making and to favor those close to the government, the ruling elite apparently gives some consideration to the effects of policy on the masses of ordinary Mexicans, if not out of adherence to the revolutionary ideology, then out of fear of causing disturbances which might threaten their own privileged position. There have been important advances in social legislation, and considerable increases in spending on projects designed to improve the welfare of the population.[11] Similarly, the Mexican system has been criticized as being authoritarian. Yet, it is worth noting that, while some Latin American countries have adopted more democratic political systems for limited periods, few have been able to equal Mexico's record in evolving a formula that has been able to provide political stability and effective decision making with a minimum of repression, a large degree of freedom of dissent, and a virtual absence of military influence.

Another undoubted advantage that the Mexican political system and the revolutionary ideology provide the country is that governments have an extraordinary degree of self-confidence mixed with a strong dose of pragmatism, which have allowed successive governments to maintain a program of accelerated growth while adapting their policies to changing circumstances. Thus, in situations such as the world Depression and the fall in commodity prices in the 1950s where the governments in other countries retrenched in the face of difficult circumstances, the Mexicans continued to make the necessary policy innovations to maintain their goal of modernization.[12]

As it directly concerns the economic decision-making process, the role of the president is to set the broad outlines of official policy and settle the most important disputes that cannot be resolved at lower levels. In his leadership role, the president responds to political pressure transmitted by the ruling group, the economic realities as transmitted by the Ministry of Finance, and also to the interests of the nation as he conceives them. Once a decision is taken, he can then make use of the formal and informal political structure to mobilize support for official policy.

THE FINANCE MINISTRY AND THE BUREAUCRACY

The executive branch is a huge complex of ministries, commissions, and decentralized agencies. By its power to grant favors, to control the flow of information to the president, and to formulate policy options, some analysts have identified the bureaucracy as an independent center of power.[13]

Decisions concerning public spending have always been intensely political, even more than in other countries. The growth of public expenditure from the 1930s onward served not only the economic function of development, but also the political function of rewarding the faithful and holding potentially independent centers of power inside the framework of the political structure. The agencies of the executive rule on the petitions of business interests seeking tax reductions, tariffs, licensing, and other government support. Moreover, access to public funds and credit, as well as the prospect of receiving favorable decisions, are means of keeping business interests closely tied to government.[14]

Owing to the intense pressures that the executive branch receives and its general desire to accelerate both public works and welfare spending, there is a persistent tendency toward overspending in the public sector. Consequently, the problem of fiscal discipline, which would have been great in any case due to the lack of hard information and administrative skills, was compounded by political pressures. Even though the process of preparing the budget was formalized by the administration of Alemán (1946–1952) and further strengthened under Ruiz Cortines (1952–58), the problem has been an ongoing one.[15] The task of reconciling the claims of individual agencies of the executive branch with the level of real resources available to the government falls on the Ministry of Finance.[16] Because of his responsibilities in preparing and executing the budget, the Minister of Finance is generally regarded as the first among equals in the cabinet. Thus, the best statement of official economic policy is the annual speech by the Finance Minister to the convention of the Bankers Association.

The stabilizing role of fiscal policy is somewhat restricted. There has traditionally been little flexibility on the revenue side; few major changes in tax law have been enacted. As a result, whatever stabilizing role fiscal policy has played, and whatever leeway in discretionary measures exists, have been on the expenditure side. Even on the expenditure side, however, the flexibility of the authorities is limited. Government spending tends to follow a "political cycle," rising in the middle and the end of the six-year presidential terms without regard to the business cycle.[17] Nevertheless, since the total volume of government expenditure influences the level of monetary aggregates, the absolute level of public expenditure is a critical determinant of economic activity.[18]

In broadest terms, the Ministry of Finance is something of a link between the political system and economic reality. The Finance Ministry receives pressures for increased spending, some of which may be backed by powerful political forces or which may be destined for projects where needs appear pressing. The Finance Ministry must allocate government projects according to an established set of priorities, and must keep expenditure within the limits compatible with the objectives of stabilization policy. Moreover, the alliances that exist within the public sector may affect the outlook of the Finance Ministry and hence the course of stabilization policy. If the Finance Minister aligns himself with the agencies of the government that wish to accelerate public investment, the country will in all likelihood follow the inflationary pattern of growth. On the other hand, if the Finance Minister sides with these organizations favoring stable growth, principally the Bank of Mexico, he will then accept strict budget constraints and keep public spending within the capability of the financial system to provide noninflationary finance.

THE BANK OF MEXICO

The Bank of Mexico is legally subordinate to the Finance Ministry and hence in the last analysis must support government policy. However, the Bank enjoys considerable prestige for its technical competence and nonpolitical nature. The prestige that the Bank painstakingly cultivated over the years has given the Bank an appreciable leverage in formulating policy, especially after 1954 when price stability became a major objective.[19]

The fact that the Bank of Mexico is a nonpolitical institution in a highly politicized environment does not mean that the central bank has no point of view or does not compete for influence in the decision-making structure. The Bank is nonpolitical only insofar as it has no constituency in the nation at large and its judgments are thus taken as representing the honest opinion of a highly competent staff. Nevertheless, the central bank must be politically astute, and it must also skillfully apply the arts of bureaucratic infighting. In order to effectively influence policy, the Bank must gauge the political circumstances that limit the kind of advice that the executive branch is willing to accept. In addition, the central bank must be close enough to the administration politically to convince the executive branch that political and monetary objectives are compatible.

The Bank of Mexico was founded in a period of monetary collapse and charged with the responsibilities of restoring confidence in the Mexican currency and building an effective financial system at a time when the public had lost confidence in the country's financial management. This origin has colored the outlook of the Bank of Mexico in later years.[20] While presidents and finance ministers have wavered between the objectives of growth and reform on the one hand, and stability on the other, the Bank of Mexico has single-mindedly taken a stance in favor of stability within the limits allowed by the government. As Rodrigo Gómez, the Director General of the Bank from 1953–1970, said, "The primary role of the Bank has been to struggle to maintain the internal and external purchasing power of the peso."[21] During the adminstrations of Cárdenas and Ávila Camacho, when there was no possibility of noninflationary finance for infrastructure expenditure, the central bank mainly supported the growth of bank activity through rediscount operations, which helped increase the lending of the banking system. When the rising costs of inflation became apparent in the postwar period, and made such a position politically viable, the Bank of Mexico argued forcefully for a policy of price stability.

The major operative concern of the Bank of Mexico is to finance the government deficit in a noninflationary way through the banking system. In order to accomplish this, it manipulates reserve requirements in order to hold the level of private investment within the amount compatible with the needs of the government sector and the capacity of the banking system.[22] Hence, government expenditure must be controlled enough to permit the central bank to carry out this task. If the programmed level of public sector financing is excessive, the Bank of Mexico can persuade the Finance Ministry to hold expenditure within agreed-upon limits. The Finance Ministry, in turn, can press individual ministries of decentralized agencies to reduce spending.[23] Similarly, in cases where the operations of the private banking system are squeezed excessively, the central bank can transmit these pressures back to the Finance Ministry. In addition to its influence over operational matters, the Bank of Mexico, through its contacts with government, can generally advocate stability as a goal of economic policy and thus, by its presence in official circles, move the entire decision-making structure toward a more stability-oriented posture.

Because of the experience of financial collapse in its early years, the Bank of Mexico, even more than other central banks, perceives its task as that of maintaining confidence in the financial system. Thus, the Bank of Mexico is particularly sensitive to the role of expectations. For example, the central bank stands ready to purchase virtually all fixed-income securities at par.[24] On the external side, the Bank of Mexico believes that, in view of the complete convertibility of the peso, the possibility of speculation has at times severely hampered the ability of the domestic financial system to attract funds. Therefore the central bank sees the public perception of the exchange risk as a constant threat to the stability of the domestic financial system and strongly supports a stable exchange rate.[25]

NOTES

1. Frank R. Brandenburg, *The Making of Modern Mexico* (Englewood Cliffs, N.J.: Prentice-Hall, 1959), pp. 141–165; and L. Vincent Padgett, "Mexico's One-Party System: A Re-evaluation," in *American Political Science Review*, Vol. LI (December 1957), pp. 995–1008.

2. The most systematic attempt to apply the concepts of political economy in explaining the long-term success of Mexico in promoting industrialization and economic development is Roger D. Hansen, *The Politics of Mexican Development* (Baltimore: Johns Hopkins University Press, 1971). A discussion of the motivations of Mexican officials can be found in chapters 5 and 6, pp. 97–163.

3. Political scientists differ over the exact distribution of power among the president, the ruling elite, and the bureaucracy. Nevertheless, there is wide agreement on the outlines of the power structure. For a review of ideas on the structure and some idea of the controversies over its functioning see: Carolyn Needleman and Martin Needleman, "Who Rules Mexico: A Critique of Some Current Views of the Mexican Political Process," in *The Journal of Politics*, Vol. XXXI (November 1969), pp. 1011–1034.

4. For a case study involving the government's decision to introduce profit-sharing for employees in private firms, see Susan Kaufman Purcell, "Decision Making in an Authoritarian Regime: Theoretical Implications from a Mexican Case," in *World Politics*, Vol. XXVI (October 1973), pp. 28–54.

5. Brandenburg, *op. cit.*, pp. 83–118.

6. Raymond Vernon, *The Dilemma of Mexico's Development* (Cambridge, Mass.: Harvard University Press, 1963), p. 12.

7. For a detailed statement of the revolutionary ideology, see Brandenburg, *op. cit.*, pp. 7–8.

8. Raymond W. Goldsmith, *The Financial Development of Mexico* (Paris: OECD Development Centre, 1966), p. 13.

9. For a defense of this point of view and a contrast with others see William B. Glade Jr., "Revolution and Economic Development," in *The Political Economy of Mexico*, William P. Glade and Charles W. Anderson (eds.), (Madison: The University of Wisconsin Press, 1963), pp. 11–12.

10. Oscar Lewis, "Mexico since Cárdenas," in *Social Change in Latin America Today* (New York: Vintage Books, 1966), pp. 320–347; and John J. Johnson, *Political Change in Latin America: The Emergence of the Middle Sectors* (Stanford, Calif.: Stanford University Press, 1965), pp. 128–154.

11. Xavier de la Riva Rodrígues, "Salubridad y Asistencia Médico-Social," in *México: Cincuenta Años de Revolución*, Vol. II, *La Vida Social* (Mexico: Fondo de Cultura Económica, 1961), pp. 383–443; and Miguel García Cruz, "La Seguridad Social," in *ibid.*, pp. 501–570.

12. Manning Nash, "Economic Nationalism in Mexico," in *Economic Nationalism in Old and New States*, Harry G. Johnson (ed.), (Chicago: University of Chicago Press, 1967), pp. 71–84.

13. For example, see: Needleman and Needleman, *op. cit.*, pp. 121–127; and Vernon, *op. cit.*, pp. 13–15.

14. Robert E. Scott, "Budget Making in Mexico," in *Inter-American Economic Affairs*, Vol. IX (Autumn 1955), pp. 8–12; Rafael Izquierdo, "Protectionism in Mexico," in *Public Policy and Private Enterprise in Mexico*, Raymond Vernon (ed.), (Cambridge, Mass.: Harvard University Press, 1964), p. 235; Charles W. Anderson, "Bankers as Revolutionaries," in *The Political Economy of Mexico*, William P. Glade and Charles P. Anderson (eds.), (Madison: University of Wisconsin Press, 1963), pp. 129–178; Miguel S. Wionczek, "Incomplete Formal Planning: Mexico," in *Planning Economic Development*, Everett E. Hagen (ed.), (Homewood, Ill.: Richard D. Irwin, Inc., 1963), pp. 150–181; and Frank R. Brandenburg, "Organized Business in Mexico," in *Inter-American Economic Affairs*, Vol. VII (Winter 1952), pp. 26–50.

15. Scott, *op. cit.*, pp. 4–8.

16. For discussion of the functions and organization of the Ministry of Finance, see Rosa María Tirado de Ruiz, "La Hacienda Pública y sus Funciones Económicas," in *Revista de Administración Pública*, No. 11 (January–March 1959), pp. 69–82; Jose Alvarado, "El Extraño Caso de la Secretaría de Hacienda," in *Problemas Agrícolas e Industriales de México*, Vol. V (January–March 1955), pp. 163–168.

17. Dwight S. Brothers and Leopoldo Solís M., *Mexican Financial Development* (Austin: University of Texas Press, 1966), pp. 52–71; and John E. Koehler, "Information and Policy-Making: Mexico," (unpublished Ph.D. dissertation, Economics Department, Yale University, 1967), pp. 12–16. Koehler uses a variety of statistical tests to reject the hypothesis of a stabilizing fiscal policy and also supports the existence of the "political cycle" in government spending that was intuitively accepted by Mexicans.

18. The process by which the authorities finance government spending will be discussed in a later chapter. For discussion of the importance of government spending see: Koehler, *op. cit.*, pp. 16–21; Gilberto Escobedo, "The Responsiveness of the Mexican Economy to Policy Action," in *Federal Reserve of St. Louis Review*, Vol. LX (July 1973), pp. 19–20; and B. Griffiths, *Mexican Monetary Policy and Economic Development* (New York: Praeger, 1972), pp. 22–29.

19. Raúl Martínez Ostos, "El Banco de México," in *Banca Central*, M. H. de

Kock (ed.), (Mexico: Fondo de Cultura Económica, 1970), pp. 392–396; Frank Tamagna, *La Banca Central en America Latina* (Mexico: CEMLA, 1963), pp. 500–509; and Koehler, *op. cit.*, pp. 61–62.

20. Virgil M. Bett, *Central Banking in Mexico: Monetary Policy and Financial Crises, 1864–1940* (Ann Arbor: University of Michigan Press, 1957), pp. 23–51. For a discussion of the founding of the Bank of Mexico amidst the collapse of the financial system, see: Rodrigo Gómez, speech at University of Chile, February 1958, in *Textos de Rodrigo Gómez* (Mexico, D.F.: Gráficas Panamericanas, 1967), p. 123.

21 *Ibid.*, pp. 60–62.

22. Koehler, *op. cit.*, pp. 34–40.

23. The techniques of monetary management will be explained in Chapter VII.

24. Martínez Ostos, *op. cit.*, pp. 401–405.

25. Rodrigo Gómez, speech to CEMLA participants (August 1957) in *Textos de Rodrigo Gómez*, pp. 107–108.

Chapter IV

Inflationary Development, 1946–1954

CONTINUED INFLATIONARY GROWTH

In the immediate postwar years, the growth of the Mexican economy continued to be characterized by heavy infrastructure spending financed by a generous expansion of bank credit. In 1946, Manuel Ávila Camacho was replaced as president by Miguel Alemán, who continued the general line of his predecessor's policies, with respect both to his lower priority given to social reform projects in favor of industrialization and the inflationary means of financing that program. The thrust of policy under Alemán was to foster the growth of domestic industry and capital formation. As Table IV-1 indicates, government capital outlays rose about twice as fast as real national income, which grew at slightly more than 6 percent annually.

At the same time the government adopted a distinctly pro-business outlook, partly out of a desire to foster industrialization and partly out of pure corruption. Owing to the extremely friendly attitude of the Alemán regime to domestic industrialists, the Mexican private sector flourished as the government provided a secure market and ample credit. The process of import-substituting industrialization that had begun spontaneously in World War II became an explicit objective of government policy. Through a combination of tax incentives, tariff protection, and credit, official policy sought to encourage the growth of domestic industry to satisfy demands that had hitherto been met by imports.[1] As a spur to industrialization, the Alemán administration sought to promote higher levels of investment.

Table IV - 1.

Public Expenditure Policies by Presidential Term, 1935 - 1952

(percentages)

Period	Annual growth rate of real public investment	Sectorial distribution of public investment				Social Progress[1]	Other
		Economic development					
		Total	Agriculture	Industry	Transport and com-munications		
Cárdenas 1935 - 1940	10.8	78	17	9	51	8	14
Ávila Camacho 1941 - 1946	8.6	78	16	10	52	13	9
Alemán 1947 - 1952	13.5	81	22	19	40	13	6

[1] Schools, hospitals, etc.

Source: Roberto Santillán López and Aniceto Rosas Figueroa, *Teoría General de las Finanzas Públicas y el Caso de México*, Appendices.

In this highly protected environment, a new generation of Mexican businessmen appeared, closely aligned with the government, and thus constituting an additional base of support for the ruling group. At the same time, the private sector developed basic managerial skills.[2] The public credit institutions, especially Nacional Financiera, gained the ability to engage in sectorial planning by identifying key sectors in the economy and directing credit and other resources to those sectors.[3]

Although the Alemán government is most identified with the policies of import substitution and industrialization, the country also made notable advances in agriculture and exports. Indeed, a satisfactory performance in these sectors allowed the country to pursue its other aims. The sizable investments in agriculture in earlier years paid off as real agricultural output grew at 6.5 percent per year between 1945 and 1952, roughly the same rate as the growth of national income. Unlike many Latin American countries where a stagnant agricultural sector held back growth as increases in income in other sectors merely led to higher food prices and rising food imports, Mexican agriculture was able to support the growth of other sectors by providing an elastic food supply and a source of support for the balance of payments. Rising agricultural production increasingly replaced previously imported goods and also provided export revenue.[4]

Although exports grew by less than during the Second World War they managed to keep pace with the growth of nominal income. Between 1946 and 1952 the value of visible exports grew by 14.9 percent yearly while total receipts on current account grew by an average annual rate of 11.9 percent. Visible exports grew in response to expanding output and generally firm prices for agricultural and mineral products, while tourism, border transactions, and workers' remittances provided the main source of invisible earnings. The export sector also received additional expansionary pushes in the period by the devaluations of the peso in 1948–1949 and by the boom in commodity prices following the outbreak of the Korean War in 1950.

INFLATIONARY FINANCE OF DEVELOPMENT

Since domestic investment, prodded by official policy, continued to expand well in excess of the possibilities of voluntary domestic savings, and since access to foreign capital was rather limited, Mexico's economic ex-

Table IV - 2

Distribution of Credit by Sectors, 1945 - 1952
(millions of pesos)

Year	Total Credit Out-standing	Total	Private sector						Public sector
			Total	Production		Mining	Foreign Trade	Domestic Trade	
				Industry	Agriculture				
1945	3,882.5	2,746.2	2,031.5	1,194.0	812.0	9.3	16.2	714.7	1,136.3
1946	4,689.0	3,349.0	2,497.3	1,646.9	791.7	16.7	42.0	851.7	1,340.0
1947	5,677.6	4,198.2	3,218.2	2,223.0	948.5	15.8	30.9	980.0	1,479.4
1948	6,906.8	5,020.9	3,895.6	2,850.8	986.4	15.4	43.0	1,125.3	1,885.9
1949	8,091.4	5,749.1	4,515.0	3,321.4	1,006.7	17.7	169.2	1,234.1	2,342.3
1950	8,858.0	6,689.2	5,018.1	3,664.5	1,150.2	23.7	179.7	1,671.1	2,168.8
1951	10,544.2	8,436.4	6,708.2	5,022.8	1,468.4	26.6	190.4	1,728.2	2,107.8
1952	11,570.4	9,327.2	7,423.4	5,482.8	1,729.8	20.5	190.3	1,903.8	2,243.2
Annual average rate of growth 1946 - 1952	20%	22%	24%	28%	14%	14%	50%	18%	12%

Source: **Bank of Mexico,** *Annual Report, 1954.*

pansion continued to be financed by inflation. The official monetary stance reflected the official desire to maintain the flow of resources to the economy rather than considerations of price stability. In 1948 and 1949, the Bank of Mexico introduced a system of "selective credit controls" under which reserve requirements were selectively applied to commercial banks according to the different categories of borrowers, thus giving the authorities an additional means of channeling credit to key sectors of the economy.[5] However, little was accomplished in restraining the overall growth of credit. Under Alemán, central bank financing of the budget deficit continued to expand rapidly. These injections of high-powered money into the system allowed for a rapid expansion of bank credit to the private sector. As Table IV-2 indicates, the rapid expansion of bank credit to the private sector was unrestrained, with industry receiving the biggest share.

Because monetary policy aimed at supplying credit for public spending and industrial expansion with little regard for stability, the money supply expanded rapidly, as shown in Table IV-3. In 1949 and 1950, foreign exchange inflows and increases in the peso value of foreign assets, both of which resulted from currency depreciation, contributed to the expansion of money supply. Since the rate of growth of the money supply was nearly three times faster than the rate of growth of real output, inflationary pressures remained intense, with wholesale prices rising by an average of 11.6 percent per year.

While the inflationary process proved disruptive in many aspects, it helped the authorities to fulfill their objective of growth. The problem that confronted the authorities was to finance ambitious public investment programs and growing private investment in agriculture and industry despite only small amounts of voluntary domestic savings. Only a limited amount of foreign resources were available in the form of direct private investment or official loans. However, plainly a considerable shift of resources from consumption to investment was occurring, as can be seen in Table IV-4.

Believing that there was little possibility of expanding domestic savings through financial markets, the effect of official policy was to promote forced savings through inflation. Such a policy implies a transfer of real income from those who are likely to consume to those who are likely to invest. In effect, this means a transfer of resources away from wage earners and other low-income groups to the industrialists and the state, pro-

Table IV - 3

Sources of Monetary Expansion, 1946 - 1952
(millions of pesos)

Year	External Factors[a]	Internal Factors[b]			Increase in assets of banking system	Money supply absorbed[c]	Net variation in money supply	Aggregate money supply (M1)	Wholesale prices 1950 = 100
		Total	Public sector	Private sector					
1946	..	..	..	..	..	..	..	3,514	73.5
1947	-460	1,010	185	825	550	-564	-14	3,500	77.8
1948	- 32	1,278	488	790	1,246	-752	494	3,994	83.4
1949	667	612	380	232	1,279	-781	498	4,492	91.4
1950	-1,512	'491	-166	657	2,003	-331	1,672	6,164	100.0
1951	-214	1,548	- 50	1,598	1,334	-551	783	6,947	124.0
1952	53	1,453	445	1,008	1,506	-1,179	327	7,274	128.6
Annual average increase 1946 - 1952		20%	12%	22%		—	—	16.8%	11.6%

a Change in peso value of foreign exchange holdings.
b Change in credit to public and private sector.
c Increase in nonmonetary liabilities of banking system.

Source: ECLA, Economic Survey of Latin America, 1953, and Bank of Mexico, Annual Reports.

Table IV - 4

Gross National Product and Gross Domestic Investment, 1939 - 1954
(million of pesos at 1950 prices, unless otherwise noted)

Year	Gross National Product Total	Gross National Product Increase	In %	Gross domestic investment	Investment as a percentage of GNP	Marginal capital output ratio[a]
1939	22,339	—		1,169	5.2	—
1940	22,588	249	1.1	1,600	7.1	—
1941	24,751	2,163	9.5	2,006	8.1	1.25
1942	26,291	1,540	6.2	1.728	6.6	1.14
1943	27,471	1,180	4.4	1,730	6.3	1.22
1944	29,676	2,205	8.0	2,206	7.4	1.47
1945	30,494	818	2.7	3,191	10.5	2.33
1946	32,319	1,825	5.9	4,391	13.6	3.00
1947	33,496	1,177	3.6	5,034	15.0	3.40
1948	34,987	1,491	4.5	4,712	13.5	3.07
1949	37,108	2,12	6.1	4,240	11.4	2.05
1950	40,577	3,469	9.3	4,828	11.9	1.66
1951	43,621	3,044	7.5	6,242	14.3	2.18
1952	45,366	1.745	4.0	6,483	14.3	4.52
1953	45,618	252	0.6	6,243	13.7	4.46
1954	50,391	4,773	10.5	6,509	12.9	2.02

[a] Adjusted by means of three year moving averages.
Source: Enrique Pérez López, "The National Product of Mexico, 1895 - 1964," in *Mexico's Recent Economic Growth,* p. 32.

vided that the state uses its increased share of income to promote investment. The inflationary financing of development involved the state bidding resources away from the private sector, using its power to issue unlimited quantities of money in exchange for real goods and revenue. Spending increased until real official expenditures reached the desired level with the private sector experiencing a loss of real income through price increases. At the same time, private industry increased savings in the form of reinvested earnings, as real wages lagged behind profits which rose in response to price increases. Such a strategy assumes that those whose real consumption falls have insufficient market power to maintain their real income shares. The possibility of financing economic development under these conditions was advanced by W. Arthur Lewis who hypothesized that in an economy with a large reserve of underemployed workers in agriculture or services, capitalists in the modern sector can attract an elastic supply of labor by offering a subsistence wage. Moreover, if inflation causes the real wage level to fall, business enterprises can increase profits and increase investment by reinvesting those profits. As the real wage level falls, real consumption falls; savings and investments are brought into balance at higher real levels, and a redistribution of income takes place.[6]

There is considerable evidence that what occurred in Mexico since 1940 closely followed the Lewis model. There are, unfortunately, insufficient data to directly estimate the real level of total wages, but virtually all indirect data support the conclusion that real wages were falling. The best measure of real wages, the level of minimum wages, points in that direction. According to the Constitution, the minimum wage is that level that is capable of sustaining a laborer and his family at a subsistence level. Minimum wages are revised every two years in order to offset increases in the cost of living. At present, there are 105 districts in Mexico, in which a commission made up of government, business, and labor representatives agree on minimum wage levels in their respective districts. In earlier years, procedures were more irregular, but the outlines of the system were essentially the same. Minimum wage laws are legally binding on all employers, but in fact, the laws are only enforced in large enterprises. Large numbers of workers in small businesses, household services, and agriculture earn less than the minimum wage. In 1974, the Minimum Wage Commission estimated that 80 percent of the labor force work for the minimum wage or less. In earlier years, the proportion was almost certainly higher.[7]

Table IV-5 shows the evolution of minimum wages in the period 1939–1965, both in nominal terms and in real terms deflated by the cost of living for Mexico City. As the table clearly shows, there was a marked tendency for real wages to fall through the early 1950s, with some improvement registered thereafter. In effect, the low-income classes were unable to defend their real wages throughout the 1940s and early 1950s, given the virtually elastic supply of unskilled and semiskilled labor.[8] In

Table IV - 5

Minimum Daily Wages, 1939 - 1965
(pesos)

Year	Current urban average	Current rural average	Urban average (1954 prices)	Rural average (1954 prices)
1939	1.81	1.28	8.58	6.07
1940	1.91	1.34	8.96	6.29
1941	1.91	1.34	8.64	6.06
1942	1.85	1.29	7.22	5.03
1943	1.85	1.29	5.52	3.85
1944	2.44	1.54	5.79	3.66
1945	2.44	1.54	5.41	3.41
1946	3.11	2.01	5.51	3.56
1947	3.11	2.01	4.89	3.17
1948	3.54	2.43	5.25	3.61
1949	3.54	2.43	4.99	3.42
1950	4.07	2.87	5.41	3.81
1951	4.07	2.87	4.79	3.38
1952	5.70	3.87	5.88	3.99
1953	5.70	3.87	5.97	4.06
1954	8.22	5.71	8.22	5.71
1955	8.22	5.71	7.08	5.78
1956	8.44	6.14	6.94	5.05
1957	8.44	6.14	6.56.	4.77
1958	9.84	7.11	6.87	4.96
1959	9.84	7.11	6.69	4.84
1960	11.73	8.46	7.60	5.48
1961	11.73	8.46	7.48	5.40
1962	14.30	9.79	9.02	6.17
1963	14.30	9.79	8.96	6.13
1964	17.98	12.72	11.02	7.80
1965	17.98	12.72	10.63	7.52

Source: King, *Mexico: Industrialization and Trade Policy*, p. 26.

addition, the Alemán Administration was actively pro-business, especially to businesses that were willing to collaborate with government. In order to increase profits, the government actively sought to keep wages down, at times using repression in an attempt to prevent the formation of powerful independent unions. The effect of government policy was to encourage capital formation by allowing price increases to lower real wages, thereby encouraging high profits and a high level of self-finance in Mexican enterprises.[9]

The effect of the decline in real wages was to make the distribution of income increasingly unequal. A number of studies of the distribution of income made at the time support the conclusion that the real wage level was falling and the distributional effect of government policy was extremely regressive.[10] The sharp increase in the investment share of national income registered in the decade also suggests that the income shares of lower income groups were diminishing. Indeed, it would be difficult to advance an alternative explanation for the rise in the investment share of national income that occurred in the 1940s.

Although the share of income of the least favored groups in society was shrinking, there were other developments in the economy which cushioned the impact of this development. In the first place, the level of real income was growing rapidly and many groups experienced a rise in absolute real income, along with a fall in the share of real income. Furthermore, owing to dynamic changes in the structure of employment, the level of total real earnings was increasing markedly even as the minimum wage was falling. There was a sizable migration from subsistence agriculture to more modern sectors that tended to increase total wages at the same time (See Table IV-6.) In addition, there was a general shift in the composition of employment to higher paying occupations.[11] Thus, there was a considerable increase in opportunity for upward mobility that partly compensated for the falling wage rate.

In discussing the inflationary finance of development, it is essential to draw a distinction between the Mexican inflation and that of other Latin American countries which also experienced persistent price increases. In most cases other than Mexico, inflation resulted from budget deficits that reflected excessive current government expenditures that mainly represented subsidies to consumption. These expenditures included items such as maintaining increasingly high levels of public sector employment and generous welfare payments. On a political level, these

Table IV - 6

Changing Occupational Structure of the Labor Force, 1940 - 1965

Year	Population and labor force (thousands)		Occupational distribution of labor force (percentages)							
	Population	Labor Force	Agriculture	Mining	Construction	Commerce	Transport	Service	Industry
1940	19,654	6,055	63	2	2	9	2	10	11
1950	25,791	8,345	58	1	3	8	3	15	12
1960	34,923	11,332	54	1	4	9	3	14	14
1965	42,689	13,427	51	1	4	10	4	14	15

Source: Nacional Financiera, *Statistics on the Mexican Economy:* and Dirección General de Estadística, *Anuario Estadístico Compendiado,* various issues.

spending programs usually resulted from pressures from trade unions and similar organized groups trying to maintain the real income shares of low income groups, especially urban workers, while governments were powerless to break the inflationary cycle.[12] In Mexico, on the other hand, inflation resulted from an accelerated investment program which was subsidized by reducing real consumption.[13] Politically, it displayed the strength of a government which was able to maintain itself in office despite a considerable and prolonged fall in real wage levels.

EXTERNAL IMBALANCE

Mexico's inflationary growth pattern, combined with the end of wartime conditions, immediately led to severe dislocations in the country's balance of payments. In the years following World War II, the balance of payments was characterized by a current account that tended toward deficit as excess demand led to sharply rising imports and inflation diverted resources away from exports to domestic consumption. At the same time, capital inflows were increasing but had not yet reached the magnitude where they could offset the current account deficit. (See Table IV-7.) Since no exchange controls existed, the only policy instruments available were import controls and devaluation.

The value of visible exports rose by an annual average rate of 9.9 percent between 1946 and 1954, with most of the growth concentrated between the end of the war and the Korean War boom of 1950–1952. As Table IV-8 shows, Mexican exports of goods were rather diversified, especially compared to the Latin American countries which usually depended upon one or two commodities for export receipts. The commodity composition of Mexican exports was constantly changing, with agricultural products gaining at the expense of minerals.[14] It is clear from the diverse composition of Mexican exports that there was considerable elasticity of export supply in response to relative price and exchange rate changes. (This will be demonstrated empirically in a later chapter.) A variety of products, especially foods and manufactured goods, could be exported or consumed domestically, therefore, the devaluations of 1948, 1949 and 1954 also stimulated export growth. Other goods might be imported or produced domestically.

Mexican imports, demand for which had been pent up during the war, rose sharply in volume with the removal of export controls in the

Table IV - 1

The Balance of Payments, 1946 - 1954
(millions of dollars)

	1946	1947	1948	1949	1950	1951	1952	1953	1954
I. Current Accounts Balance	-174	-166	- 56	53	40	-215	-107	-118	- 45
A. Exports of goods and services	570	714	716	701	827	918	984	964	1,048
1. Exports of goods	319	424	419	407	493	592	625	559	616
2. Tourism	86	81	87	100	111	111	115	109	86
3. Border transactions	66	66	107	86	122	148	163	202	247
4. Workers remittances	34	29	22	18	19	30	29	34	28
5. Other	16	54	26	41	31	23	22	23	24
B. Imports of goods and services	744	880	772	648	787	1,133	1,090	1,082	1,094
1. Imports of goods	601	720	591	514	597	889	829	808	789
2. Border transactions	50	50	79	49	77	88	102	128	162
3. Investment income	58	75	64	51	66	102	108	83	75
4. Debt service	2	3	6	10	11	10	10	11	11
5. Other	19	18	20	19	27	32	29	36	42
II. Capital Account	21	68	33	19	130	126	75	54	63
A. Long-term	49	71	24	37	70	99	85	53	112
1. Direct investment	38	62	33	31	72	121	68	42	93
2. Development credits (net)	33	23	7	17	11	14	43	33	41
3. Other	- 22	- 14	- 16	- 11	- 13	- 36	- 26	- 22	- 49
B. Short-term	- 29	- 3	9	- 38	60	27	- 9	1	- 49
III. Errors and omissions	52	- 12	- 17	- 27	2	82	11	23	-144
IV. Changes in official reserves	-100	-111	- 41	45	172	- 8	- 21	- 42	- 26
V. Level of official reserves[e] (end of year)	256	145	104	149	321	314	293	251	225

[e] estimated.
Source: Banco de México, S.A.

75

Table IV - 8

Commodity Composition of Exports, 1945 - 1948
(percent of total)

Minerals	61.9
Base metals	38.7
Petroleum	15.1
Gold and silver	8.1
Agricultural products	31.3
Henequen	3.5
Coffee	3.4
Cotton	6.0
Raw hides	0.2
Cattle	0.1
Vegetables	0.1
Miscellaneous	18.0
Industrial products	5.0
Chemical and	
pharmaceutical products	0.2
Textiles	3.6
Miscellaneous	1.2
Other	1.8
Hardwoods	0.6
Chicle	0.7
Miscellaneous	0.5

Source: ECLA, *Economic Survey of Latin America,* 1949.

United States. In addition, the removal of price controls in the United States in 1946 sharply raised the price of Mexican imports. In 1946, there was not only an increase in import volume, but the total value of imports increased strikingly. In response to the deterioration in the trade balance, as well as to domestic pressures, the government introduced measures in 1947 which raised tariffs and prohibited the import of many items. The list of controlled imports was constantly adjusted thereafter, and import controls thus became a major policy tool.[15] Imports dropped following the 1948–1949 devaluation and began rising again in 1950. Consumer goods represented a declining proportion of imports, while raw materials and capital goods represented an increasingly larger share.

Spending by tourists, mainly from the United States, and the remittances of Mexican seasonal workers in the United States also represented considerable net inflows. The Mexican balance of payments also contains an item called "border transactions" in which there is a sizable two-way trade. On the debit side, this account reflects mainly purchases of relatively cheaper goods, especially consumer durables, by Mexican residents living in border areas who are exempt from import restrictions. On the credit side, it reflects the items purchased in Mexican border towns by U.S. residents of those Mexican goods and services which are relatively cheaper.

Capital inflows were small, but growing in importance. Direct investment grew as import-substituting policies and high rates of return on investment opened up possibilities for foreign investors, both independently and in joint ventures with Mexican capital. Similarly, the borrowings for economic development projects by the public sector, especially Nacional Financiera, began to increase in importance. That institution started borrowing from the Eximbank in 1942 and from the IBRD in 1948. Net short-term capital flows were small, and tended to be negative at times of general instability, specifically when devaluation seemed possible. Errors and omissions, which included smuggling and unrecorded short-term capital movements, also tended to turn sharply negative when the Mexican currency appeared overvalued.

As a result of the tendency toward deficit, reserves were under constant pressure following the end of the war, when the United States listed controls on exports and later removed price controls. Imports almost doubled between 1945 and 1947, thus moving the current account balance into deficit. The tightening of import controls in 1947 and 1948 reduced imports somewhat, and net capital inflows, especially those representing direct foreign investment, increased somewhat. Nonetheless, the balance of payments as a whole was in deep deficit.

By mid-1948, most of the international reserves accumulated during World War II were lost, and the nation experienced its first postwar balance of payments crisis. In June 1948 the Bank of Mexico had to abandon support of the peso in the exchange market.[16] (See Table IV-9.) Owing to the low level of reserves, the exchange rate continued to float downward for several months. There were some attempts to support the rate late in 1948, but when pressures intensified in early 1949, the central bank once again stepped aside and allowed the rate to depreciate further.[17] The authorities consulted with the International Monetary Fund in order to arrive at an appropriate exchange rate for the peso. In view of the continued inflationary policies being pursued in Mexico, the Fund argued that the exchange rate should have been undervalued in anticipation of future price increases, suggesting a parity of ten pesos per dollar. The government, however, decided that since devaluation was an unpopular political step, the rate would be fixed where it was floating at 8.65 per U.S. dollar.[18] On June 17, 1949, the monetary authorities fixed a new parity of 8.65 pesos per dollar and began supporting this rate in the exchange market. The new parity represented a devaluation of 78.4 percent in terms of dollars from the pre-1948 rate.[19]

Table IV - 9

Exchange Rates for the Mexican Peso, 1948 - 1949
(monthly averages, pesos per U.S. dollar)

	1948	1949
January	4.859	6.879
February	4.857	6.969
March	4.859	6.974
April	4.857	6.998
May	4.859	8.062
June	4.859	8.218
July	6.450	8.645
August	6.835	8.647
September	6.893	8.641
October	6.893	8.642
November	6.892	8.641
December	6.879	8.640

Source: Bank of Mexico, *Annual Report, 1950.*

Although the fluctuations in demand in the United States may have aggravated the situation, the devaluation resulted from inflationary finance of Mexico's development program. The increases in money supply contributed directly to the imbalance on current account by raising demand for imports and making Mexican goods less competitive with imports. Furthermore, since excess demand resulted in higher prices in Mexico than in the United States, it also tended to widen the current account deficit by shifting resources away from the export sector. The incentive to export was reduced as domestic purchasers competed with foreign demand for Mexican goods. The devaluation, on the other hand, strengthened Mexico's competitive advantage, thus leading to a considerable expansion of exports and a contraction of imports.

As the foregoing discussion implies, the policy instruments available to Mexican authorities were limited. Deflationary demand management policies were ruled out as incompatible with the domestic goal of growth. The authorities in Mexico had also decided as a matter of long-term policy not to employ exchange controls. The thinking of Mexican officialdom concerning exchange controls has long been the same. As early as 1939, the Bank of Mexico had stated that exchange controls require such strict surveillance of individual behavior and close scrutiny of virtually every transaction as to make such a system intolerable.[20] Most Mexican officials believe that, given the long unpatrolled border with the United States, an unmanageable black market in dollars would inevitably emerge. Nearly half of current account transactions consists of invisibles, the most difficult kind of transaction to police. In addition, Mexican visible exports are highly diversified. The closeness of the United States already gave rise to a considerable problem of smuggling of goods. Exchange controls or multiple exchange rates would increase corruption without stemming outflows of dollars. Furthermore, the complete convertibility of the peso is viewed as a positive achievement. Although capital flight has been a problem at times of uncertainty, Mexico has avoided the constant outflows of flight capital that have plagued many Latin American countries that have exchange controls. To be sure, some economists from outside official circles have from time to time advocated exchange controls.[21] The majority of Mexican officials, however, remain unconvinced, whatever their views on other policy issues.

Nor could international credits be used to defend the peso. The resources available in addition to the country's international reserves, the IMF credit *tranche,* and the standby agreement with the U.S. Treasury were inadequate in the face of the fundamental disequilibrium of the Mexican balance of payments. The total Mexican borrowing facility in the IMF credit then was $113 million, of which the authorities had already drawn $23 million available under the automatic gold *tranche* facility.[22] In order to qualify for further credit, the authorities would have had to agree to an IMF-sponsored stabilization program, including an agreement to reduce expenditure which was unacceptable to the government.[23] In 1947, Mexico concluded a "swap" agreement with the U.S. Treasury for $50 million, under the Exchange Stabilization Fund, and by 1948 the Mexicans had drawn $37 million from this fund.[24] Thus, the possibility of defending the peso with the support of credits from foreign governments or international institutions was likewise extremely limited.

The 1948–1949 experience of an uncontrolled depreciation deeply impressed Mexican financial policy makers, especially in the Bank of Mexico. The lack of exchange controls exposed the vulnerability of the peso to movements of short-term capital. Once a movement against the peso had begun, the central bank could only supply all dollars demanded in the market or allow the exchange rate to depreciate, while the lack of foreign lines of credit left the country with narrowly circumscribed resources to withstand pressures on the exchange rate. Thus, once the margin for tightening import restrictions was exhausted, the only available policy option was an adjustment in the exchange rate. Furthermore, virtually the entire adjustment had to be made on current account. The exchange-rate adjustment had to be large enough to push the current account back into surplus. The problem can be restated in terms of national income analysis by saying that domestic investment in excess of domestic savings could only be sustained by drawing down past savings in the form of reserves. When the latter were depleted, a cycle of building up savings through a current account surplus was necessary in preparation for another period of investment in excess of domestic savings.

Domestic policy remained essentially the same after the 1949 repegging of the peso. As a result, the same kind of pressures that led to the 1948 devaluation began to reappear. The growth of demand for imports intensified, and the current account, which has been in surplus in 1949 and 1950, moved back into deficit. The process of inflationary growth in Mexico was clearly leading to renewed balance of payments pressures, which culminated in the devaluation of the peso in 1954.

DEVALUATION AS AN EXPANSIONARY POLICY INSTRUMENT

Although the depreciation of the exchange rate created problems for Mexican officials it was a logical extension of domestic policies which included a rapid rate of export growth and a rapid increase in investment generated by inflation. Inflationary domestic policy required a willingness to accept exchange-rate adjustments. Inflation led to excess domestic consumption and a diversion of goods from export markets, as reflected in the current account deficit. By shifting resources away from domestic consumption back to the export sector, devaluation allowed the country to increase exports as a means of stimulating the further growth of the economy. At the same time, it gave an added measure of protection to domestic industry, which was another major objective. More generally, by stimulating both the export and import-substituting sectors, it aided the process of capital formation.

Taken as a whole, the exchange-rate policy that Mexico pursued was the most suitable, given the country's pattern of growth. Just as the Mexican inflation, which promoted investment, contrasts with those of South American countries, where inflation resulted from government spending subsidies to consumption, such as transfer payments or support of large amounts of workers on the public payrolls, the policy of devaluation stands in sharp contrast to the exchange-rate practices of those countries. The policy, pursued by many South American countries, of maintaining overvalued exchange rates, coupled with exchange controls, subsidized consumption, drained income away from the export sector, and thus retarded capital formation. While these policy instruments may have been necessary on political grounds, since they softened working-class hostility to government policy, they also resulted in economic stagnation. Thus, in retrospect, the policy of devaluation appears to have fitted in perfectly with Mexico's other policy instruments and objectives.

However, while Mexico's policy of inflationary growth coupled with devaluation made a great deal of sense on purely economic grounds, it was bound to arouse the hostility of those whose real incomes were reduced. For as will be argued in the next chapter, the internal struggle over income shares was a critical factor in the authorities decision to change their policy.

NOTES

1. Tomme Clark Call, *The Mexican Venture* (New York: Oxford University Press, 1953), pp. 39–44; Timothy King, *Mexico: Industrialization and Trade Policies Since 1940* (London: Oxford University Press, 1970), pp. 32–35; and Saúl Trejo Reyes, "Los Patrones del Crecimiento Industrial y la Sustitución de Importaciones en México," in *La Economía Mexicana* Leopoldo Solís (ed.), Vol. I. *Análisis por Sectores y Distribución* (Mexico: Fondo de Cultura Económica, 1973), pp. 152–161.

2. Sanford A. Mosk, *Industrial Revolution in Mexico* (Berkeley: University of California Press, 1950), pp. 32–53 and 109–173.

3. Oscar Fraustro, "Nacional Financiera, S.A.," in *Revista de Administración Pública*, No. 5 (January–March 1957), pp. 19–28; and Calvin P. Blair, "Nacional Financiera: Entrepreneurship in a Mixed Economy," in *Public Policy and Private Enterprise in Mexico*, Raymond Vernon (ed.), pp. 211–240; Daniel Carl Falkowski, "Nacional Financiera, S.A., de México: A Study of a Development Bank," (unpublished Ph.D. dissertation, Department of Economics, New York University, 1972).

4. ECLA, *Economic Survey of Latin America, 1949* (E/CN. 12/164/Rev. 1, January 1951), (New York, 1951), pp. 391–400 and pp. 432–455; Carlos Tello, "El Sector Agrícola y el Desarrollo Económico de los Paises Latinoamericanos," in *El Trimestre Económico*, Vol. XXXII (January–March 1965), pp. 89–116; Leopoldo Solís, "Inflacíon, Estabilidad y Desarrollo: El Caso de México," in *El Trimestre Económico*, Vol. XXV (July–September 1968), pp. 487–504; Horacio Flores de La Pena, "La Mecánica del Desarrollo Económico," in *Revista de Economía*, Vol. XXV (August 1962), pp. 301–302; Richard W. Parks, "The Role of Agriculture in Mexican Economic Development," in *Inter-American Economic Affairs*, Vol. XVIII (Autumn 1964), pp. 3–27; and F. Dovring, "Papel de la Agricultura dentro de las Poblaciones en Crecimiento: Mexico, Un Caso de Desarrollo Reciente," in *El Trimestre Económico,* Vol. XXXV (January-March 1968), pp. 25–50.

5. Brothers and Solís, *op cit.*, pp. 72–78; and Mario Ramón Beteta, "The Central Bank: Instrument of Economic Development in Mexico," in *Mexico's Recent Economic Growth*, Tom E. Davi (ed.) (Austin: University of Texas Press, 1967), pp. 71–87.

6. "Economic Development with Unlimited Supplies of Labour," in *Manchester School of Economic and Social Studies*, Vol. XXII (May, 1954), pp. 139–191. For

a discussion of the general problem of development finance, see: Lester D. Thorow, "Development Finance in Latin America: Basic Principles," in *Financing Development in Latin America,* Keith Griffin (ed.), (London: Macmillan, 1970), pp. 26–50. For a specific treatment of inflationary finance, see: Rosemary Thorp, "Inflation and the Financing of Economic Development," in *ibid.,* pp. 182–224.

7. Interview with Saúl Trejo Reyes, Technical Director, National Commission of Minimum Wages, April 24, 1974.

8. For example see: Emilio Mujica M., "Los Salarios en la Industria," in *Revista de Economía,* Vol. XV (September 1952), pp. 276–284. The author discusses the decline of wages resulting from urban under-employment and migration of unskilled and semiskilled labor from subsistence agriculture. The Bank of Mexico conducted a survey of its own wage levels and those of some major financial and industrial institutions and found that wage increases tended to lag significantly behind price increases in the 1940s and late 1950s. Interview with Sergio Ghigliazza, Assistant Director of Economic Research, Bank of Mexico, March 22, 1974.

9. Hansen, *op. cit.,* pp. 113–116.

10. Adolf Sturmthal, "Economic Development, Income Distribution and Capital Formation in Mexico," in *Journal of Political Economy,* Vol. LXIII (June 1955), pp. 187–197; and I. M. de Navarrete, *La Distribución del Ingreso y el Desarrollo Económico de México* (Mexico: Universidad Nacional Autónoma de México, 1960), pp. 55–100. Navarrete and Sturmthal use data from the World Bank study of 1953 which showed a sharp decline in the share of wages and salaries in national income along with a sharp rise in the share of profits and other forms of investment income. Although the reliability of the data has been challenged, the authors conclude that there has been a significant redistribution of income shares away from low income groups. Also see: Hansen, *loc. cit.;* the author uses Bank of Mexico data to show that the results of economic growth in terms of income distribution has generally been regressive.

11. Diego G. López Rosado and Juan F. Noyola Vásquez, "Los Salarios Reales en México: 1939–1950," in *El Trimestre Económico,* Vol. XVIII (April–June 1951), pp. 205–209; King, *op. cit.,* pp. 25–30; and Horacio Flores de la Pena and Aldo Ferrer, "Salarios Reales y Desarrollo Económico," in *El Trimestre Económico,* Vol. XVIII, (October–December 1951), pp. 617–628.

12. For some case studies, see: David C. Redding, "The Economic Decline of Uruguay," in *Inter-American Economic Affairs,* Vol. XX (Spring 1967), pp. 55–72; John Thompson, "Argentine Economic Policy under the Ongania Regime," in *Inter-American Economic Affairs,* Vol. XXIV (Summer 1970), pp. 51–75; Roberto T. Alemann, "Argentina," in *Economic Development Issues: Latin America* (New York: Committee for Economic Development Supplementary Paper No. 21,

1967), pp. 1–58; Tom E. Davis, "Eight Decades of Inflation in Chile, 1879–1959: A Political Interpretation," in *Journal of Political Economy,* Vol. LXXI (August 1963), pp. 389–397; and G. Maynard and W. Van Rijckeghem, "Argentina, 1967–70: A Stabilization Attempt that Failed," in *Banca Nazionale del Lavoro Quarterly Review,* No. 103, (December, 1972), pp. 396–412.

13. For a discussion of the sole of inflation in Mexican economic development, see Leopoldo Solís, "Inflación, Estabilidad y Desarrollo: El Caso de México," pp. 483–516. The hypothetical possibility of inflation promoting economic development by reducing real consumption is considered in Martin Bronfenbrenner and F. D. Holzman, "Survey of Inflation Theory," in *American Economic Review,* Vol. LIII (February, 1966), pp. 609–613. For a further discussion of the possibility of raising investment and productivity through an inflationary redistribution of income, see Nicholas Kaldor, "Economic Growth and the Problem of Inflation," Parts I and II in *Económica,* Vol. XXVI (August 1959 and September 1959), pp. 212–226 and 287–298.

14. Timothy D. Sweeney, "The Mexican Balance of Payments, 1947–50," in *IMF Staff Papers,* Vol. III (April 1953), p. 133.

15. *Ibid.,* pp. 143–147.

16. Bank of Mexico, *Annual Report 1949,* p. 13.

17. The Mexican authorities and some nonofficial economists have portrayed the 1948 devaluation as part of the worldwide series of parity adjustments that took place in that year. For example, see Bank of Mexico *Annual Report 1949,* pp. 9–15. This was only true inasmuch as the authorities, noting the actions of other countries, decided to act at that time. The fact that the decision to float downward occurred in response to an exhaustion of reserves strongly suggests that the move was in reality forced upon the authorities by pressing circumstances. Their inability to defend a new rate further suggests that the authorities were acting under pressures beyond their control.

18. Antonio Carrillo Flores, *Homenajes y Testimonios* (Mexico: By the author, 1967), pp. 145–147. For contemporary views of the devaluation, see John S. De Beers, "El Peso Mexicano, 1941–1949," in *Problemas Agrícolas e Industriales de México,* Vol. V. (January–March, 1953); Enrique Padilla, "La Devaluación del Peso Mexicano: Cuatro Conferencias," in *El Trimestre Económico,* Vol. XV (October–December 1948), pp. 396–412; Anibal de Iturbide, "La Devaluación del Peso Mexicano y sus Antedentes," in *Revista de Economía,* Vol. XI (August 1948); Virgil Salera, "The Depreciation of the Mexican Peso," in *Inter-American Economic Affairs,* Vol. III (Autumn 1949); and Elaine Tanner, "The Devaluation of the Mexican Peso," in *Inter-American Economic Affairs,* Vol. III (Summer 1949).

19. Bank of Mexico, *Annual Report 1950,* pp. 29–30.

20. Bank of Mexico, *Annual Report 1939,* p. 18.

21. For example, see Alberto Noriega Herrera, "Posibilidad de Establecer Controles de Cambio en México" Thesis: Escuela Nacional de Economía, Universidad Nacional Autónoma de México, 1965.

22. IMF, *International Financial Statistics* (1972 Supplment).

23. Rodrigo Gómez, *Economic Growth and Monetary Stability* (Washington: The Per Jacobson Foundation, 1964), p. 30.

24. Bank of Mexico, *Annual Report 1948,* p. 20.

Chapter V

The Transition from Inflation to Stability

After successfully implementing the techniques of inflationary finance for nearly two decades, Mexico in the years following the 1954 devaluation completely changed its pattern of economic development. The country turned from an inflationary domestic financial system accompanied by depreciation of the peso to a domestic financial system that depended on domestic price stability and a stable exchange rate for its efficient operation. There was no single reason for this change of policy. A whole constellation of forces, some economic and others political, some within Mexico and others in the world economy, were at work, which made the change of policy both necessary and feasible.

Inflation was eroding real wages. Therefore, the less privileged classes were bearing a disproportionate share of the burden of Mexican growth. The decline of the purchasing power of the working class was becoming a divisive political issue that threatened to undermine the legitimacy of the regime which depended in part upon its image of reaching across class lines. As a result, the government decided that the inflationary course of action was both socially intolerable and politically dangerous. At the same time, the country's most important financial officials became convinced that alternative sources of savings could be found to support an economic development program. Provided the proper policies were introduced, higher domestic savings could be mobilized through a dynamic financial system while foreign savings in the form of long-term loans from international lending agencies could be raised. Two official institutions concerned with stability and the planning of economic development—the Bank of Mexico and the Nacional Financiera—

gained increasingly prominent roles in policy-making. The need for foreign capital was especially acute. In the 1950s, Mexico suffered deterioration of its terms of trade; therefore, new sources of foreign exchange were essential as the national interest was increasingly defined in terms of price stability. The efforts to restructure the system of development finance were enhanced by the long-term growth of the power of the central government relative to local political leaders and the private sector.

THE POLICY DEBATE

Mexican economists and policy-makers, who tried to conceptualize the problem of development finance and propose solutions, were pulled in two opposite directions. Conventional economic thinking backed by the experience of the developed countries asserted that growth ought to take place in a context of price stability, and that the financial system should be able to efficiently transfer the savings of the community to investors. Moreover, a dynamic and highly competitive private sector could be the leading factor in economic growth. On the other hand, the hard experience of the previous twenty years seemed to suggest that inflation and devaluation had efficiently worked to increase investment beyond the capability of voluntary savings. In addition, there was a wide disenchantment with the workings of the market economy, which had generated wealth for foreigners and for a limited number of Mexicans but left the majority still locked into subsistence agriculture and urban underemployment.[1] Formidable barriers on the external side, such as the decline in the terms of trade after the Korean War boom and the paucity of foreign development lending, further eroded confidence in the desirability of leaving development to the free play of market forces. The policy debate became extremely sharp in the period of the 1954 devaluation.

The disappointment with market-oriented patterns of development was not confined to Mexico. During this period, the so-called "structuralist" school of thought achieved widespread acceptance in Latin America. Basically, the structuralists argued that the monopoly power of powerful entrenched groups in Latin America made economic performance unresponsive to conventional policy instruments. The backwardness prevailing in the region including the unequal distribution of income, the lack of basic infrastructure and the low level of popular consciousness all stood in the way of development by creating inelasticities of supply that made the economy unresponsive to changes in demand management. Because of inelasticities of supply, increases in demand led to price rather than real income increases.

On the financial side, the structuralists argued that there was little possibility of directing existing savings to productive investment through policies aimed at developing financial markets. The observed preference of Latin American wealth holders for real goods and foreign exchange was attributed to historical experiences that had produced a defensive risk-averting mentality. The structuralists argued that savings were inelastic with respect to yields on financial assets. Savings were, in any case, unlikely to be channeled to sectors where needs were most critical. The continued or even accelerated growth of the economy along traditional lines would merely enrich the traditionally favored sectors and leave most of the population still outside the mainstream of economic activity. Therefore, the state had to appropriate resources and direct them into the most socially useful fields. In the long run, development could be attained by overcoming bottlenecks in the economy through investments in human and physical capital to transform the structure of the economy. Since savings, either in the form of voluntary domestic savings or foreign capital flows, were inadequate to finance development, the structuralists postulated a fundamental and inevitable "development disequilibrium" resulting from efforts to foster needed investment aimed at changing the structure of the economy and the lack of real resources that could be mobilized through conventional means. The result of the development disequilibrium was inevitably inflation. Mexican structuralists cited the Mexican public works spending program as the main case in point. The program had produced inflation and currency depreciation, but had nonetheless been indispensable in providing a basis for the development of the country. Inflationary spending was also likely to create balance-of-payments disequilibrium by generating excess demand for foreign exchange. Accordingly, the structuralists usually advocated exchange controls. In addition, the structuralists held that a long-term trend for the terms of trade of producers of raw materials tended to aggravate the existing "development disequilibrium." Imports, especially of capital goods for economic development, grew with national income, while the prices of raw materials tended to stagnate or fall.[2]

The structuralist hypothesis of a structural gap between the requirements of economic development and the potenial for noninflationary finance was not merely a matter of academic concern. Although the structuralists tended to be younger men entering government service, the monetarist-structuralist split existed at all levels of the bureaucracy. Moreover, every man who had served as Finance Minister between 1926 and 1952 publicly took a position in the debate on inflationary finance.

The most prominent official advocate of inflationary development was Eduardo Suárez who, as Finance Minister from 1935–46, was responsible for the inflationary policies of Cárdenas and Ávila Camacho. In 1951, he advanced a theory of "productive inflation" in which he argued that owing to the low elasticity of savings there was no other means of continuing economic growth:

> Contrary to the way of thinking of those who argue that an economy without stable money is abnormal, there is another opinion which is gaining in prestige. Money has a much more important role than a means of payment and a yardstick of value. Although it does not constitute investment, it is, in our present society, the means of creating it. If because of a lack of savings, unemployment should appear and resources are underutilized, it is legitimate and even necessary to create money; by means of the printing press, if need be—even if this implies a rise in the price level. For it would be a far greater evil for society to accept a waste of human resources and impoverishment. . . . When the country has achieved a certain degree of industrial development, this will permit on the one hand an increase of individual savings and on the other hand higher tax revenues with which it will be possible to finance a program of public investment with real resources.[3]

On the other side of the debate on inflation, many economists and government officials, often called "monetarists," believed that price stability was compatible with a high rate of growth and that inflation was preventing the country from attaining other important national objectives. The monetarists argued that inflation and accompanying currency depreciation were causing a persistent fall in the standard of living of the least privileged classes, and that this method of promoting development was both unacceptable and socially dangerous.[4] (The structuralists agreed that inflation had effectively worked against low-income groups, but favored controls and subsidies to offset the worst effects of inflation.)

The second major "monetarist" criticism of inflationary policy was that, in an environment of stability, voluntary savings could be mobilized to support development; but constant inflation and devaluation of the peso had made the development of efficient financial markets impossible, since investment in Mexican financial assets was not competitive with alternative outlets for investment. The better-off classes in Latin America tended to invest in socially unproductive assets such as real estate and foreign exchange, not because of any psychological peculiarities, but because official policy had undermined the proper development of financial markets. Investment had flowed into real estate, a hedge against price increases because inflation had made yields on financial assets low or even negative in real terms. Similarly, Mexicans tended to place funds in dollar-denominated assets because experience had shown that with constant depreciation of the peso, those who placed their holdings in dollars had obtained higher yields than those who held pesos. An additional problem was the difference in yields within the capital market. Even with inflation (and indeed partly because of inflation), investors could obtain large returns from direct investment, despite the low or negative return on investment in financial assets. The total level of investment, according to the monetarists, had to be raised by reducing inflation and thereby encouraging the development of indirect investment through financial markets.

The balance-of-payments problem, in the monetarist framework, resulted from the creation of excess demand which in turn led to rising imports, weakened the competitive position of Mexican exports, and caused a constant outflow of Mexican capital as the public correctly foresaw the need for devaluation. The monetarists believed that as long as the public could profit from devaluation by placing funds abroad, the domestic financial system would remain weak and the balance of payments would be unstable.[5]

The devaluation of 1954 intensified the debate over inflation.[6] The government received criticism from both sides in the monetarist-structuralist controversy, with the monetarists arguing that inflation was unnecessary and that devaluation was an inevitable consequence of the government's policy, while the structuralists contended that inflation was inevitable, but that the devaluation again demonstrated the need for exchange controls.[7] The devaluation revealed divisions within the ruling group and at all levels of government. The debate among former finance ministers grew more intense. Indeed, the very fact that high officials were placing themselves in public opposition to official policy is a measure of the discord that existed.

To be sure, the debate over the issues concealed a great deal of the political preferences of individual debaters and was partly a reflection of former officials trying to defend their performance while in office.[8] Nevertheless, there were important conceptual and policy questions at issue. Specifically, the structuralists claimed that demand for financial assets was inelastic with respect to yields on financial assets, and hence the country could either pursue inflationary policies and introduce exchange controls or accept stagnation. The monetarists, on the other hand, held that the portfolio decisions of the public would change in response to a rise in returns on real assets and that the resulting development of the financial markets and the additional foreign resources available would allow the country to maintain a high rate of growth with price and balance of payments stability. As will be seen in another chapter, in the later experience of Mexico, private sector holdings of financial assets rose as a result of the introduction of price stability and the country thereby was able to maintain growth with stability.

One of the essential points in the argument over external imbalance was the structuralists' claim that devaluation was ineffective as a policy instrument. The structuralists held that the current account balance changed in response to external demand and the growth of income in Mexico, rather than to relative prices in Mexico and the outside world.[9] This became a lively issue after the 1954 devaluation. Specifically, it was charged that the devaluation resulted from decreased world demand for Mexican exports stemming from the 1953 recession in the United States, and that the end of the recession rather than the devaluation was the major reason for the improvement in the current account balance that followed the devaluation. The view was widespread that the devaluation was an overreaction by the authorities to speculation and pressures from export interests and that, owing to the excellent harvests that were already forecast, the devaluation could have been avoided.[10]

In addition to specific criticism of the 1954 devaluation, many structuralists questioned the overall effectiveness of devaluation as a means of achieving balance of payments equilibrium. The best-known exposition of this view was the 1957 report of ECLA on external disequilibrium in Mexico, which contended that external imbalance resulted from the changes in the structure of the Mexican economy coupled with a tendency toward deterioration in the terms of trade, rather than from inflationary policies in Mexico.[11] The study took 1937 as a base year, since the peso had been floating freely for a prolonged period, and used the concept of the purchasing power parity theorem. The ECLA calculations are shown in Table V-1. As the table shows, although prices had generally risen faster in Mexico than in the United States, devaluation had more than offset the difference in price increases, and therefore the Mexican peso had in fact been undervalued on a basis of simple purchasing power parity in all but four years between 1937 and 1955. In other words, Mexico had a tendency towards external disequilibrium over and above that which could be explained by relative price increases. The document, therefore, concluded that rising and inelastic Mexican demand for capital goods, coupled with falling demand for Mexican exports, was the fundamental cause of the long-term depreciation of the peso. Thus the ECLA report contained the three elements of the structuralist position in the debate over exchange-rate policy: the terms of trade argument, the inelasticity argument and the resulting conclusion of the ineffectiveness of devaluation as a policy tool.

An official spokesman, Josué Saenz, attempted to refute the argument on two essential points.[12] He pointed out that, in the period between 1937 and 1955, the Mexican balance of payments had experienced several swings from surplus to deficit and back again, thus indicating that the currency may have at times been undervalued and at other times overvalued. Yet, the ECLA study showed the peso as constantly undervalued. Moreover, he questioned the validity of calculating a purchasing power parity over a period of nineteen years, which neglected the importance of dynamic change in the economy. Even using the methodology of the ECLA projections, Saenz still found room for disagreement. He used 1941, the first full year since the Depression in which the peso was fixed, as a more recent base for estimating the evolution of relative purchasing power. (See Table V-2.) With this new index, the peso appeared constantly overvalued, and thus the devaluation was a proper response to the overvaluation. Even after the 1954 devaluation, the degree of undervaluation was so slight as to leave the balance of payments

Table V - 1

ECLA Calculation of Mexican Purchasing Power Parity

Year	Price Index (1937=100)		Exchange Rate (pesos per dollar)			Index of under/ or overvaluation of the peso
	Mexico	U.S.	Relation (A) (B)	Existing (C)	Equilibrium (C/100)3.60 (E) (D)	(E) (D)
	(A)	(B)	(C)	(D)	(E)	(F)
1937	100	100	100.0	3.60	3.60	100.0
1938	106	91	116.5	4.52	4.19	92.7
1939	107	89	120.2	5.18	4.33	83.6
1940	108	91	118.7	5.40	4.27	79.1
1941	114	101	112.9	4.86	4.06	83.5
1942	125	114	109.6	4.85	3.95	81.4
1943	153	119	128.6	4.85	4.63	95.5
1944	191	121	157.9	4.85	5.68	117.1
1945	208	123	169.1	4.86	6.09	125.3
1946	240	140	171.4	4.86	6.17	127.0
1947	254	176	144.3	4.86	5.19	116.8
1948	272	191	142.4	5.73	5.13	89.5
1949	298	180	165.6	8.01	5.96	74.4
1950	326	189	172.5	8.64	6.21	71.9
1951	404	209	193.3	8.65	6.96	80.5
1952	419	302	206.4	8.63	7.43	86.1
1953	411	201	204.4	8.62	7.35	85.3
1954	450	201	223.9	11.53	8.06	69.9
1955	511	201	254.2	12.49	9.15	73.3

Source: ECLA, *El Desequilibrio Externo en el Desarrollo Latino-americano,* Vol. I, p. 75.

in a precarious situation. Indeed, according to Saenz's calculations, the peso had already become overvalued before the end of 1955.

Obviously, the choice of base years is critical, and there is no compelling reason to choose either year. The rate was floating in the entire period 1937–1940, and all rates were therefore, by definition, equilibrium rates. Furthermore, the rate floated both upward and downward,

Table V - 2

Recalculations of Estimations of Purchasing Power Parity
(base 1941, parity 4.85)

Year	Price indexes Mexico	USA	Relation A/B	Exchange rate (pesos per dollar) Existing	Equilibrium	Index of under/or overvaluation
	(A)	(B)	(C)	(D)	(E)	(F)
1941	100	100	100	4.85	4.85	100
1948	238	189	144	4.85	6.98	144
1949	262	178	167	7.30	8.09	111
				8.65	8.09	94

(base 1950, parity 8.65)

Year	Price indexes Mexico	USA	Relation A/B	Existing	Equilibrium	Index
1950	100	100	100	8.65	8.65	100
1951	124	116	107	8.65	9.35	108
1952	128	107	119	8.63	10.20	118
1953	126	106	119	8.62	10.20	118
1954	138	106	130	12.49	11.20	90
1955	157	106	148	12.49	12.76	102

Source: Saenz, *op. cit.*, p. 537.

apparently influenced by expectations and capital flows as much as by the current account balance. It will be seen later in this chapter that there is no basis for concluding that the terms of trade deteriorated between 1937 and the early 1950s, which is the underlying assumption of the ECLA argument. At the same time, using the 1948 rate, which was also an equilibrium rate fixed under conditions similar to those prevailing in the early 1950s, as a base, the rate clearly appears overvalued. However, even if one accepts the ECLA argument that an excess demand for foreign exchange was present, the policy remedy is not clear. One could consistently hold that Mexico had developed excess demand for foreign exchange precisely because the government had subsidized inefficient domestic industry while neglecting the export sector. In any event, while the authorities might have been willing to accept the structuralist argument on conceptual grounds, they were not ready to accept the structuralist policy recommendation which invariably was to introduce exchange controls.

The inelasticity argument is more amenable to direct measurement. In order to evaluate conflicting positions on the relative importance of price and income in the performance of the current account, ordinary least-square regressions were used to estimate elasticities of exports and imports of goods and services. The elasticities measured were the growth of exports in response to the business cycle in the United States, price performance and changes in the exchange rate. On the import side, imports of goods and services were related to the growth of national income in Mexico, relative price performance and exchange-rate adjustments. (It would have been preferable to express exports and imports as volume rather than value; however, the figures were not available.)

The equations are as follows:

$$\log X = a_0 + a_1 \log Y_{us} + a_2 \log \frac{P_m}{P_{us}} + a_3 \log \frac{R_o}{R_t}$$

Where Y = the level of real GNP in the United States
X = the dollar value of exports

$\frac{P_m}{P_{us}}$ = the ratio of wholesale price index in Mexico to the same index in the United States

$\frac{R_o}{R_t}$ = the exchange rate in 1946, divided by the current exchange rate

The export regression yielded the following results:

	Elasticities	Standard error	t-Statistic
$a_1 =$	1.73	0.55	3.17
$a_2 =$	-0.56	0.60	-9.22
$a_3 =$	-0.53	0.22	-2.36
$R^2 = 0.94$			DW $= 2.05$

$$\log M = b_0 + b_1 \log Ym + b_2 \log \frac{P_m}{P_{us}} + b_3 \log \frac{R_0}{R_t}$$

Where M = the dollar value of imports
YM = GNP in Mexico

The results for imports were:

	Elasticities	Standard error	t-Statistic
	$b_1 = 0.82$	.26	3.11
	$b_2 = 0.71$	.46	1.55
	$b_3 = 0.36$	.19	1.91
$R^2 = 0.93$			DW = 1.70

The magnitude and signs of the coefficients were credible and the R^2 coefficients indicate that the results are significant. Both imports and exports are clearly more income-elastic than price-elastic.[13] The relatively higher income elasticity and lower price elasticity of exports compared to imports probably reflects that the former consisted mainly of primary commodities and the latter manufactured goods. Moreover, the imports of Mexico may be somewhat less elastic due to the prevalence of controls. At the same time, although inelastic, the coefficients indicate some responsiveness to price and exchange-rate changes, especially if one recalls the magnitudes of the changes that actually occurred. The range of variance of GNP growth has generally been on the order of 7 percent, between 0–6 percent in the United States and 3–10 percent in Mexico. At the same time, price increases in Mexico averaged 9 percent per year between 1946 and 1954 and the peso depreciated by an annual average rate of 11 percent. Thus, despite the relative price and exchange-rate inelasticity of trade one can conclude that price and exchange rate factors probably affected the current account by as much as income changes in the inflationary period. However, after 1954 when price and exchange-rate stability was achieved, the current account responded mainly to income changes.

In the narrowest sense, the data do not support the structural disequilibrium hypothesis; exports are more elastic with respect to the growth of real GNP in the United States than are imports with respect to Mexican GNP. If both countries were to grow at their full potential, Mexico at roughly 6.5 percent and the United States at about 4.5 percent, there need not be any tendency toward imbalance. However, a limited form of the structural disequilibrium hypothesis is plausible. In particular, since during the period under consideration the United States had a tendency toward less than full capacity growth, Mexico encountered a shortfall of external demand that placed pressures on the current account balance. The United States entered a prolonged period of slow growth, with the yearly growth of real GNP averaging only 2.8 percent between 1952 and 1962. Therefore, in that period the Mexican current account suffered a continuous widening owing in large part to the uneven performance of the United States economy.

The significance of the policy debate that surrounded the devaluation goes beyond the relative intellectual merits of either side. The criticism from virtually all quarters places the authorities squarely on the defensive. Probably the Mexican government, which wants to operate on a broad consensus, can withstand less criticism than a government which openly competes for votes and where parties alternate in office. It was clear that the earlier line of policy had pleased no one. Those who favored development with stability attacked the policy for undermining the financial system. The structuralists, who were more tolerant of inflation, rejected devaluation as a policy instrument and called for exchange controls. Thus, the government was confronted with opposition from both sides.

REAL WAGES AND THE PROBLEM OF INCOME DISTRIBUTION

The debate over policy was on an intellectual plane and of itself would surely not have caused a reversal of policy. The inflation did not begin for ideological reasons. It continued because it produced acceptable results and because the inertia of government practice supported it. It ended when it became a divisive political and social problem. The inflation-devaluation cycle was arousing mounting opposition in major organized sectors of the economy, culminating in a fierce public outcry against the 1954 devaluation.

The financial community, including the private financial sector and the Bank of Mexico, favored price stability since they believed that inflation made the public reluctant to hold peso-denominated assets while the exchange risk made foreign assets more attractive than domestic placements.[14] The Bank of Mexico argued in official councils for more emphasis on stability, while private financial institutions also pressed this point of view on public officials, both through public statements and by unofficial persuasion.[15] In 1953, the nation's largest private bank, Banco Nacional de México, published an article calling on the government to introduce a policy of price stability. The document concluded that "an inflationary policy cannot be used indefinitely as a means of promoting economic development." While such a policy "can be justified in an early state of economic development, in which the fundamental objective is to undertake important public works such as irrigation, energy development . . . Mexico is in a later stage of development in which such a policy is no longer justified."[16]

The position of Mexican industry was more equivocal. On the one hand, domestic industrialists had been the most favored group in society since 1940. The government had been very generous in providing protection, tax incentives, and credit to support the expansion of this sector. Moreover, the government's inflationary policies and devaluation helped the advance of this sector by lowering real wages and providing an extra measure of protection against foreign competition. However, even though the manufacturing sector had proven itself capable of thriving in an inflationary environment, domestic industrialists were not necessarily in favor of continued inflation and devaluation. Mexican industrialists, who were major importers of capital goods, saw the prices of imported goods rise sharply as a result of the devaluation.[17] In the weeks following the devaluation, numerous industrial groups began to request price increases, and on April 23 the Federal Chamber of Commerce asked for a general easing of price controls in order to offset the increased costs brought on by the devaluation.[18] True, the devaluation increased effective protection to domestic manufacturers, but the latter were mainly concerned with assuring protection through tariffs, quotas and licensing.[19] Of all domestic producers, only exporters had a clear interest in continued devaluation. With this exception, the attitude of the private sector toward inflation and devaluation ranged from ambivalence to strong advocacy of stability.

The attitude of organized labor was most hostile to inflation and devaluation. It was argued in an earlier chapter that Mexican economic development followed the pattern of an elastic labor supply with a falling real wage level and a tendency for real consumption to fall. The inflationary process, at least from 1940 on, heavily favored profits and thereby allowed industry to finance itself through retained earnings. The price

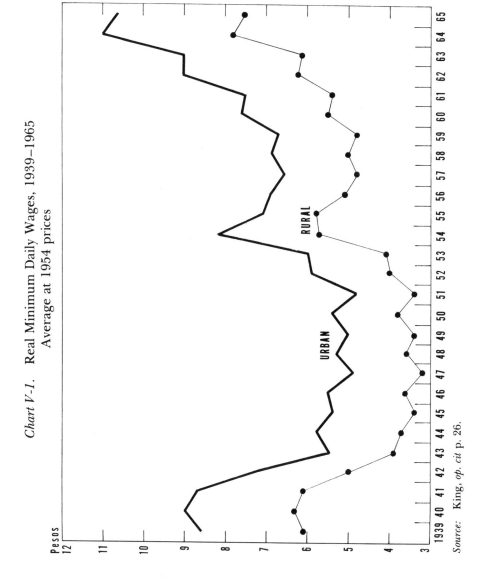

Chart V-1. Real Minimum Daily Wages, 1939–1965
Average at 1954 prices

Source: King, *op. cit* p. 26.

of this pattern of development was a sharp decline in real wages, which is visible in Chart V-I. The fact that the least privileged classes were bearing an inordinate share of the burden of development became an important political issue. One representative critic took the government to task for allowing a general deterioration of the wage level and neglecting what he considered elementary fairness, and warned that "to continue with policies which reduce the standard of living and purchasing power of groups that make up the majority of the population will surely lead to disturbances that will jeopardize the future development of the country."[20] Similarly, a document submitted to the government by the largest trade union group, the Confederation of Mexican Workers (CTM), studied a wide sampling of minimum wages in relation to the cost of living index. It concluded that the real minimum wage had been falling for many years, and that the minimum wage was not enough to sustain a family on a diet consisting mostly of beans and corn.[21]

The government itself was convinced that real wages were falling, and many officials were uneasy about it. The government claimed to base itself on a popular uprising, to be an all-inclusive grouping that cut across class lines, and to aim to achieve an ideal of social justice. Yet, since 1940, the effect of official policy had been the exact opposite. As early as 1947, the Finance Minister, Ramon Beteta publicly admitted that growth had generated profits for a small group of industrialists, while inflation had lowered the living standards of the masses.[22] Beteta restated his misgivings about government policy to the 1951 Bankers' Convention:

> The group to which we belong is a privileged minority. . . . While there exist misery, unemployment, economic insecurity, while the possession of wealth not only gives its owner control over goods, but over the lives of others . . . [other] social groups fear equally depression, which deprives them of the means of subsistence or an artificial prosperity based on inflation, high prices and lower real wages. . . . These men are hoping for a change, any change which will offer them a way out.[23]

Late in Alemán's presidential term, the government's policies—above all the widespread corruption, the favoritism to priviledged industrialists, and the activities to suppress unions and maintain low wages—led to a reaction by high level political figures. According to some sources, Alemán was threatened with forcible removal from office unless he agreed to soften his policies.[24] In any event, the new government in 1953 committed itself to arresting the decline of real wages. President Ruiz Cortines was reportedly chosen as a compromise candidate, following a dispute between Alemán, who favored continued development of the economy along lines of his Administration with emphasis on heavy public works spending and with industry continuing to receive preferred treatment by the government, and Cárdenas, who wanted a return to the social reform of the 1930s.[25] As a result, Ruiz Cortines had a mandate to stop the decline in real wages, but not to do so at the expense of domestic industrialists. With this growing political commitment to higher real wages, the new Finance Minister, Antonio Carrillo Flores, was able to spell out the government's intent to the 1953 Bankers' Convention:

> The development program, in the thinking of the Chief of State . . . must continue in a way that advances rather than retards social justice, contributing to full employment with rising levels of real wages. . . . Studies and analyses made recently show that between 1939 and 1952, salaries, wages and the income of small enterprises, have risen much less than profits, interest and investment income. The proportion of the latter in national income has risen at the expense of the former. . . . Clearly, the recent high investment of the private sector in urban construction and agriculture have been made possible by an increased capacity for savings which resulted from this redistribution of national income. However, after a decade of this process of intensive capital formation, it is now necessary to widen and strengthen the domestic market. The State considers this necessary not only from the point of view of social justice . . . but also because a further fall in the income of the majority of the population would cause a fall in economic activity.[26]

The Ruiz Cortines administration began to back away from the pro-industrialist position of the Alemán years. With the start of the Ruiz Cortines administration, the real wage level began a steady improvement, even though real wages did not regain their prewar levels until the early 1960s.

The position of Mexican trade unions is critical for understanding the erosion of real wages that occurred in the 1940s, as well as the events that followed the devaluation. In the first place, only a small minority of the Mexican labor force was ever organized, as can be seen in Table V-3. Even though the proportion of workers belonging to unions was rising in industry and services, total membership never accounted for much

Table V - 3

Labor Force and Trade Union Membership, 1950 - 1965

Population (A)   Labor force (B)
(thousands)

			B/A
1950	25.891	8,345	32%
1960	34,923	11,332	32%
1965	42,689	13,427	31%

Sectorial distribution of labor force
(percentages)

	Total	Agriculture[a]	Industry[b]	Services[c]
1950	100	58	16	26
1960	100	54	19	26
1965	100	51	20	28

Trade union membership
(thousands)

	Total	Agriculture[a]	Industry[b]	Services[c]
1953	864	144	414	307
1955	979	147	490	342
1960	1,298	124	759	414
1965	1,697	136	1,006	554

Trade union membership as percentage of labor force

	Total	Agriculture[a]	Industry[b]	Services[c]
1950[e]	10	3	29	13
1955[e]	11	3	29	15
1960	11	2	36	14
1965	13	2	36	15

[a] - includes hunting, forestry and fishing.
[b] - includes mining, construction and manufacturing.
[c] - includes transport, commerce, and services.
[e] - estimated.

Source: Dirección General de Estadística, *Anuario Estadístico Compendiado,* various issues.

more than 10 percent of the labor force. Moreover, most Mexican trade unions have been closely tied to the government, and many key trade union leaders owed their positions to the government rather than to their own rank and file.[27] Trade unions form an integral part of the official party, while business organizations are specifically excluded from participation. However, since a great deal of decision making takes place by means of direct contact between businessmen and government officials, business was better able to press its points of view on government.[28] Therefore, union leaders were in an ambiguous position. They could represent their membership's point of view inside government councils, but once a decision was made they had to mobilize support for government policy within the unions. When governments became pro-business in the 1940s, the leverage of the union officials on the wage panels was curtailed while they were unable to openly confront the authorities on wage policy. In any case, given the conditions of a virtually elastic supply of cheap unskilled labor, the market power of organized labor was small. In effect, the official union leaders were reduced to pleading the cause of their membership with no means of putting real pressures on the employers or the government.

The workers, who had proven to be the group in society that was least able to defend itself against inflation, tended to oppose inflationary policies. Since devaluation was identified with the inflationary cycle, devaluation aroused special resentment among the working class. Moreover, it seems reasonable to believe that devaluation indeed lowered the real wage of the working class. In the first place, devaluation led directly to higher domestic prices as businesses passed on increased costs of imported capital goods to consumers or as higher-priced domestic goods were substituted for imports. Mexico imported sizable quantities of food and raw materials and the inflationary impact of devaluation was felt immediately. Owing to the diverse commodity composition of Mexican exports, the decrease in domestic price of exportable goods also tended to lower the real incomes of the working classes.[29] Probably at least two thirds of Mexican exportable goods could also be consumed at home, especially items such as cotton, coffee, sugar, meat, fish, processed foods and textiles. (See Table V-6). In more general terms, devaluation represents a transfer of resources from domestic consumption to the export sector. Hence devaluation is a stimulus to saving and a deterrent to consumption. Generally speaking, one would expect the real income of exporters to rise and the real consumption of all other sectors to fall.[30]

It is quite true that there were secondary income effects of devaluation that partly offset the adverse price effect, i.e., the shift of resources to investment may result in a higher level of real national income than would have been possible in the absence of devaluation. There is some validity to this argument, especially since GNP grew by 10 percent in the year following the devaluation. However, the experience of Mexico had been that increases in national income tended to be accompanied by decreases in the wage level and increases in total employment. Thus, those workers who were already employed still were likely to experience a decline in real income despite the improved outlook for total employment. Under any conditions, it is difficult to convince workers to accept a decline in real present income in exchange for any future benefits.

The 1954 devaluation highlighted the divided loyalties of the union leaders. Independent commentators seized upon the effects of the devaluation, claiming that it was a spur to profits but a loss in real purchasing power for the working class. Rank-and-file members reacted violently against the measure. The official union leaders, on the other hand, called an emergency meeting of the central committee of the Confederation of Mexican workers and issued a statement supporting the devaluation as a "patriotic and courageous act."[31] With industrialists petitioning the government for an easing of price controls, Fidel Velásquez, Secretary-General of the CTM, supported the devaluation but asked the government for assurance that adequate measures would be taken to protect the interests of the working class, especially that price controls on articles of mass consumption be maintained.[32] The announcement of the devaluation provoked a panic reaction from the public. Within a day, panic buying began as shopkeepers increased prices sharply and unrest began in the working-class districts.[33] As prices rose sharply, the government was obliged to make strenuous efforts to hold prices down by arresting merchants who violated price control regulations and by direct sales of foodstuffs in poorer areas from government stocks.[34] The dimensions of the crisis became apparent, as agitation accelerated and rumors began to circulate that the introduction of exchange controls was imminent, leading to a capital flight.

As the authorities seemed to be losing control of the situation, the CTM continued to back official policy. On April 26, the CTM placed a full-page advertisement in *Excelsior* supporting the government and attacking "profiteers" who used the devaluation as an excuse to raise prices. Meanwhile, the actions of independent union leaders and the pressures from the rank and file were placing the CTM in an increasingly awkward position. Immediately following the devaluation, the independent leader of the electrical workers' union, Rafael Galván, threatened to strike if wage contracts, which were normally renegotiated every two years, were not revised to compensate for the devaluation. After some resistance, the government agreed to allow for negotiations.[35] Other independent unions and some unions affiliated with the CTM began to issue strike threats.

As pressures from all directions mounted, Velásquez was forced to modify his initial pro-government stance. In a speech to the central committee of the CTM on June 8, Velásquez raised the possibility of a general strike, demanding significant wage increases to compensate for the devaluation, and asking the government to come forth with a package of measures to protect the working class from increases in the cost of living.[36] On the following day, the central committee of the CTM voted to stage a general strike on July 12 if wages were not increased by 24 percent.[37]

In the next two months, the rank and file clamored for increased wages and independent unions struck individual employers. Some CTM-affiliated unions broke away from Velásquez's leadership and struck on their own. Velásquez and the national committee, however, effectively worked to dissipate the bargaining power of organized labor by encouraging individual unions to settle wage disputes and by backing away from their initial militant posture. Following meetings with Adolfo López Mateos, the Secretary of Labor, Velásquez stated that he was not seeking conflict with the government or with employers, but that he had to defend the interests of the workers.[38] By June 16, the CTM was already divided, with many uions beginning direct negotiations with their respective employers.[39] On the following day, some major settlements were announced.[40] As individual unions continued to submit demands for the initial 24 percent wage increase, the negotiations continued, and by the end of June it was announced that more than half of the outstanding disputes had been settled, with reported settlements averaging about 10–12 percent.[41]

On July 8, *Excelsior* reported that the danger of a general strike had passed, and the following day the National Committee of the CTM announced that the deadline for the general strike would be postponed until the 23rd of the month. In the ensuing weeks, negotiations continued. The government made some concessions to the workers: minimum wages in seventeen states of the republic were raised by 17–22 percent. On July 23, the deadline for the strike, a whole list of settlements were announced, and the issue of wage increases was totally defused. Only two affiliated unions actually struck.[42]

It is the opinion of virtually all observers of the Mexican scene that, even if he sincerely wanted to, Velásquez did not have the power to oppose the government. Nevertheless, the government was clearly unprepared for the opposition that the devaluation aroused in the working class.[43] Indeed, the working class reaction might have been the highest political cost that the authorities incurred as a result of the devaluation. Moreover, the fact that the official trade-union leaders had acted as agents of the government instead of defending the interest of their membership undermined their credibility. Such an open disply of ineffectiveness could eventually have led to a rank-and-file rejection of leadership and possibly open hostility of the working classes toward the government. Thus, even though labor was perhaps the least able of all organized groups to immediately affect government policy, it did have the ultimate power to reject its leaders and pass into open opposition. Since the government eschewed outright repression as a political tactic, the interests of the working class had to be recognized as a major influence in future government calculations. Moreover, the union leaders' faithful defense of government policy probably gave them some claim to consideration.

In addition to the shifts in power alignments, it must have been extremely embarrassing for the authorities, who claimed to be ideological heirs of the 1910 revolution, to engage in actions that were clearly aimed at weakening the effective power of the working class, the more so since government officials had already rejected the development strategy based on falling real wages. Having decided that the policy should foster a rise in real wages, the government was given a strong incentive to maintain price stability. While it is true that real wages could conceivably be maintained through an overt tilt toward labor in legislation and on minimum wage panels (which would alienate domestic industrialists), it was probably not an acceptable alternative. Such a posture would have led to growing power and real independence for the trade unions, a development the government did not wish to encourage. In practice, a policy of raising nominal wages would have been unenforceable since many employers did not pay the minimum wage, and there were always workers willing to accept lower wages. Thus, a policy of raising nominal wages could only protect the well-organized workers, who were only a small minority. Inflation would produce strife between organized and unorganized labor and between skilled and unskilled workers.[44] Furthermore, since the authorities had decided to renounce the practice of fomenting forced savings through inflation, it was imperative to find alternative sources of savings by increasing domestic savings through the development of the financial system and to increase inflows of foreign capital. Both of the sources of savings depended upon the maintenance of stability.

THE CHANGING INTERNATIONAL ENVIRONMENT

Deterioration in the Terms of Trade

Foreign trade, which had been a stumulus to economic growth in the immediate postwar years, began increasingly to become an obstacle to growth in the 1950s. Despite the intensive efforts at import substitution, demand for imports grew steadily as the authorities maintained a rate of growth of real output of over 6 percent per year. However, Mexican capacity to pay for those imports with export earnings began to encounter difficulties. The value of visible exports had grown by an average of about 18 percent yearly in the period 1946–1950. This rate of growth slowed to 8 percent in 1951–1955 and then further weakened to only 3 percent in the period 1956–1960. As Table V-4 suggests, the development of exports was even less favorable when one considers that, after peaking in 1956, revenue from visible exports did not regain its 1956 level until 1962. Only the continued growth of tourist income and border transactions prevented an absolute decline in current account earnings.

There are many indications that sluggish external demand played a large role in the stagnation of export earnings. As Table V-5 shows, this trend toward slower export growth was the rule and not the exception in

Table V - 4

Current Account Earnings, 1954 - 1965
(millions of dollars)

	1954	1955	1956	1957	1958	1959	1960	1961	1962	1963	1964	1965
Total	1,048	1,208	1,324	1,257	1,268	1,320	1,372	1,463	1,587	1,709	1,848	1,980
Merchandise exports	616	739	807	706	709	723	739	804	906	936	1,022	1,110
Tourism	76	118	134	129	134	145	155	164	179	211	241	270
Border transactions	247	262	278	313	316	354	366	392	407	446	463	500
Workers remittances	23	25	38	33	36	38	36	84	32	31	29	12
Other	24	24	25	24	24	30	28	28	26	35	46	44

Source: Banco de Mexico, S.A.

Table V - 5

Growth of Exports of Latin American Countries, 1946 - 1965
(annual averages in percent)

Country	1946 - 1950	1951 - 1955	1956 - 1960	1961 - 1965
Mexico	17.5	8.2	3.0	5.1
Argentina	16.2	-5.5	0.4	5.2
Bolivia	1.4	1.1	6.0	4.2
Brazil	18.7	5.9	-3.0	1.1
Chile	9.3	7.8	1.0	4.1
Colombia	20.9	13.8	-0.07	0.2
Costa Rica	30.0	13.3	1.4	4.4
Dominican Republic	17.4	7.9	4.3	1.7
Ecuador	24.0	16.2	6.2	2.1
El Salvador	207.7	15.2	4.1	5.4
Guatemala	24.5	7.6	3.8	5.3
Haiti	21.0	8.4	-4.0	0.5
Honduras	42.5	4.0	2.2	6.2
Nicaragua	21.0	24.0	4.3	10.5
Panama	47.2	17.3	11.3	12.0
Paraguay	13.5	3.2	1.5	5.5
Peru	20.9	9.0	6.3	12.1
Uruguay	17.3	3.5	10.1	4.1
Subtotal	17.3	4.6	0.2	4.0
Venezuela	29.5	12.2	9.4	0.4
Total	19.0	6.1	2.6	3.0

Source: (1946 - 1960) ECLA *External Financing in Latin America* and (1961 - 1965), International Monetary Fund, *International Financial Statistics.*

Latin America. Doubtless, the policies of many Latin American countries of maintaining overvalued exchange rates and neglecting the export sector aggravated the trend. Nevertheless, the deterioration is so pervasive that it appears to affect virtually all countries in the region, regardless of the policies they pursued. Moreover, the data discussed earlier indicate that Mexican exports are high elastic in response to the economic growth in the United States, which absorbed about 70 percent of Mexican exports. At that time, the United States entered a period of slow growth that lasted until the early 1960s. Therefore, it is hard to avoid the conclusion that external market conditions were largely responsible for the

Table V - 6

Commodity Composition of Exports, 1951 - 1965

	Percentage share of total			Average annual rate of change in percent
	1951 - 1955	1956 - 1960	1961 - 1965	
Agricultural products	53.3	48.7	43.2	5.8
Cotton	31.8	29.2	23.4	4.7
Henequen	1.2	.5	.6	.64
Grain	1.6	1.8	4.5	62.7
Coffee	13.7	12.6	8.7	7.1
Others	4.9	4.7	5.9	6.4
Meat	2.3	5.6	7.7	58.1
Fish	3.9	4.8	6.0	7.3
Mineral Products	33.3	27.9	21.3	2.6
Copper	8.4	5.7	2.2	-3.6
Zinc	5.7	4.7	4.1	9.1
Lead	11.3	6.1	3.5	-4.6
Petroleum	6.0	5.0	4.5	5.9
Others	1.9	6.4	7.0	65.0
Manufactured goods	8.1	12.9	21.8	13.9
Processed food	2.0	4.9	11.0	25.0
Textiles	3.9	3.9	4.5	5.0
Chemicals	0.9	1.9	2.8	20.7
Others	1.1	2.1	3.4	21.4

Source: Banco de Mexico, S.A.

lackluster performance of Latin American exports in general and Mexican exports in particular.

The ability of Mexicans to develop new products for export further suggests that external demand may have been partly at fault. In the period 1945–1948, minerals represented more than 60 percent of Mexican exports, while agricultural products accounted for about 30 percent and manufactured products were still only 5 percent. As Chart V-2 indicates, the commodity composition of Mexican exports was constantly changing, with agricultural products and manufactured goods gaining, while minerals declined in importance. Moreover, the broad distribution of export growth by individual products indicates that within the context of weak external demand Mexican exporters took advantage of opportunities in export markets, despite generally unfavorable conditions. (See Table V-6.)

Further support for the proposition that external demand was the cause of the poor export performance in the 1950s can be seen in the behavior of the export volume and prices. Table V-7, which shows the development of Mexican export prices and volume, gives a more complete picture of the factors underlying the weakening of the export performance. After increasing at an annual average rate of 9.1 percent between 1948 and 1955, export volume stagnated at 1.5 percent per year between 1955 and 1961. There was some recovery after 1961, with export value increasing at a yearly rate of 6.2 percent in 1961–65. At the same time, export prices remained soft throughout the late 1950s before recovering somewhat in the early 1960s.

Although this problem is often referred to as the deterioration in the terms of trade, it is more complicated than that. The terms of trade refers to the relation between export prices and import prices.[45] A country developing a new manufactured product, for example textiles or transistor radios, may be able to expand exports through aggressive price cutting. In these circumstances, its terms of trade may be declining, but export revenues may still be growing rapidly. The country exporting primary commodities, however, is in a different position. If demand for its exports softens, this will result, not only in a decrease in price, but in a decrease in the quantity demanded. As a result, a fall in demand leads to a sharp decline in export value.[46]

Since Mexico was encountering sluggish demand for its exports com-

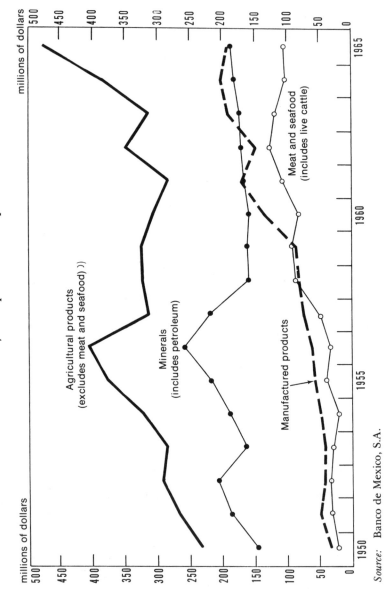

Chart V-2. Commodity Composition of Exports, 1950–1965

millions of dollars

500
450
400
350
300
250
200
150
100
50
0

Agricultural products
(excludes meat and seafood))

Minerals
(includes petroleum)

Manufactured products

Meat and seafood
(includes live cattle)

1965
1960
1955
1950

millions of dollars

500
450
400
350
300
250
200
150
100
50
0

Source: Banco de Mexico, S.A.

Table V - 7

Terms of Trade and Related Indices, 1948 - 1965

(1963 = 100)

	1948	1949	1950	1951	1952	1953	1954	1955	1956	1957	1958	1959	1960	1961	1962	1963	1964	1965
Exports[a]																		
Value	38	39	54	66	68	61	65	81	83	75	76	78	78	85	94	100	106	116
Volume	44	50	57	58	60	63	64	79	81	74	80	87	86	88	99	100	101	112
Prices	85	78	94	113	113	95	101	102	102	101	94	89	92	90	95	100	105	103
Imports[a]																		
Value	37	36	45	66	65	63	63	71	86	93	91	81	96	92	92	100	120	126
Volume	69	60	71	92	90	87	86	93	109	113	108	100	106	97	92	100	109	114
Prices	54	59	63	72	72	75	74	77	79	82	84	81	90	95	100	100	110	110
Terms of Trade	157	132	149	157	157	127	136	132	129	123	112	110	102	101	95	100	95	94

[a] - merchandise trade.
Source: ECLA, *Statistical Bulletin for Latin America* (Vol. VIII, 1971).

bined with rising import prices in the 1950s, a strategy of devaluation to improve the trade balance would have been less effective in the mid-1950s than in earlier years. Such a policy would have involved shifting increasing amounts of resources into the export sector, despite weak foreign demand. Devaluation would have had to be larger than in earlier years to increase export earnings by equivalent amounts. In effect, Mexico would have had to adopt a strategy of competitive devaluation, that is of trying to undercut other suppliers. Such a policy would undoubtedly have been opposed by international organizations, especially the IMF and GATT. Furthermore, by its inflationary and distributional effects, such a policy would have deepened the social tensions which the government already perceived as a difficult problem.

The Growing Availability of Foreign Capital

While the prospects of increasing foreign exchange earnings on current account were dimming, a variety of new sources of capital flows appeared that presented alternative means of financing economic growth, not only the shortfall of import needs over export earnings, but of domestic investment over domestic savings as well. Mexicans had been keenly aware of the possibilities of foreign loans to ease their growth problems for several years. Moreover, the public sector had already established a presence in international financial markets. The government, having committed itself to repay its external debt in 1942, began borrowing from Eximbank in 1942 and the IBRD in 1948. In 1949, Mexico began operations with the Bank of America and in the following year with several other commercial banks in the United States.[47]

The Mexican institution that was most deeply involved in external borrowing was the Nacional Financiera (Nafin). As the nation's development bank, this institution had acquired substantial experience in carrying out economic and engineering feasibility studies of the economy by sector, identifying critical "bottleneck" areas of the economy and then centering its activities on these key areas of the economy.[48]

Nafin had taken the lead in borrowing from foreign credit institutions, realizing that foreign credit would supplement domestic resources in the country's economic development program. By the beginning of the 1950s, Nafin was actively seeking to broaden its access to foreign official lending agencies and increase its line of credit. In 1950, Nafin's official publication *El Mercado de Valores* began discussing the possibility of increasing the volume of long-term loans from overseas sources. In August of that year, the Nafin's director general, Antonio Carrillo Flores, was able to report "the international credit rating of Mexico is improving. Mexico has obtained sizable resources from Eximbank, the IBRD, and the U.S. private banks including Bank of America and Chase National Bank."[49]

With these successful operations behind them, Nafin's management wanted to expand the scope and size of its operations with international lending agencies. The World Bank (IBRD), originally established to finance European reconstruction, seemed an especially promising source of funds. The IBRD and the Eximbank earmarked most of their resources for specific projects that were proven to be technically feasible, economically sound and not likely to be financed through private capital markets.[50] Since Nafin had nearly twenty years' experience in creating projects and channeling funds in precisely the same areas, there was a great identity of interest between it and the World Bank; as a result, it was especially well equipped to take advantage of expanding World Bank facilities.

In 1953, Mexico was the subject of a study by economists from the Bank of Mexico, Nafin and the IBRD. The resulting report, addressed to both the president of the IBRD and the director general of Nacional Financiera, specifically disavowed any commitment on either side to any specific program, but the intent was clear.[51] Nacional Financiera and the IBRD were thinking in terms of more systematic use of long-term foreign loans to aid in the development of Mexico. The report surveyed the past performance of the various sectors of the economy and forecast the potential for growth in each one, while at the same time evaluating the capacity of each sector to effectively utilize foreign loans in the future. The report concluded that it would be difficult to raise domestic savings above the existing level and that, to maintain the pace of development, Mexico would have to rely increasingly on foreign capital. In addition, the report drew up a tentative medium-term plan for foreign borrowing based on the country's projected need for foreign loans and its capacity to repay.[52] While the World Bank held the promise of large-scale international support for Mexican development, it also implied that the ability to obtain such financing would be contingent upon Mexican willingness to adopt sounder financial policies. This is a matter of World

Bank policy. In its 1953 statement of policy, that institution spelled out its position on the financial responsibilities of borrowers:

> It happens not infrequently that the Bank's examination of general economic conditions in the borrowing country reveals the existence of economic or financial practices or policies which so adversely affect the financial and monetary stability of the country that, if continued, they would endanger both the productive purposes and the repayment prospects of the Bank loan. In such cases, it is the policy of the Bank to require, as a condition of Bank financing, that the borrowing country institute measures designed to restore stability to its economy. The Bank does not, of course, insist that all remedial measures which may appear necessary in the case of any given country be completed before that country may qualify for a loan. On the other hand the Bank is not normally willing to rely simply on a representation that such remedial measures will in due course be taken. The Bank's position is midway between these extremes; it requries concrete evidence that the government is actually taking appropriate steps to establish stability, but, once given such evidence, it is usually willing to make a loan concurrently with the execution of the measures adopted.[53]

The report advocated less reliance on inflationary finance and increased taxes on the domestic side.[54] Externally, the report endorsed an increase in public official borrowing and favored an external policy that combined continued import substitution and export promotion to maintain manageable current account deficits.[55] Less abrupt shifts in the current account balance were needed for the country to maintain an acceptable level of international reserves to sustain its credibility as a stable credit risk. The problem of the level of reserves was important in Mexico, which had no exchange controls. Countries with exchange controls could use existing reserves as proof of their capability of meeting obligations. In cases where overall demand for foreign exchange became excessive, exchange controls could be tightened and the central bank could cease to use reserves to support nonessential transactions. In Mexico, on the other hand, which was committed to supporting all transactions at a single rate, debt service could have no special claim. A speculative run on the currency could easily result in a default on debts. Consequently, the authorities had to maintain a large reserve for contingencies and pursue policies to forestall speculation against the currency.

The requirements that the IBRD proposed were probably not inflexible. Considering the close and developing relationship between Mexico and the World Bank, the essential requirement was that Mexico convince the World Bank that its policies were sound from the points of view of development and stability.

In addition to increasing borrowing from public agencies such as IBRD and Eximbank, the government wished to develop closer ties with private financial institutions. As with official institutions, Mexico had to convince potential private creditors that it was pursuing sound policies and that there was little risk of default.[56]

Shortly after the 1954 devaluation, the authorities began to articulate a new balance of payments strategy. In June 1954, Octaviano Campos Salas, chief of research at the Bank of Mexico, outlined a policy of creating a network of international financial relationships that would avoid future recourse to devaluation. The collapse of the Korean War boom had created a new problem for the balance of payments. The current account deficit had to be held within manageable limits, through intensified import substitution and export promotion. The remaining current account deficit would be financed through increased external borrowing. In order to pursue this policy, the country would need to maintain a high level of reserves and to actively seek foreign credits.[57] Later in the year, the finance minister, Carrillo Flores, said that it was an explicit goal of government policy to seek general purpose loans to support the balance of payments and increase foreign exchange reserves.[58]

In the years immediately following the devaluation, official economic thinking went beyond the abstract need for foreign funds and began to concentrate on the problems of raising more funds in international markets and of working out an operational doctrine of efficiently utilizing foreign funds inside a financial system based on stability. For example, Ruben Gleason Galicia of the Nacional Financiera, outlined the role of external credit in the development of specific sectors of the economy, indicating that foreign loans were becoming an integral part of development planning.[59] Aflredo Navarrete of Nacional Financiera elaborated a modified pattern of economic development, in which the financial system would mobilize greater domestic savings and international borrowing would be increased. One of the underlying problems of policy would be to assure a constant flow of necessary imports while maintaining stability of the balance of payments. The country would need increasing and dependable flows from the international lending agencies such as Eximbank and the IBRD and private financial institutions.[60]

THE POLICY-MAKING PROCESS

As both internal and external forces converged to make the need for stabilization evident, the determination of the government to resist inflation grew steadily. The government had, at its outset, committed itself to price stability, for it perceived inflation as a threat to the viability of the broad-based coalition from which it drew its support. The extreme divisiveness of inflation became even more evident in the wake of the devaluation. At the same time, the inertia of past behavior and claims of powerful economic groups were pulling the authorities toward a continued inflationary policy. There was also still considerable belief at fairly high levels of government in the concept of development through inflation, and individual ministries still were able to use the need for spending on social and infrastructure projects as a means of eliciting government spending.

The changes of personnel that took place in 1953 were significant. The new president, Adolfo Ruiz Cortines, was considerably less corrupt than his predecessor.[61] The change in administration brought Antonio Carrillo Flores to the post of finance minister. As a member of the cabinet, he shared the president's commitment to price stability on social and political grounds. In addition, because of his involvement with Nacional Financiera, he was especially aware of the need for comprehensive development planning, which in turn depended on a stable flow of external resources. Carrillo Flores immediately aligned himself with the group favoring stability. When the administration changed hands, Rodrigo Gómez was named director general of the Bank of Mexico. Gómez was a classic central banker who personified the stability-oriented outlook of the Bank of Mexico. In later years, when Mexico had successfully maintained a high rate of growth without inflation, Gómez emerged as an international spokesman for development with stability and thereby greatly enhanced the prestige of the central bank and hence its ability to effect policy. Yet, it would be a mistake to overemphasize the role of the Bank of Mexico at the outset of the stabilization effort. The central bank advocated a policy of stabilization and, once the stabilization process had begun, its expertise was instrumental in developing the financial system. But, the Bank of Mexico's effectiveness depended on the government's willingness to listen to its advice.[62]

With a group favoring stabilization gaining ascendancy, the national interest was identified with price and exchange-rate stability, and the authorities reaffirmed the national interest over the claims of particular interests. From the outset, the Ruiz Cortines administration moved to restrain inflationary forces. Control over public sector expenditures was essential. In the summer of 1953, the president ordered the ministries of Finance and Economy to prepare an investment program for the entire duration of his administration (1953–1958). A permanent Investment Committee composed of representatives from these ministries as well as the Bank of Mexico and the Nacional Financiera gathered data, formulated projects, and submitted an investment program to the president.[63] This body became the chief coordinating and planning body in the country. The presence of representatives of the Bank of Mexico and Nafin on the committee indicated that the commission would take into account the efficient allocation of resources and the stabilization effects of government expenditure.

Years later, Rodrigo Gómez, who undoubtedly was speaking for the government as well, described the situation facing the authorities in the early 1950s:

> With the increase in social responsibilities in the modern state, the most difficult pressures for the monetary authorities to resist are those that come from the public sector. . . . Such is the case with large irrigation projects, railroads, highways, port facilities, potable water, sewage and other urban facilities, as well as, in most underdeveloped countries, electric power, telecommunications, hospitals, schools, markets and low-cost housing.
>
> It is understandable, because it is natural and human, that government officials in charge of solving these urgent needs want to make as much progress as possible in their respective fields during their terms of office—even at the cost of hindering other departments of the administration or causing budgetary deficits that may induce inflation. . . . Moreover, it is very difficult for Ministers of Finance to convince other ministers in the government that the most effective way to betray their noble cause is through uncontrolled spending, and that, in the long run, monetary stability—the product of disciplined spending—provides many more real

resources to solve the problems of infrastructure, education, health, and economic activity in general. Monetary authorities must also struggle with the deficits of certain government-controlled enterprises. Because of easy access to public funds, government enterprises are frequently lax in their efforts to reduce costs and operate efficiently. The resulting deficits of the public sector have to be financed by the central bank.[64]

Operating through the Investment Commission, the Finance Minister aimed to order government spending programs according to a set of priorities that would hold the sum of government spending within limits compatible with the capacity of the banking system for noninflationary finance of the deficit.

As was seen in earlier chapters, the expansion of credit to the private sector had been growing far more rapidly than credit to the public sector. Stabilization would require tighter control over credit expansion to domestic industry, particularly since the private banking system would be called upon to finance the government deficit. Gomez also touched on this problem:

> But the private sector also creates strong inflationary pressures which are exerted mainly on the central bank. This is not only true of an important part of the industrial, agricultural and commercial sectors but also of the banking sector itself. Some private bankers believe that through the elimination or loosening of some legal reserve requirements or through unlimited rediscounts, the central bank should provide all the banking system with abundant, cheap and opportune credit for all economic activities. These pressure groups frequently allege that credit to increase production is not inflationary, or that the central bank's stabilization policies slow down the country's progress. And there are countless plans to establish banks for the granting of loans to specific economic activities. They overlook the fact that—in the absence of developed money markets—if these banks do not obtain sufficient deposits from the public, it is the central bank that is resorted to in demand of rediscount. The stand taken by the central bank is that what is lacking is voluntary savings for the granting of more credit, not more banks. Every day new solutions are offered to real or imaginary problems. Some favor the suppressing of taxes, others the granting of subsidies, still others want both. At the same time, it is thought that public investment should be increased in order to keep up economic activity and raise the country's productive capacity. In addition, there is constant pressure on the central bank of the country to back different

types of low-interest loans on the grounds that entrepreneurs are not in a position to pay the high rates of interest prevailing on the market.[65]

Although the government was determined from the outset to introduce a stabilization program, the hostile reaction from virtually all interest groups to the 1954 devaluation played a role in fortifying the government's resolution to persevere in its stabilization efforts. Rodrigo Gómez summarized the feelings of Mexican officials when he said, "The strong unfavorable reaction to all sectors gave the Ministry of Finance and the Bank of Mexico sufficient strength successfully to overcome inflationary forces." [66]

Underlying the Ruiz Cortines administration's ability to assert the primacy of the national interest was the fact that, with the passage of time, the balance of power was passing toward the central government. It is worth remembering that the inflationary policies of Mexico were partly a political response to the conditions of anarchy and civil war that prevailed during the revolution and its aftermath. With the memory of the revolutionary bloodshed and the unbridled factionalism of 1919–1930 still fresh in mind, Cárdenas's spending program had the political objective of placating local chieftains and military leaders, who might have been able to mount a threat to the authority of the central government. Consequently, whatever stabilization objectives the government had were subordinated to the greater goal of establishing social peace and centralizing power in the presidency. Local potentates were made clients of the federal government. The military were stripped of their power as the government held military expenditures at low levels and refused to expand manpower or modernize equipment. Likewise, the new class of industrialists that the government had nurtured was uniquely dependent on the government for its well-being and indeed its existence. By the early 1950s, however, a quarter century had gone by since the authority of the central government had been seriously challenged. The power to mount a new challenge had faded from those who may have held it earlier. Institutions that the government originally needed for support ultimately became dependent upon the government for their survival.

All this is not to say that the government could treat interest groups with disdain. The political process involved in budget-making still required constant placating of pressure groups and a careful balancing of interests. Nevertheless, the government's ability to increasingly place the national interest, which it increasingly saw as tied to price and exchange-rate stability ahead of individual and group interests, clearly indicates that the preponderance of power had subtly tipped in favor of the national government.

SUMMARY

Mexican economic policy underwent a profound change in the 1950s, in which the entire basis for financing economic development shifted from forced savings through inflation and devaluation to the more conventional policy of financing development through domestic and international financial markets. The government made a specific decision to stop inflation that lowered the real income of the working class because continued lowering of the real purchasing power of the majority threatened to provoke a working-class backlash which could have endangered the stability of the regime. At the same time, the policy of devaluation would probably have been less effective owing to the decline in the country's terms of trade at the time. However, as external demand for Mexican products weakened, the country became increasingly adept at raising funds in international capital markets.

The process of stabilization was aided by a political system that was able to react effectively to the changes in domestic and international economic forces and to make the necessary adjustments. The increased power of the national government facilitated the transition from inflation to stability by enabling the authorities to exercise increased control over inflationary spending and expansion of credit.

NOTES

1. The best overall summary of the currents of economic thought in Mexico can be found in Leopoldo Solís, "Mexican Economic Policy in the Post-War Period: The Views of Mexican Economists," in *American Economic Review*, Vol. LXI (June 1971), *Supplement: Survey of National Economic Policy Issues and Policy Research*, pp. 3–67, especially pp. 28–42, where the monetarist-structuralist controversy is examined. For a view of the controversy in the context of Latin America, see Werner Baer and Isaac Kerstenetzky (eds.), *Inflation and Growth in Latin America* (Homewood, Ill.: Richard D. Irwin, Inc., 1964), especially article by Dudley Seers, "Inflation and Growth: The Heart of the Controversy," pp. 89–

103. For individual works by Mexicans arguing the structuralist point of view, see Víctor L. Urquidi, "Obstáculos al Desarrollo Económico," in *Revista de Economía,* Vol. XIV (February 1951), pp. 18–25. Juan P. Noyola Vázquez, is considered the definitive spokesman for the structuralist school in Mexico; see "Desequilibrio Fundamental y Fomento Económico en México." (Thesis: Escuela Nacional de Economía, Universidad Nacional Autónoma de México, 1949), especially, pp. 19–23, and "El Desarrollo Económico y la Inflación en México y Otros Paises Latinoamericanos," in *Investigación Económica,* Vol. XVI (fourth Quarter 1956), p. 616 ff, Horacio Flores de La Pena, "La Mecánica del Desarrollo Económico," in *Revista de Economía,* Vol. XXV (August 1963), pp. 229–307, "Los Obstáculos al Desarrollo Económico: El Desequilibrio Fundamental" (Thesis: Escuela Nacional de Economía, Universidad Nacional Autónoma de México, 1955), and "La Elasticidad de la Oferta y el Desarrollo Económico," in *El Trimestre Económico,* Vol. XXII (January–March 1955), pp. 1–12.

2. Most structuralists accepted the terms of trade agreement and the inevitability of balance-of-payments disequilibrium. For example, see Alfredo Lagunilla Iñarritu, "Un Desequilibrio Fundamental de Desarrollo," in *Comercio Exterior,* Vol. V (December 1955), pp. 495 ff. Generally, the structuralists believed that foreign official capital could ease the problems of development, but doubted that sufficient funds would be forthcoming. For example, see Urquidi, *op. cit.,* pp. 24–25. In a similar statement Alfredo Navarrete of Nacional Financiera accepted the hypothesis of "development disequilibrium." Navarrete, however, rejected exchange controls and instead advocated periodic devaluations; see "Una Hipótesis Sobre el Sistema Económico de México," in *El Trimestre Económico,* Vol. XVIII (January–March 1951), pp. 21–55, especially pp. 54–55.

3. Quoted in Antonio Manero, *La Revolución Bancaria en México* (Mexico: Talleres Gráficos de la Nación, 1957), pp. 274–275. There was a recurrent tendency among many structuralists to identify a conservative monetary policy with prolonged deflation. The structuralists often tried to argue that the restriction of demand in a given year was the equivalent to permanently reducing the rate of growth. Thus Suárez later used the example of the deflationary policies of Great Britain and other European countries in the 1920s in attempt to discredit orthodox monetary policies. See *ibid.,* pp. 291–295.

4. See Solís, *op. cit.,* pp. 38–40. One of the more severe orthodox critics of inflation was Luis Montes de Oca, Finance Minister 1929–1931 and former Director General of the Bank of Mexico, see Manero, *op. cit.,* pp. 279–283.

5. For example, see Sabas Robledo, "Causas de las Devaluaciones en México Desde 1938," in *Revista de Economía,* Vol. XVIII (July 1955), pp. 167–173; and Leopoldo Hernández Lara, "Las Devaluaciones Monetarias y la Política del Banco de México." (Thesis: Escuela Nacional de Economía, Universidad Nacional Autónoma de México, 1966).

6. Two former Finance Ministers were the most prominent orthodox critics of government policy. Montes de Oca renewed his earlier attacks on government policy, blaming the excessive creation of money and the resulting inflation for the devaluation. In 1955, Alberto Pani, Minister of Finance from 1929 to 1933, published a book in which he identified the lack of confidence of the public in Mexican money caused by inflation and devaluation as the "supreme problem" of the country; see: *El Problema Supremo de México,* (Mexico: Inversiones A.R.P.A., 1955), pp. 45–69. His attack on excessive spending by the Alemán government, which he held responsible for the 1954 devaluation, was extremely bitter. The introduction of price stability would permit the domestic financial system to channel resources to productive activities and would not require any loss in real output. The promises and the early acts of Ruiz Cortinez to slow inflation represented a hopeful sign. However, in the future, he believed, the government would have to increase efforts to bring expenditures under control and hold the growth of money supply within the limits of the growth of potential output. More generally, Pani argued that Mexican private industry had reached the point where it could assume a more dynamic role in the economic growth process and that the excessively activist and inflationary role of government could be diminished. Suárez attempted to counter Pani's argument. Replying directly to Pani's charges, he said, "The supreme problem of Mexico is not to achieve monetary stability but to raise national output and per capita income. . . . While pursuing this goal, we should try to have as much monetary stability as possible. Unfortunately, the forces which operate to produce the former also operate to destroy the latter, and to balance them requires a supreme skill in managing economic policy" (Manero, *op. cit.,* p. 295).

7. Ramón Beteta, who had been finance minister under Alemán (1946–1952), jointed the debate taking a position somewhere midway between the two extremes. "In the first place, he denied that government infrastructure was as inflationary as both the critics and defenders of inflationary policy had assumed. Instead, he claimed that the expansion of banking system credit was the true source of inflation. (In fact, as was seen in the last chapter, Beteta was partly correct. Private sector investment had been growing considerably more rapidly than public investment and credit by the banking system to the private sector expanding about twice as rapidly as credit to the government sector. Nevertheless, this was at least partly due to the creation of high powered money by the central bank, which, in turn resulted from the government deficit.) Secondly, Beteta said, perhaps inflation had not had as pernicious an effect on the masses as many believed, since consumption of staple items such as beans, rice, corn, and sugar had risen along with the growth of population. Without specifying whether Mexico had yet arrived at that stage of development, he said that when productive capacity had been enlarged enough to make inflationary finance un-

necessary, the country could be able to have stable prices and stable exchange rate. See *ibid.,* pp. 296–300. For a more elaborate statement of Beteta's views see Ramon Beteta, *Tres Años de Política Haciendaria,* (Mexico: Secretaría de Hacienda y Crédito Público, 1951), especially chapters IV and V, pp. 40–111.

8. In addition to the verifiable conflicts over elasticities, the structuralists believed that a development led by state activism was preferable to one based on generating large profits for domestic industrialists and a permissive attitude toward foreign capital, while the monetarists believed that stability and the development of private enterprise were desirable. At the risk of oversimplifying, one could say that the monetarists were to the classical liberals, while the structuralists were on the political left.

9. The difference is one of degree. The Bank of Mexico, which was the embodiment of the monetarist position, often used the external business cycle as a explanation of Mexican export performance. The structuralist position was that price and exchange-rate changes had virtually no effect on the balance of payments.

10. This view is still widely held by many Mexicans. For some exposition of this viewpoint, see Guillermo Ramos Uriarte, "La Devaluación y el Comercio Exterior," in *Revista de Economía,* Vol. XVIII (July 1955), pp. 162–166; Walter J. Sedwitz, "Mexico's 1954 Devaluation in Retrospect," in *Inter-American Economic Affairs,* Vol. X (Autumn 1956), pp. 24–29; and Carlos Carranza Edwards, "La Devaluación Monetaria de 1954: Análisis de sus Causas y Consecuencias." (Thesis: Escuela Nacional de Economía, Universidad Nacional Autónoma de México, 1967), especially pp. 110–116.

11. ECLA, *El Desequilibrio Externo en el Desarrollo Económico Latinoamericano: El Caso de México* (E/CN. 12/48). (La Paz, Bolivia, 1957), Vol. I, pp. 72–78.

12. "Problemas Monetarios," in *Comercio Exterior,* Vol. VII (October 1957), pp. 535–538. The methodology and conclusions of the ECLA report are also challenged in Ifigenia M. de Navarrete, "Desequilibrio Externo y Desarrollo Económico," in *Comercio Exterior,* Vol. VII (November 1957), pp. 592–595.

13. B. Griffiths arrived at similar conclusions, using somewhat different equations. His study covered the period 1940–1967. His export equation combined the price and exchange rate terms into a single term. In estimating import elasticities, the price term was import prices divided by Mexican prices, which also takes exchange-rate changes into account. Griffiths' results were similar to those presented in the text. The elasticities of exports with respect to the growth of income in the United States and the price equation were 1.48 and -0.52 respectively. The import elasticities in the period 1946–50 were 0.85 with respect to the growth of Mexican GNP and 0.36 with respect to relative prices. See: *Mexican Monetary Policy and Economic Development* (New York: Praeger, 1972), pp. 86–88.

14. For a statement of the Bank of Mexico's view at the time, see Rodrigo

Gómez, Speech to 1953 Bankers' Convention, in *Textos de Rodrigo Gómez* (Mexico Gráficas Panamericanas, 1967), pp. 5–8.

15. Interview with Javier Márquez, Director of CEMLA (1952–73) and Adviser to Bank of Mexico, April 19, 1974. Interview with Antonio Carillo Flores, Finance Minister 1952–58, July 15, 1974.

16. Banco Nacional de México, "La Experiencia Monetaria y de Crédito en México," in *Revista Bancaria*, Vol. II (November–December 1953), p. 592.

17. Edmundo Moyo Porras, "Efectos de la Devaluación en la Industria de Transformación," in *Revista de Economía*, Vol. XVII (May 1954), p. 142.

18. *Excelsior*, April 24, 1954.

19. Interview with Jorge Heyser, formerly Chairman, National Chamber of Manufacturing Industry, April 30, 1974.

20. Emilio Mujica, "Los Salarios en la Industria," in *Revista de Economía*, Vol. XV (September 1953), p. 276.

21. Edmundo Moyo, *et al.*, "Análisis Sobre Salarios Mínimos Elaborado por la CTM," in *Revista de Economía*, Vol. XVI (December, 1953), pp. 359–367.

22. Jorge Espinosa de los Reyes, "La Distribución del Ingreso Nacional," in *La Economía Mexicana*, Leopoldo Solís (ed.), Vol. I, *Análisis por Sectores y Distribución* (Mexico D.F.: Fondo de Cultura Económica, 1973), p. 332.

23. Quoted in *ibid.*, p. 333. Also see Beteta, *op. cit.*, pp. 82–124.

24. Brandenburg, *op. cit.*, pp. 103–107.

25. *Ibid.*, pp. 106–107.

26. Quoted in Espinosa de Los Reyes, *op. cit.*, p. 334.

27. Victor Alba, *Politics and the Labor Movement in Latin America* (Stanford University Press, 1968), pp. 300–317; and Roger D. Hansen, *The Politics of Mexican Development* (Baltimore: Johns Hopkins University Press, 1971), pp. 113–116.

28. For a study of the means that businessmen have evolved to influence government policy, see Frank R. Brandenburg, "Organized Business in Mexico," in *Inter-American Economic Affairs,* Vol. XII (Winter 1958), pp. 26–50.

29. Countries whose exports are less diversified might find devaluation less disruptive. For example, if most exports consisted of products in which home consumption did not compete with export markets, for example, coffee in Colombia, or tin in Bolivia, the main effect would be to increase the incomes of exporters without affecting domestic consumption. In those cases, the resulting profits could be taxed away, either directly or through a special exchange rate.

30. Although some independent commentators believed the devaluation was necessary, virtually all considered it as likely to make the distribution of income less equal. Sabas Robledo, for example, called it "harmful to the poorest sectors of the economy." See "Comercio Exterior, Desequilibrio de Fomento y Devaluación," in *Revista de Economía*, Vol. XVII (June 1954), p. 183; and "Devaluación," editorial in *Revista de Economía*, Vol. XVII (May 1954), pp. 133–134. Similar

points of view can be found in Ernesto Huergo H., "Causas, Fines y Efectos de la Devaluación," *Revista de Economia,* Vol. XII (June 1954), pp. 177–179; Sabas Robedo, "Efectos de la Devaluación en el Desarrollo Económico," *Revista de Economía,* Vol. XVII (May 1953), pp. 137–141; Gustavo Romero Kolbeck, "La Devaluación Monetaria," in *Revista de Economía,* Vol. XVII (May 1954), pp. 135–137; and Elena Ferreirro P., "Devaluación y Consumo," in *Revista de Economía,* Vol. XVIII (July 1955), p. 178.

31. *Excelsior,* May 20, 1954.

32. *Excelsior,* April 22, 1954.

33. *New York Times,* April 19, 1954, p. 24; *New York Times,* April 26, 1954, p. 7.

34. *New York Times,* April 23, 1954, p. 6.

35. Interview with Rafael Galván, Secretary-General, Union of Mexican Electrical Workers, April 25, 1974.

36. *Excelsior,* June 9, 1954.

37. *Excelsior,* June 10, 1954.

38. *Excelsior,* June 16, 1954.

39. *Excelsior,* June 17, 1954.

40. *Excelsior,* June 18, 1954.

41. *Excelsior,* June 20–26, 1954.

42. *Excelsior,* July 23, 1954.

43. President Ruiz Cortines had approved the devaluation in the belief that the working class was mainly interested in the prices of basic foodstuffs rather than the devaluations of the peso. When the depth of working-class protest became apparent, the president and the ministers of Labor and Finance declared that they would allow wage increases compatible with the government objective of stabilization (Interview with Antonio Carrillo Flores, July 15, 1974).

44. Carlos Bázdresch hypothesizes that in subsequent years an implicit understanding evolved between the government, the unions, and the industrialists in which official economic policy was conducted so as to provide a continuous growth of national income in which industrialists were guaranteed a high return on capital and a favorable climate for investment, while the official trade unions were guaranteed a moderate, but constant, increase in real wages, see "La Déuda Externa y Desarrollo Estabilizador," mimeographed discussion paper for Mexican Economy Seminar, Stanford University (March 1974), pp. 5–8. Similarly, Rafael Izquerido argues that the balance of interest between the unions and the industrialists is the principal reason for the government's commitment to price stability, and a mainstay of the Mexican economic system (Interview, April 17, 1974).

45. This study considers only the "gross barter" terms of trade. For a discussion of alternative concepts of the terms of trade, see: Gerald M. Meier, *The International Economics of Development* (New York: Harper & Row, 1968), Chapter 3, pp. 41–65.

46. Despite this decline in terms of trade in the 1950s, it is difficult to substantiate a hypothesis of a secular tendency for Mexican terms of trade to weaken. The terms of trade in the early 1960s were still more favorable than in 1940. See, William O. Freithaler, *Mexico's Trade and Economic Development* (New York: Praeger, 1968), pp. 41–50. It is likely that wartime demand, postwar shortages and the Korean boom led to an extremely favorable performance for the terms of trade in those years, while the slow growth of the United States economy between the end of the Korean War and the early 1960s exaggerated the swing in the other direction.

47. Rubén Gleason Galicia, "Papel de los Créditos del Exterior en el Financiamiento del Desarrollo Económico," in *Investigación Económica*, Vol. XV (fourth quarter, 1955), pp. 500–503.

48. Calvin P. Blair, "Nacional Financiera: Entrepreneurship in a Mixed Economy," in *Public Policy and Private Enterprise in Mexico*, Raymond Vernon (ed.), (Cambridge, Mass.: Harvard University Press, 1964), pp. 193–204.

49. *El Mercado de Valores*, Vol. X (August 28, 1950), p. 2.

50. For a discussion of the evolution of World Bank lending policies see Martha Solano Moctezuma, "Financiamiento Externo del Sector Público de Mexico" (Thesis: Escuela Nacional de Economía, Universidad Nacional Autónoma de México, 1965), pp. 75–78; and IBRD, *The International Bank for Reconstruction and Development 1946–53*, (Baltimore: Johns Hopkins University Press, 1954), pp. 3–11. Fuller discussions of IBRD policy in the period when bank operations were centered on developing countries can be found in John A. King, Jr., *Economic Development Projects and their Appraisals: Cases and Principles from the Experience of the World Bank.* (Published for the Economic Development Institute, International Bank for Reconstruction and Development) (Baltimore: Johns Hopkins University Press, 1967), pp. 3–15; and IBRD, *Policies and Operations: The World Bank IDA, and IFC* (Washington: IBRD, 1971), pp. 29–46.

51. Combined Mexican Working Party, *The Economic Development of Mexico* (published for IBRD), (Baltimore: Johns Hopkins University Press, 1953), pp. ix–x. (The report is the best single source of statistical data on the Mexican economy for 1939–1950).

52. *Ibid.*, pp. 13–18 and pp. 111–139.

53. IBRD, *The International Bank for Reconstruction and Development 1946–53*, pp. 53–54.

54. *Ibid.*, pp. 190–191 and pp. 30–61.

55. Combined Mexican Working Party, *op cit.*, pp. 103–110 and 137–156.

56. Alfredo Navarrete, who was director of research of Nacional Financiera at that time, said that, as the country edged toward stabilization, there was a general feeling at the policy-making level of the Nacional Financiera that new sources of external finance, including funds from private institutions, would become avail-

able if Mexico maintained policies of price stability. Interview, April 25, 1974. Similarly, Raúl Martínez Ostos, who as assistant director of Nacional Financiera negotiated many credits for the Nacional Financiera in ensuing years, said that Mexican economic policies of stability were indispensable to the country's position in negotiating credits from international organizations and private foreign institutions. Interview, April 30, 1974.

57. "Una Política de Relaciones Económicas Internacionales," in *Comercio Exterior,* Vol. IV (June 1954), pp. 219–224.

58. *El Mercado de Valores,* Vol. XIV (October 11, 1954), pp. 361–362.

59. Gleason Galicia, *op. cit.,* pp. 497–558.

60. Alfredo Navarrete, "El Sector Público en el Desarrollo Económico," in *Investigación Económica,* Vol. XVII (first quarter, 1957), pp. 43–47; and "Las Relaciones Financieras Internacionales de México," in *Investigación Económica,* Vol. XV (second quarter, 1955), pp. 179–190.

61. Ruiz Cortines made repeated promises to halt the corruption of the Alemán years during his election campaign. James R. Wilkie, *The Mexican Revolution: Public Expenditure and Social Change since 1910* (Berkeley: University of California Press, 1967), pp. 85. (Although elections in Mexico always result in the election of the PRI candidate, the candidate always campaigns vigorously for popular support.) Many Mexicans believe that one of the reasons for the cutbacks in public spending that took place in 1953 was to punish contractors who had profited from corruption under Alemán.

62. An incident at the 1958 Bankers' Convention illustrates the degree to which the public had credited the Bank of Mexico with the success of the stabilization program. On the last day of the convention, Carrillo Flores made an emotional speech in which he alluded several times to the public's underestimation of the Finance Ministry's role in bringing about stabilization, and also meaning that the public overestimated the role of the Bank of Mexico. He then began to outline the government's accomplishments and the success of the stabilization effort. Secretaría de Hacienda, *Discursos Pronunciados por los cc. Secretarios de Hacienda y Crédito Público en las Convenciones Bancarias Celebradas del Año 1934 a 1958.* (Mexico: 1958), pp. 283–285.

63. Miguel S. Wionczek, "Incomplete Formal Planning: Mexico," in *Planning Economic Development,* Everett E. Hagen (ed.) (Homewood, Ill.: Richard D. Irwin, Inc. 1963), pp. 157–165.)

64. *Economic Growth and Monetary Stability: Lectures Delivered by Maurice Frere and Rodrigo Gómez* (Washington: The Per Jacobson Foundation, 1964), pp. 32–33.

65. *Ibid.,* pp. 33–34.

66. *Ibid.,* p. 34.

Chapter VI

The 1954 Devaluation

Although the changeover from inflation to stability was a gradual process, the 1954 devaluation marked a clear turning point in economic policy. The authorities' awareness of the potential dangers of continued inflation and of the possibilities of development with stability grew over a period of years; but the adverse political reaction to the devaluation strengthened their will to proceed with stabilization. Policies to stabilize the economy were gradually introduced in the years after the devaluation; but the emphasis in policy changed at that time. Until the devaluation, the authorities were trying to formulate short-term policy in the face of an underlying balance of payments instability, but after that time they began actively building a financial system based on price stability and a stable exchange rate. Because of its importance in the historical evolution of Mexican policy, the devaluation is worthy of some detailed study, particularly since, even in Mexico, the events are not well known.

THE DEVALUATION

Both domestic policy and external conditions led to the devaluation. Continued inflationary finance in Mexico had left the peso overvalued. With this underlying instability, the balance of payments problem was pushed to the crisis point by a fall in the prices of Mexican export products stemming from the 1953 recession in the United States.

Immediately after the 1949 devaluation, Mexico resumed its inflationary growth pattern (see Table VI-1).

Table VI - 1

Indicators of Inflationary Pressure, 1950 - 1956
(percentage change)

Year	Real GNP	Foreign[a] position	Domestic credit	Money supply	Wholesale prices	Imports[b]
1950	9.4	98	12	38	9	21
1951	7.3	-9	19	14	24	44
1952	4.1	-2	10	4	4	-4
1953	0.4	-11	12	8	-2	-1
1954	10.5	20	28	14	9	1
1955	8.7	100	6	21	14	8
1956	6.2	15	11	11	5	22

[a] - Net foreign assets of Bank of Mexico and commerical banks in pesos.

[b] - Value in dollars, goods and services.

Sources: IMF; International Financial Statistics; Nacional Financiera, *Statistics on the Mexican Economy;* and Bank of Mexico.

Net domestic credit expansion was moderate in 1950, but the sizable balance of payments surplus stemming from a boom in export earnings and an inflow of capital following the outbreak of the Korean War in that year led to a large increase in the assets of the banking system. In 1951, the external sector proved to be less of a stimulus to monetary growth, but the authorities permitted an extremely high expansion of domestic credit, thus continuing the rapid growth of money supply. Owing to the large increases in domestic demand and the sizable rise in the price level, the current account moved into large deficit. (See Table VI-2.) Capital inflows were already growing, but not nearly by enough to offset the current account deficit. As a result, the country began to lose reserves steadily. In 1952 the authorities, fearing that a continued expansion would lead to a balance of payments crisis, shifted to a restrictive policy. The growth of bank credit and money supply was sharply reduced. While inflationary pressures abated, the pace of real growth also slackened considerably.[1]

In December 1952, Adolfo Ruiz Cortines became president, inheriting a precarious balance-of-payments situation. The peso showed clear signs of being overvalued. The exchange rate had been fixed at an equilibrium level in 1949. Between that year and 1952, wholesale prices had risen by 36 percent in Mexico, but by only 11 percent in the United States. Therefore, equilibrium could be maintained only if the growth of domestic demand were severely restrained and demand for Mexican exports remained buoyant. The new president chose Antonio Carillo Flores as finance minister. Carillo Flores later said that he hesitated to accept the post, since he believed that a devaluation of the peso was all but inevitable and that such a step was likely to be a highly unpopular measure.[2]

Table V - 2

The Balance of Payments, 1950 - 1956
(millions of dollars)

	1950	1951	1952	1953	1954	1955	1956
Current account	40	-215	-107	-118	- 45	22	-123
Exports[a]	827	918	984	964	1048	1208	1324
Imports[a]	-787	-1133	-1090	-1082	-1094	-1186	-1447
Capital account	130	126	75	54	63	222	218
Long-term	70	99	85	53	112	129	150
Short-term	60	27	- 9	1	- 49	93	68
Errors and omissions	2	82	11	23	- 44	- 44	- 32
Change in official reserves[e]	172	- 8	- 21	- 42	- 26	200	63
Level of official reserves[e]	321	314	293	251	225	425	488

[a] Goods and services.
[e] Estimates.
Source: Banco de Mexico, S.A.

The situation became more foreboding in 1953 when the United States entered a recession, causing demand for Mexican exports to fall. With a relatively low level of international reserves and few sources of credit available from the world financial community, the finance minister and high officials of the Bank of Mexico now believed that the exchange rate could be maintained only if the country were willing to sacrifice other important objectives. This impression was confirmed by an IMF report of 1953, which concluded that the only way to avoid a devaluation was by a sizable reduction in public expenditure.[3] The scope for such a policy was limited, however, since the president believed it was politically intolerable to have two years of slow real growth in succession. Thus, the Ruiz Cortines administration at first continued the deflationary policies of the last year of Alamán's term. In mid-1953, however, the magnitude of the economic slowdown became apparent, and the government abruptly shifted gears and began moving toward an expansionary spending policy. Public expenditure accelerated sharply while tax revenue stagnated.[4] As a result, reserve losses continued and the country was clearly headed toward another foreign-exchange crisis.

Carillo Flores was convinced that devaluation had become inevitable as soon as the decision to accelerate public spending was taken. Given the inevitability of such a measure, he believed it would be best to devalue as soon as possible, rather than stage a prolonged defense of the exchange rate. Rodrigo Gómez and Antonio Carillo Flores, who had participated in the decision making that preceded the establishment of a new parity in 1948–1949, did not wish to repeat the experience of that period when after having exhausted all reserves, the authorities could not control the downward float of the peso. In 1949 the exchange rate had been fixed at an equilibrium level, and consequently the rate quickly became overvalued as the country continued to pursue inflationary policies. This time the authorities wished to stop reacting defensively to external imbalance and introduce a comprehensive stabilization program. This could be done only if the exchange rate were clearly undervalued in order to give the authorities enough breathing room to gradually introduce stabilization. Another important consideration was that it was still relatively early in the presidential term, and enough time remained for the administration to regain some of the prestige it would lose by devaluing if it could produce solid economic results.[5] Accordingly, on January 11,

Carillo Flores asked Rodrigo Gómez to have the staff of the Bank of Mexico prepare a study of an appropriate exchange rate for the peso in case of devaluation.[6]

The devaluation would be an extremely unpopular move in any case, and hence the finance minister needed to develop as wide as possible a consensus both within the government and in the public at large that the devaluation was needed. On the one hand, this involved trying to persuade as many as possible that the peso was overvalued, and that devaluation was a suitable remedy. Simultaneously, the authorities had to make concrete efforts to restore external balance without devaluation in order to show that all alternatives had been exhausted. In February 1954, the authorities tried to postpone the inevitable by raising all tariffs by 25 percent. The current account deficit, nevertheless, continued to widen while a gathering speculative movement out of pesos placed additional strains on official reserves.[7] In the early days of April, the speculative outflow quickened. The authorities were now faced with the possibility of a near total depletion of reserves which would have made it impossible to defend the existing exchange rate or a new rate should the currency be devalued. The Finance Minister decided that the time had come to devalue. After presenting the case for devaluation to the president, Carillo Flores received final approval. The move would have to be taken swiftly and in the strictest secrecy in order to forestall speculation and avoid political charges that the government allowed its friends to profit from the devaluation while imposing sacrifices on the majority of the population. Easter Week was approaching, at which time the banks would be closed from Wednesday afternoon through Sunday. The long holiday would give the authorities enough time to take the needed step secretly. At this point, only four men knew of the decision to devalue: President Ruiz Cortinez, Antonio Carrillo Flores, Rodrigo Gómez, and the President of the National Mortgage Bank.

At the time the decision to devalue was made, Raúl Martínez Ostos, Assistant Director General of the Nacional Financiera and formerly Mexican executive director in the International Monetary Fund, was in the United States negotiating long-term credits from potential creditors.[8] Summoned back to Mexico on Saturday April 10th. 1954, Martínez Ostos was asked to carry on the negotiations because of his personal acquaintance with key individuals in the United States government and the IMF. The country would need the support of the International Monetary Fund or it might face isolation from the international financial community. Since the United States at that time had more than 30 percent of the voting power in the IMF, Washington's support for the move was essential.[9]

The banks in Mexico closed on Wednesday for the remainder of the Easter Week, thus freeing the hands of the authorities.[10] The same Wednesday, at noon, Martínez Ostos began negotiations at the United States Treasury and later at the International Monetary Fund to convince the officials in those institutions to support a large devaluation. At first, the U.S. Treasury opposed the devaluation on the grounds that such a large parity adjustment would be a competitive devaluation, designed to give Mexican exports an unfair competitive advantage over those of other countries. Martínez Ostos tried to persuade the U.S. Treasury that the adjustment was large enough to anticipate price increases and thereby allow the authorities to gradually introduce a stabilization program. He pointed out that the authorities planned to introduce taxes on exports which would remove the competitive edge to Mexican exports. After some hesitation, the Fund staff supported the Mexican position that the move was necessary. Finally, at about 3:30 P.M. on Friday, April 16, the United States Treasury agreed to support the Mexican devaluation. The devaluation was announced in Mexico on Saturday, April 17.

The authorities gave the following rationale for the devaluation:

> . . . the maintenance of a moderate anticyclical and development policy with financial and external equilibrium. The new exchange rate was chosen to stimulate private investment and to maintain imports within the level of our foreign-exchange receipts, and through higher taxes on exports and a general increase in tax collections increase government revenue to the point that will permit the balancing of the government budget at a reasonable level of public spending.[11]

Along with the announcement of the devaluation, the government imposed taxes of 25 percent on the value of Mexican export products, designed to both increase government revenues and to serve as a kind of "windfall profit" tax, by limiting the transfer of income to the export sector.[12] The increase in export taxes was also aimed at allaying criticisms that the devaluation aimed at permanently establishing an undervalued exchange rate in order to improve Mexico's trade at the expense of other countries. At the same time, the authorities required the commercial banks to surrender their existing foreign exchange holdings at the earlier exchange rate, in order to prevent the banks from profiting from the exchange-rate adjustment.[13] The official statement also disavowed any intentions of competitive devaluation:

> The government of Mexico did not decide to adjust the exchange rate as a competitive expedient in order to increase the share of Mexican exports in foreign markets at the expense of other countries. Mexico has always disapproved such practices, which it considers illegal. Moreover, in present circumstances, such practices would fail in any case, given the deterioration in the terms of trade of our country, to produce any considerable increase in the value of exports.[14]

Along with the agreement of the U.S. Treasury and the IMF to support the devaluation, the IMF extended a package of credits totaling $50 million, consisting of $22.5 million from the Mexican gold *tranche* in the Fund plus an additional $27.5 million "stand-by" agreement.[15] The $75 million "swap" line with the U.S. Treasury also remained in effect. In addition, commercial banks in the United States extended some credit to Mexico. In combination with roughly $200 million of international reserves, the country's lines of credit raised total resources available to support the peso to over $350 million.

As was mentioned earlier, Carillo Flores had long been convinced that there was no alternative to devaluation. On a political level his task was to persuade the public and the ruling group that the devaluation was the best possible course of action under existing circumstances, and that all possible steps to avoid devaluation had been taken. According to a statement to the press by Carillo Flores, the government had been left with four options:[16]

1. to drastically reduce public spending which, by decreasing the rate of growth, would reduce imports. This option was rejected as incompatible with the country's overall objective of maintaining a high rate of growth. Moreover, the authorities believed that such action would be ineffective because private investors would have realized that sooner

or later the government would have to expand demand and abandon the exchange rate. Thus, such a decision would have provoked a capital flight in any case.

2. to introduce controls on capital exports. However, the opinion of those who would have to administer the controls (presumably the Bank of Mexico) was that this would be unworkable and would further undermine confidence in the peso. In the words of an official statement by the Ministry of Finance:[17]

> It is true that in certain circumstances, some less desirable elements in society can abuse the freedom [of capital movements] and seek a profit, when in the process they do damage to society as a whole. However, this bad effect, which the penal law punishes with severe sanctions, is smaller than the harm which would come from complicated, and in Mexico, ineffectual systems, which, while unable to prevent illegal manipulation, given the size of our frontiers, the great variety of our exports, and the importance of tourist expenditures would deprive our economy of the capital resources it needs for the continuation of economic development.

3. to continue supporting the peso in the exchange market with existing international reserves. The authorities believed that a massive capital flight would have begun. Furthermore, if the recession in the United States did not end quickly, the country would still be forced to devalue the currency under less favorable conditions.

4. to devalue the peso immediately. This solution would im prove the current account balance. Moreover, it would preempt a capital flight by making a sizable parity adjustment, thus removing any incentive to speculate against the peso. The authorities decided that under the circumstances, this was the best available option.

Despite the efforts to portray the devaluation as necessary and despite the improved outlook for the current account, the Mexican public panicked at the announcement. A fierce speculative movement out of pesos occurred in the week after the devaluation.[18] The devaluation also met with dismay in the foreign press which generally believed that the devaluation was not necessary and that the authorities should have continued to defend the peso.[19] The climate of confusion, the capital flight, and the extreme public reaction against the devaluation gave rise to widespread rumors that the introduction of exchange controls was imminent, which further aggravated the run on the peso.[20] The government was faced with sharp criticism in the Mexican press, and a deep political turmoil continued for several months. As the public reaction grew more intense, the president decided that Carillo Flores would have to absorb all criticism for the aation. In defense of his policy, Carillo Flores persisted in arguing that there was no alternative to devaluation other than exchange controls.[21]

By the end of June, reserves were down to about $100 million. At that time, however, the domestic political situation quieted and the threat of a general strike disappeared. The movement out of pesos subsided, and some reflow of funds developed in the second half of that year.[22]

In explaining the 1954 devaluation, the Bank of Mexico emphasized the influence of the international economic system on the country's growth. The less-developed countries could only continue to sustain an acceptable rate of growth if they could continue to pay for their imports through stable export earnings and predictable flows of foreign capital. "However, when there are disturbances in the world of such magnitude as have been seen in recent years, development can only continue successfully if they can escape economic crisis."[23] The recession in the United States had led to a fall in the prices of exports from developing areas. Since offsetting capital flows were not forthcoming, the less-developed countries either had to face external disequilibrium or introduce deflationary policies at home.[24] In the official Melxican view, the dependence of their country on the United States business cycles forced their country to either slow its rate of growth in response to balance-of-payments pressures or accept devaluation as a remedy.

POLICY CHANGES ACCOMPANYING THE DEVALUATION

The public outcry against the devaluation and the changes in the international economy all seemed to reaffirm the government's conviction that future devaluation was to be avoided. An alternative strategy had to be found that would allow the country to withstand a drop in export receipts without recourse to devaluation. Such a strategy first of all required a high level of reserves to defend the peso and thereby allow the domestic economy to expand even if conditions in the rest of the world were unfavorable. Since the authorities were also willing to forego the benefits of devaluation to the current account, such a policy would have to give greater emphasis to the capital account. In June 1954, Octaviano Campos Salas, chief of the Research Department of the Bank of Mexico, outlined a new international economic strategy, which involved both preventing excessive current deficits and increasing capital flows. The current account deficit would be controlled through continued export promotion and import substitution as well as a more effective use of demand management policies. At the same time, the authorities would create a network of international financial relationships that would provide enough external long-term credit to offset current account deficits and thereby alter the pattern of the balance of payments. Furthermore, the country would need access to short-term lines of credit to enable the authorities to withstand exceptional pressures on the exchange rate.[25] While their public statements emphasized the dependence of Mexico on external business cycles, the authorities were fully aware that the uncontrolled growth of demand at home had also played a large role in the inflation-devaluation cycle.

With political momentum gathering behind the idea of stabilization, the authorities now wished to elaborate a full-fledge set of stabilization targets and guidelines, and hence turned to the IMF for technical assistance. At that time, most countries had not yet arrived at the stage where monetary policy was conducted with regard to the growth of monetary aggregates; central bank operations were oriented toward market conditions. Thus, the IMF mission of 1955 was a ground-breaking attempt to systematically formulate demand management objectives and policies with respect to broad macroeconomic indicators such as the rate of growth of national income, money supply, or government spending. In drawing up the stabilization program of 1955, the authorities established the link between the level of public sector investment and the growth of the money supply which was to become the foundation of Mexican stabilization policy in the years to come. (See Chapter VII.)

The outcome of the IMF study of the Mexican economy was a report prepared in 1955 that spelled out a set of underlying objectives and medium-term targets with regard to the broad outlines of international economic policy. The report agreed that exchange controls would be ineffective in Mexico and held that the best means of preventing capital flight was to maintain a stable growth of the economy.[26] In addition, the experience of recent years had shown that the country would have to make an increase in international reserves in order to ride out short-term emergencies. Table VI-3 shows the Fund estimate of potential reserve needs. Overall contingency needs were estimated at $200–300 million, but since no country would wish to approach total exhaustion of its reserves, the IMF suggested an additional $100 million, thus fixing the target for reserves at $400 million.[27] Reserves reached this figure, equal to some six months of visible imports, in 1955. The report states that the peso had probably been overvalued since 1952 or 1953.[28] Since the 1949 devaluation, prices had risen about 30 percent in Mexico as opposed to 10 percent in the United States. The 45 percent devaluation thus left the peso undervalued by some 25 percent. Mexico had been able to maintain equilibrium in its balance of payments only with the exceptionally favorable circumstances of the Korean War boom and hence the need to establish the exchange rate at a more defensible level was obvious.[29] In order to prevent future devaluation, Mexico should aim at purchasing power parity with the United States. The IMF staff estimated when the wholesale price index rose 38 percent, the peso would be at a purchasing power parity with the dollar.[30] As the price level approached that point, the degree of monetary discipline would have to be much greater.

Table VI - 3

IMF Estimates of Mexican Contingency Needs
(millions of dollars)

Crop failure	30
Export decline	40 - 50
Seasonal variations	30 - 40
Capital flight	80 - 100
Budget deficit	40 - 80
Total	220 - 300

Source: IMF Report, p. 8.

The IMF assumed that real output would grow at 5 percent per year, hence monetary expansion would have to be held to 66 million pesos per year, which, given the size of the Mexican money supply in 1955, represented an expansion of roughly 6 percent.[31] The report concluded that the only means to control monetary expansion was to maintain strict limits on the growth of bank credit and the level of public sector investment.[32] With respect to public sector spending, the general level of fiscal discipline would have to be improved and the role of the Investment Commission would be especially important in the overall move toward stabilization.

It is essential to emphasize the voluntary nature of Mexico's relations with the Fund especially in view of the criticism that IMF programs have received particularly in Latin America.[33] The IMF participates actively in the formulation of stabilization programs in member countries. Acceptance of stabilization programs is required for access to Fund borrowing facilities. Such policies have been strongly criticized on the grounds that the Fund's resources and prestige are used to force countries in balance of payments distress to adopt measures that are in keeping with the Fund's preference for orthodox policies.[34] The critics of the IMF allege that the recipient countries accept stabilization programs merely to become eligible for short-term loans and to remain in good standing with other international lenders, and that these programs are based on a fundamental misreading of the aspirations of Latin America and the development process in Latin American countries which are often oriented toward inflationary finance and extensive use of controls.[35] Whatever the overall merits of this criticism, it is plainly not valid in the Mexican case. Undoubtedly, the Fund's influence had some role in Mexico's decision to ask for technical assistance. Since the country wished to broaden contacts with other potential lenders such as the IBRD, the Eximbank, and private commercial banks, Fund approval of Mexican policies was extremely useful, if not necessary. By the same token, defenders of the stability-oriented policy within the Mexican bureaucracy probably used the IMF reports to try to influence government policy. Nevertheless, the desire to introduce price stability arose not out of alien pressures, but because the Mexican authorities had decided that, for reasons of domestic political and social stability, inflation had to be contained. Therefore, it is more accurate to speak of a coincidence of interest between Mexico and the IMF rather than manipulation by either party.

NOTES

1. ECLA, *Economic Survey of Latin America,* 1954 (E/CN/12/362/Rev. 1), (New York: United Nations, 1955), pp. 174–175. The fact that disequilibrium was evident even before the sharp fall in export prices occurred in 1953 indicates that Mexican policies were sufficient to give rise to a balance of payments crisis, although the situation was aggravated by a deterioration in the terms of trade.

2. Interview with Antonio Carillo Flores, July 15, 1974.

3. Antonio Carrillo Flores, *Homenajes y Testimonios* (Mexico: By the author, 1967), p. 152.

4. ECLA, *loc. cit.*

5. Interview with Carrillo Flores. See also: Rodrigo Gómez, Speech to Participants in CEMLA program, August, 1957. In *Textos de Rodrigo Gómez,* (Mexico: Gráficas Panamericanas, 1967), pp. 107–108. Rodrigo Gómez reportedly also believed that a devaluation was inevitable and would be a distasteful step. Hence, he believed that another devaluation might be impossible for perhaps a generation. Therefore, devaluation would have to be accompanied by measures to introduce stability.

6. Carrillo Flores, *op. cit.,* pp. 152–153.

7. Bank of Mexico, *Annual Report,* 1955, p. 21.

8. Except where otherwise noted, the chronology of the negotiations leading to the devaluation is based on an interview with Raúl Martínez Ostos, April 30, 1974, and a letter from Martinez Ostos dated September 4, 1974.

9. The United States held 31.08 percent of total voting power in the International Monetary Fund, *Annual Report of the Executive Directors,* 1954, p. 143.

10. In Mexico, as in many Latin American countries, the banks close at noon Wednesday of Easter Week.

11. *Excelsior,* April 18, 1954.

12. *El Mercado de Valores,* Vol. XIV (April 26, 1954), pp. 137–138.

13. *Ibid,* p. 141.

14. *Ibid,* p. 137

15. Bank of Mexico, *Annual Report,* 1955, p. 20.

16. *El Mercado de Valores,* Vol. XIV (April 26, 1954), pp. 138–141.

17. Secretaría de Hacienda, press release, April 18, 1954.

18. *The New York Times,* April 26, 1954, p. 59.

19. Miguel S. Wionczek, "Las Opiniones Extranjeras Sobre La Devaluación," in *Revista de Economía,* Vol. XVII (May 1954), pp. 148–152.

20. *The New York Times,* April 26, 1954, p. 59.

21. *The New York Times,* April 20, 1954, p. 20.

22. Bank of Mexico, *Annual Report,* 1955, pp. 22–24.

23. *Ibid,* p. 15

24. *Ibid,* pp. 16–22.

25. "Una Política de Relaciones Económicas Internacionales," in *Comercio Exterior,* Vol. IV (June 1954), pp. 219–220.

26. "Financial Policy and Economic Development in Mexico: Report of a Mission of the International Monetary Fund," (Washington: June 24, 1955), p. 7.

27. *Ibid,* p. 8.

28. *Ibid,* p. 78.

29. *Ibid,* p. 41.

30. *Ibid,* pp. 41–43.

31. *Ibid,* p. 4.

32. Ibid, pp. 57–65.

33. For a discussion of the requirements of the IMF for stand-by agreements, see: Alexandre Kafka, "Some Aspects of Latin America's Financial Relations with the International Monetary Fund," in *Socio-Economic Change in Latin America,* Alberto Martínez Piedras (ed.), (Washington: Catholic University of America Press, 1970), pp. 96–97.

34. Miguel S. Wionczek, "Diez Años del Banco Internacional y del Fondo Monetario," in *Comercio Exterior,* Vol. VI (October 1956), p. 474.

35. For a statement of this view, see: Wolfgang Konig, "International Financial Institutions and Latin American Development," in *Latin America in the International Economy,* Victor Urquidi and Rosemary Throp (eds.), (New York: John Wiley and Sons, 1973), pp. 116–163.

Chapter VII

Financial Policy Under
Conditions of Stability

BACKGROUND OF STABILIZATION POLICY

In the years after the 1954 devaluation, the authorities proceeded to construct a new system of finance based upon price and exchange-rate stability. As Table VII-1 shows, the rate of price increase was substantially reduced while maintaining a satisfactory rate of growth of output. Although the process of stabilization was continuous, the period from devaluation to 1965 can be conveniently broken into two parts. The years 1954–1958 can best be understood as a transition period during which the basis of a system of noninflationary growth was established; after 1958, development proceeded with the pattern of noninflationary growth already established.

It is somewhat arbitrary to select 1958 as the watershed year of the period, for as will be seen shortly, individual economic variables began to respond to the change in policy at different times. Nevertheless, 1958 was a year in which many indicators began to respond favorably to policy changes. Moreover, according to official calculations, 1958 was the first full year in which the peso, which had been deliberately undervalued in 1954, was at purchasing power parity with the dollar. As discussed in the preceding chapter, the plan of action worked out with the IMF mission of 1955 called for more stringent control over public expenditure, while gradually reducing the rate of monetary expansion. It was estimated that

Table VII - 1

Key Economic and Financial Indicators, 1954 - 1965
(percent change per annum)

	Real GNP	Money supply	Domestic credit	Foreign assets	Wholesale prices	Consumer prices
1954	10.5	11.9	17.0	24.8	9.3	4.8
1955	8.7	19.5	- 2.0	99.6	13.6	15.9
1956	6.2	11.2	11.0	14.9	4.6	4.5
1957	7.7	6.6	12.9	- 4.4	4.2	5.3
1958	5.5	7.4	22.2	-14.6	4.4	12.2
1959	2.8	15.6	9.6	14.6	1.2	2.4
1960	7.9	9.3	14.9	-11.6	5.0	4.8
1961	3.4	6.5	12.9	- 5.4	0.9	1.7
1962	4.8	12.1	14.3	4.8	1.8	1.1
1963	6.2	16.1	10.9	34.5	0.5	0.6
1964	10.0	17.6	14.5	8.2	4.2	2.2
1965	5.3	5.6	15.6	- 9.7	1.8	3.6
Annual Averages						
1946 - 1953	6.9	16.1	15.6	—	8.9	8.5
1954 - 1958	7.7	11.2	12.0	—	8.5	8.5
1959 - 1965	6.0	11.8	13.2	—	2.4	2.2

Source: Bank of Mexico, *Annual Reports*; Nacional Financiera, *Statistics on the Mexican Economy*, 1966; International Monetary Fund, *International Financial Statistics*.

Mexico would arrive at purchasing power parity with the United States when Mexican wholesale prices had increased by about 25 percent. After that time, the expansion of money and credit would have to be held strictly within the limits compatible with price stability, and thus could only grow by as much as real output. Accordingly, money, credit, and the price level were allowed to reflect the increase in costs brought on by the devaluation through 1956. However, as the currency began to near parity with that of the United States, policy became more restrictive. At the 1957 Bankers' Convention, Rodrigo Gómez bluntly said that Mexico was approaching purchasing power parity with the United States and that thereafter the central bank would hold the growth of money and credit to a rate compatible with external balance.[1]

An additional reason for viewing 1958 as a key point in the stabilization process was that it marked the end of a presidential term, and a new finance minister took office who continued to implement the policies of his predecessor. Having withstood the post-devaluation backlash, Carillo Flores's task during his remaining years in office was to maintain the momentum toward stabilization begun at the time of the devaluation. The problem was to mobilize political support for a prolonged commitment to stable growth founded upon the proposition that the growth of demand had to be compatible with price and exchange-rate stability, while providing enough positive results in terms of real growth to convince the decision-making apparatus that there was no conflict between growth and stability.

In late 1958, the administration changed hands, with Adolfo López Mateos becoming president and Antonio Ortiz Mena assuming the post of finance minister. (Ortiz Mena also served in the same post in the succeeding administration, thus extending his tenure from 1959 to 1970). While there was no clear break in policy between the two administrations, Ortiz Mena formalized the policies of the earlier administration into a doctrine known as "Stabilizing Development." The objective of this policy was to continue the high rates of growth of earlier periods, but under conditions of price and exchange-rate stability. As Ortiz Mena described his policy, the government at the outset rejected the option of returning to a system of inflationary finance and decided that henceforth growth would have to be compatible with the twin objectives of price stability and the maintenance of the exchange rate at 12.50 pesos per U.S. dollar. Under "Stabilizing Development," economic development of the economy continued to be led by public investment spending and the expansion of import-substituting industry. In order to finance this expansion in a setting of stability, greater amounts of voluntary savings than in previous periods had to be mobilized through a growing domestic financial system, and the country had to gain access to a widening network of foreign credit institutions.[2] As previous discussions have made clear, these ideas were not new but were logical extentions of plans worked out in the early 1950s. The new doctrine, nevertheless, served the psychological function of hammering home to the public the idea that the stability-oriented pattern of development was not a transitory phase associated with one administration but a permanent feature of national policy. The Bank of Mexico had long held that lack of confidence in the financial market had undermined development of the system. The Finance Ministry and the Bank of Mexico were now in accord about the importance of confidence, and both institutions set about the task of altering expectations both by their public pronouncements and policy actions.

THE CHANGING PATTERN OF DOMESTIC FINANCE

New Sources of Savings and Investment

In distinct contrast to the inflationary period, the main sources of finance for domestic investment under conditions of stability were increased inflows of foreign capital and increased voluntary domestic savings channeled through a burgeoning market in fixed-interest securities, which in turn depended upon public willingness to increase holdings of financial assets. Throughout the period, the share of investment in national income was rising, which reflected the effectiveness of official policies favoring high investment activities, including credits for private industry and the government investment program. (See Table VII-2.) Apparently, this would also imply that under relative stability, resources can still be channeled efficiently into high investment activities. If the share of income represented by profits and investment income rises faster than wage income, which will still be held back by excess supplies of labor, a stabilizing system can also facilitate the transfer of resources to high investment sectors. Thus, the conflict between savings and con-

Table VII - 2

Gross Domestic Investment as a Percentage of
Gross Domestic Product, 1952 - 1965

1952	13.8
1953	13.8
1954	14.0
1955	14.3
1956	16.7
1957	16.5
1958	14.7
1959	14.2
1960	14.9
1961	14.5
1962	13.7
1963	16.7
1964	18.5
1965	18.5

Source: International Monetary Fund, *International Financial Statistics.*

sumption is separate from the conflict between inflation and stability. The investment share of income can be either rising or falling independent of the behavior of the price level.

The increased capability of foreign capital and domestic financial markets to finance domestic investment can be seen in Table VII-3. The impact of foreign capital is measured indirectly by the current account balance, which as stated earlier is equal to and opposite in sign to the flow of foreign capital. The country's capital account was roughly balanced in the period 1950–1955, mainly as a result of the devaluation-induced surpluses of 1950, 1954, and 1955. In the transition period, the country depended heavily on foreign capital inflows to finance domestic investment since domestic savings tended to respond slowly to the improvements in financial markets. In the post-1960 period, the relative dependence of the country on foreign capital declined somewhat as rising domestic savings through the financial markets became increasingly capable of financing domestic investment.

The table also compares the net increase in public holdings of fixed-

Table VII - 3

Financing Domestic Investment, 1950 - 1965

A: Foreign Capital and Domestic Investment

Current Account Balance as Percentage of Gross Domestic Capital Formation

1950	1951	1952	1953	1954	1955	1956	1957	1958	1959	1960	1961	1962	1963	1964	1965
18.7	-15.9	-2.4	-6.2	2.0	8.7	-0.6	-12.5	-10.1	-2.0	-9.1	-3.7	-1.6	-4.0	-8.3	-6.7

(annual averages)

1950 - 1955	1955 - 1960	1961 - 1965
-0.6	-6.8	-4.9

B: Capacity of Domestic Financial Markets to Finance Domestic Investment

Increase in Holdings of Fixed Income Assets as Percentages of Domestic Savings 1950 - 1969[1]

	1950	1951	1952	1953	1954	1955	1956	1957	1958	1959	1960	1961	1962	1963	1964	1965
Time deposits	3.0	8.3	1.0	6.6	13.2	3.4	2.5	2.0	1.9	10.6	10.3	6.9	9.9	10.4	13.3	9.3
Debt	20.0	13.8	10.5	10.6	7.5	9.9	5.8	10.4	7.6	9.5	15.1	9.1	9.8	14.1	26.8	41.3
Government	10.2	3.1	4.2	1.2	6.1	3.2	2.3	2.6	1.9	1.7	9.8	1.1	1.2	0.9	15.8	26.8
Decentralized agencies	6.7	9.4	2.7	9.8	-0.8	5.1	0.5	4.7	5.7	0.7	7.3	3.3	5.1	8.1	3.5	3.3
Private	3.4	6.0	3.6	-0.4	2.2	1.6	2.9	3.1	0.0	7.1	-2.0	4.7	3.5	5.1	7.5	11.2
Total[a]	22.9	22.1	11.5	17.2	20.7	13.3	8.3	12.4	9.5	20.1	25.4	15.9	19.7	24.5	40.1	50.6

(annual averages)

1950 - 1955	1956 - 1960	1961 - 1965
21.5	15.1	30.2

[a] Time deposits plus debt as percentage of domestic savings.

[1] Domestic savings = gross domestic capital formation less the current account balance.
Sources: International Monetary Fund, *International Financial Statistics*. Comisión Nacional de Valores, *Memoria Anual*.

149

interest assets, mainly time deposits and bonds, with total national savings. At the beginning of the period, the increased public holdings of fixed-interest assets were equal to about one fifth of national savings. The net contribution of the financial markets to total national savings declined somewhat in the next few years. Public holdings of fixed-yield securities were rising rapidly, but other forms of savings were rising even more rapidly—especially retained corporate earnings, a reduced current account deficit and a reduced budget deficit. After 1960, the financial markets began to increase their capability to finance higher levels of domestic investment. Although the transition period was rather long, by the mid-1960s the market in securities had arrived at a point where it was capable of mobilizing a sharply increased share of national savings. The relative importance of the financial markets varied from year to year and other forms of savings continued to play important roles in the finance of domestic investment. Clearly, however, the pattern that emerged was that the market for fixed-income securities was able to finance an increasing share of domestic investment on balance.

The system of inflationary finance had worked under the distinct disadvantage that the inflation-devaluation cycle had made it impossible for a conventional securities market to function. The private sector made little effort to utilize the securities markets since the public lacked confidence in financial assets and hence would hold domestic assets mainly for transactions purposes. Consequently, savings could only be fomented by redistributing national income through transfers of income to sectors of the economy with high propensities to save, such as industrialists and exporters. By contrast, the essential condition for the growth of the market in peso-denominated fixed-interest securities was public confidence in continued stability, which required the authorities to foster expectations that relative prices and incomes would remain stable instead of changing abruptly as a result of general price increases and devaluation. The system tended to be self-reinforcing, inasmuch as the ability to achieve stability required public confidence in the financial market, which in turn depended on a growing public experience of stability.

The Achievement of Stability

In reducing inflation, the first problem to be faced was to finance government expenditure without recourse to excessive monetary expansion. In this regard, the single most important financial innovation was the use of the private banking system to finance the government debt. To be sure, the absolute level of public spending was an important variable that required vigilance, since the control over public spending was essential to preventing excessive expansion of demand.[3] The Investment Commission had already been assigned the task of maintaining a level of government spending that was compatible with stability. The finances of public sector enterprises also were strengthened by increasing self-finance through increased charges and reduced transfers from government. In addition, the growing availability of external capital constituted an important source of funds for public investment. Moreover, the on-going struggle to keep public expenditure within the limits of the financing capability was also an essential feature of stabilization policy. Nevertheless, the major change in public finance that underlay Mexican stabilization was that the burden of financing the government debt was shifted from the central bank to the private banking system, by the use of the flexible reserve-requirement scheme under which the Bank of Mexico is empowered to: 1) vary average reserve requirements on average deposits of the banks; and 2) impose reserve requirements on average deposits of the banks and up to 100 percent on increases in deposits. These requirements can, however, be lowered if the banks invest incremental deposits in specified assets, including government bonds.[4] (Government bonds in Mexico do not pay competitive yields, and hence the banks acquire such assets merely to satisfy official requirements.)

Table VII-4 shows the evolution of the financing of the federal government debt in the period 1954-1965. Clearly, there was a profound reordering of the pattern of government finance. At the beginning of the period, the Bank of Mexico was virtually the only holder of government securities while, in most of the rest of the period, its net credit to the government was reduced. Meanwhile, beginning in 1956, the private banking system began to acquire increasingly larger amounts of government securities, and nonbank financial institutions also began to finance the government deficit. Even in 1965, when there was a surge of central bank financing of the government deficit, the Bank of Mexico purchased 38 percent of the government debt, with private financial institutions absorbing the majority.

Improvements in the pattern of government finance could only be successful insofar as central bank purchases of government debt did not

Table VII - 4

Financing of the Government Sector, 1954 - 1965
(billions of pesos)

Year	Total financial system	Total	Banking System Bank of Mexico	Commercial and savings banks	Other financial institutions
1954	2.92	2.67	2.38	.29	.25
1955	3.10	2.71	2.06	.65	.39
1956	3.01	2.40	1.54	.86	.61
1957	3.73	1.92	1.82	1.04	.72
1958	4.63	3.58	2.44	1.14	1.05
1959	4.32	3.25	1.60	1.65	1.07
1960	5.38	3.74	1.90	1.84	1.64
1961	5.54	3.77	1.38	2.39	1.77
1962	5.70	3.37	.42	2.94	2.33
1963	8.27	6.02	2.12	3.90	2.25
1964	12.96	7.72	2.53	5.19	5.24
1965	21.53	13.64	8.04	5.60	7.89

Source: International Monetary Fund, *International Financial Statistics.*

automatically cause increases in the money stock. The overall growth of money and credit still had to be kept within the limits compatible with stability. In effect, the Bank of Mexico regulated the growth of the monetary base by squeezing the commerical banks when the needs of the government sector rose, thus giving the government sector priority access to the banking system. As Table VII-5 shows, the credit to the government sector has a far higher rate of growth overall than credit to the private sector, although the rate of growth of credit to the private sector was occasionally greater in individual years. This in effect reversed the pattern of the inflationary period, when credit to the private sector grew faster. The authorities engaged in a mandatory allocation of credit, allowing credit to the private sector to increase sharply when government finance needs were low, but slowing the growth of credit to the private sector when public needs were greater.[5] Thus, the growth of high-

Table VII - 5
Monetary Expansion, 1952 - 1965
(billions of pesos, end of period)

| | Sources of expansion | | Domestic factor | | | | Sources of absorption | | | |
| | | | | | | | | | | |
Year	External factor	Total	Public sector	Private sector	Increase in assets of banking system	Percentage change in money supply	Aggregate money supply	Increase in money supply	Public holdings of other private financial assets	Percentage change in public holdings of other private financial assets
1952	-.060	0.790	0.080	0.710	0.730	4.2	7.260	0.290	4.30	8.6
1953	-.300	1.150	0.300	0.850	0.850	10.9	8.850	0.790	4.96	15.4
1954	0.580	1.370	0.600	0.770	1.950	11.9	9.010	0.960	6.95	40.1
1955	2.900	-.180	-.150	-.030	2.720	19.5	10.770	1.760	7.73	11.2
1956	0.870	1.020	-.360	1.380	1.890	11.2	11.980	1.210	8.13	5.2
1957	-.290	1.330	0.530	0.800	1.040	6.7	12.780	0.940	9.38	15.4
1958	-.930	2.580	0.860	1.720	1.650	7.4	13.720	0.940	11.14	18.8
1959	0.920	1.360	-.370	1.730	2.280	15.7	15.870	2.150	13.36	20.0
1960	-.740	2.320	0.420	1.900	1.580	9.3	17.350	1.480	19.08	42.8
1961	-.290	2.310	0.188	2.130	2.020	6.6	18.490	1.140	23.85	25.0
1962	0.260	2.890	-.400	3.290	3.150	13.2	20.930	2.440	28.25	18.5
1963	1.940	2.510	2.380	0.130	4.450	16.2	24.310	3.380	33.98	20.3
1964	0.620	3.730	1.450	2.280	4.350	17.6	28.590	4.280	41.87	23.2
1965	-.800	4.570	6.390	-1.820	3.770	5.7	30.210	1.620	50.54	20.7

Average annual increase in percent

46-52	5.5	20.	12.	22.	19.5	16.8
52-65	8.1	14.1	18.3	11.4	12.6	13.0
54-58	18.6	12.0	11.6	12.1	13.6	11.3
59-65	4.4	13.1	21.0	9.6	11.2	11.9

a increase in peso value of net foreign assets.

Sources: International Monetary Fund, *International Financial Statistics*; and Bank of Mexico, *Annual Report*.

powered money and hence the monetary aggregates were kept under control as the growth of domestic credit was sharply reduced from the pre-1954 level.

Since this chapter is concerned with the development of techniques to achieve stable growth, it does not emphasize the importance of discipline over public expenditure in the control of inflation. However, the fact that the achievement of stabilization coincided with the establishment of an innovative means of financing the government deficit should not be taken to mean that the government was able to use financial techniques as a substitute for fiscal discipline. As has been made clear in earlier chapters, the establishment of a system of growth with stable prices was accompanied by a sharply increased control over government expenditure and a heightened awareness on the part of the authorities that control over the level of public spending and the deficit were essential to maintaining fiscal and monetary control. Moreover, although monetary policy was the prinicpal means of macroeconomic management, the ability of the central bank to control the money supply is directly tied to the volume of public spending and the size of government deficits. Thus, the effective use of financial techniques requires considerable coordination between monetary and fiscal policy.

A distinguishing feature of the stabilization period was a rapid growth of the demand by the public for fixed-interest securities. The growth of the market in fixed-interest securities served to restrain inflation by lessening the inflationary impact of increases in domestic bank credit. With the growth in demand for assests other than money (see below), the public used a growing share of resources of the banking system to acquire nonliquid assets rather than expand money balances. The market in fixed-interest securities also provided an alternative source of finance to the private sector and thus enabled the central bank to slow the overall growth of credit of the banking system without depriving the private sector of financial resources.

Throughout the period, the public reacted to the change in stabilization policy by rearranging its holdings of money and nonmonetary assets. Indeed, one of the explanations for the stabilization of prices without recession lies in the rapid increase in the holdings of nonmonetary assets by the public. As the authorities became aware of the rising public demand for financial assets other than money, they were able to allow

Table VII - 6

Relation of Financial Assets to National Income, 1950 - 1965
(billions of pesos, amount outstanding at end of period)

	1950	1951	1952	1953	1954	1955	1956	1957	1958	1959	1960	1961	1962	1963	1964	1965
Nominal GNP	36.6	47.3	53.0	52.6	64.4	78.7	89.7	103.1	114.7	122.8	139.1	147.8	160.5	184.5	203.2	220.0
Money supply (M1)	6.24	6.97	7.26	8.05	9.01	10.77	11.98	12.78	13.72	15.87	17.35	18.49	20.93	24.31	28.59	30.21
Money supply (M2)[a]	7.8	9.0	9.3	10.6	12.9	15.2	16.8	17.9	19.2	23.4	27.0	29.8	34.7	41.3	50.6	56.1
Time deposits	1.52	2.00	2.08	2.58	3.94	4.40	4.82	5.16	5.48	7.51	9.69	11.28	13.78	17.02	22.02	25.92
Debt	4.702	5.502	6.338	7.145	7.915	9.276	10.240	11.971	14.193	15.092	18.278	20.376	22.840	27.257	37.327	54.663
Government	2.119	1.939	2.247	2.367	2.996	3.437	3.819	4.252	4.582	4.198	6.995	7.256	7.566	7.834	13.789	25.025
Decentralized agencies	1.244	1.878	2.093	2.840	2.756	3.453	3.543	4.331	5.293	5.419	6.955	7.708	8.988	11.543	12.835	14.220
Private	1.339	1.685	1.971	1.938	2.163	2.386	2.878	3.388	4.318	4.755	4.328	5.412	6.286	7.889	10.703	15.418
Fixed income assets[b]	6.222	7.502	8.418	9.725	11.855	13.676	15.060	17.131	19.673	22.602	27.968	31.656	26.620	44.277	59.347	80.583

Financial assets as percentages of GNP

	1950	1951	1952	1953	1954	1955	1956	1957	1958	1959	1960	1961	1962	1963	1964	1965
Money supply (M1)	17.0	14.7	13.6	15.4	14.1	13.7	13.4	12.3	12.0	13.0	12.5	12.5	13.1	13.8	14.2	13.7
Money supply (M2)[a]	21.3	16.9	15.8	18.1	17.9	17.2	16.7	15.5	14.9	17.0	17.3	18.0	19.3	21.2	22.9	23.1
Time deposits	4.2	4.3	3.9	5.0	6.2	5.6	5.3	5.0	4.8	6.2	10.0	7.7	8.6	9.7	11.0	11.8
Debt	13.0	11.7	11.7	13.7	12.4	12.0	11.5	11.6	12.5	12.3	13.2	13.9	14.3	15.5	18.3	24.9
Government	5.9	4.1	4.3	4.6	4.7	4.4	4.3	4.1	4.0	4.0	5.0	4.9	4.7	4.5	6.9	11.3
Decentralized agencies	3.5	4.0	3.9	5.7	4.3	4.4	4.0	4.2	4.6	4.4	5.0	5.2	5.6	6.5	6.4	6.5
Private	3.7	3.6	3.7	3.7	3.4	3.0	3.3	3.3	3.8	4.0	3.1	3.1	3.9	4.5	5.4	7.0
Fixed income assets[b]	17.3	15.7	15.9	18.7	18.5	17.5	16.9	16.6	17.3	18.5	20.1	21.5	22.9	25.2	29.3	36.0

[a] M2 = M1 + time deposits

[b] Fixed income assets = time deposits + bonds.

Sources: International Monetary Fund, *International Financial Statistics*, Comisión Nacional de Valores, *Memoria Anual.*

for correspondingly greater increases in total credit. The growth of public holdings of nonmonetary assets exercised a restraint on the growth of the monetary aggregates, as increases in the assets of the banking system were partly absorbed by public acquisition of nonmonetary assets.

The increase in public holdings of assets other than money underlay the success of the official policy of encouraging the development of a market in private fixed-interest securities. The goal of the policy was to alter the underlying demand of the public for financial assets. The change in the asset preferences of the Mexican public is visible in Table VII-6. In the immediate post-devaluation period, the public reduced its holdings of money as accelerated real growth combined with inflation reduced real balances in relation to income. Starting in 1958, the official squeeze on liquidity coupled with price increases put additional pressures on real balances. Later in the period, the proportion of money to national income returned to its earlier level. Meanwhile, nonmonetary fixed-income assets, including time deposits in all financial institutions and debt instruments of both the public and private sectors roughly doubled as a proportion of national income, with most of this growth occurring after 1959. Clearly, the asset preferences of the public were undergoing a fundamental change.

The shift in the asset preferences of the public in response to changes in the rate of price increases and expectations indicates that the demand for money balances was stable after the achievement of price stability while demand for other assets was growing. However, it is entirely possible that although the relation of money to national income appears stable, some shifts may have occurred among the varying motives for holding money. The reduction in inflation increased the value of real balances, thus making money balances (either broadly or narrowly defined) competitive with alternative assets. In an atmosphere of inflation, devaluation and general uncertainty, business firms may prefer to build up inventories rather than hold money balances. At the same time, the reduction in the rate of inflation, and in uncertainties associated with inflation and devaluation, lessened the precautionary demand for liquidity.

The Growth of the Securities Market

Since the option of promoting forced savings through inflation was now closed, it became a critical objective of financial policy to improve the capacity of the domestic financial system to generate other forms of savings. It was assumed that the public's asset preferences were related to the experience and expectations of inflation. Under inflationary conditions, the public would have a high preference for liquidity, and thus would want to maintain large money balances for transactions ad precautionary purposes. The reduction in the rate of inflation and in uncertainties associated with inflation and devaluation increased real balances and thus lowered the precautionary needs of the public. Increases in domestic credit were reflected in a shift in demand by the public to other assets. Moreover, domestic financial assets were becoming increasingly attractive compared to the alternative assets, such as domestic nonfinancial assets and foreign assets. Under inflationary conditions, where real interest rates are low or negative, private individuals tend to hold real assets such as real estate or place their funds abroad, while business tends to stockpile inventories or overinvest in plant and equipment in the belief that real assets will appreciate while financial assets will not. When the exchange risk is brough into the picture, the incentive to anticipate currency depreciation becomes clear. From a purely defensive point of view, businessmen will tend to step up imports of needed goods in advance of an expected devaluation. Further, the profits to be made from capital flight far exceed those of ordinary investment.

With the removal of inflation and devaluation, the gain from speculation is removed. With the increase in the real interest rate, resulting from a reduction in inflation, domestic financial assets became increasingly attractive in response to real growth. Similarly, with a stable exchange rate, the gains from foreign exchange speculation are eliminated. The differential between yields on alternative investments can be inferred from Table VII-7, which gives an idea of the opportunity costs of Mexican financial assets with respect to real domestic assets and foreign assets. In addition, financial assets compete with consumption. Since the interest rate is a reward for postponing consumption, one can infer that, with a rise in the real interest rate, a larger share of income is likely to be saved.

The yields on Mexican financial bonds, which have 10-year maturities but are in fact redeemable at any time, are compared to those on competing assets. The opportunity costs are: 1) real assets, as reflected in the wholesale price index, which will be attractive when inflation is high; and 2) foreign assets, which are attractive when there is a perceived risk of

Table VII - 7

Opportunity Costs of Investment in Mexican Financial Assets, 1946 - 1965
(percent per annum)

| | Real versus financial assets | | | Foreign versus domestic assets (without exchange rate changes) | | Foreign versus domestic assets[c] (adjusted for exchange rate changes) 1945 = 100. | |
	Interest rate in Mexico	Wholesale prices	Real int. rates	U.S. interest rates[b]	Differential	Mexico	U.S.
	(A)	(B)	(A-B)	(C)	(A-B)		
1946	10.3	15.0	- 4.7	1.2	9.1	110.3	101.2
1947	10.0	5.9	4.1	1.3	8.7	121.4	102.5
1948	9.7	7.2	2.5	1.6	8.1	133.8	123.1
1949	10.6	9.6	1.0	1.4	9.2	147.6	173.8
1950	10.7	9.4	1.3	1.5	10.2	163.1	189.2
1951	11.4	24.0	-12.6	1.9	9.5	180.9	192.9
1952	11.3	3.7	7.6	2.1	9.2	201.5	196.9
1953	10.6	1.9	2.5	2.5	8.1	224.7	201.0
1954	11.2	9.3	1.9	1.8	9.4	249.9	269.1
1955	11.3	13.6	- 2.3	2.5	8.6	278.1	303.3
1956	11.0	4.6	6.4	3.1	7.9	308.7	312.8
1957	11.2	4.2	7.0	3.6	7.6	343.2	324.1
1958	12.2	4.4	7.8	2.9	9.3	385.1	333.5
1959	11.5	1.2	10.3	4.3	7.2	429.4	347.9
1960	11.3	5.0	6.3	4.0	7.3	477.9	361.8
1961	12.1	0.9	11.2	3.6	8.6	535.8	374.8

Table VII - 7 (cont.)

	Real versus financial assets			Foreign versus domestic assets (without exchange rate changes)		Foreign versus domestic assets[c] (adjusted for exchange rate changes) 1945 = 100	
	Interest rate in Mexico	Wholesale prices	Real int. rates	U.S. interest rates[b]	Differential	Mexico	U.S.
	(A)	(B)	(A-B)	(C)	(A-B)		
1962	13.1	1.8	11.3	3.6	9.5	605.9	388.2
1963	11.8	0.5	11.3	3.7	8.1	677.5	402.6
1964	11.9	4.2	7.7	4.1	7.8	758.1	418.9
1965	11.2	1.8	9.4	4.2	7.0	843.0	436.7
Memorandum: Annual Averages							
1946 - 1953	10.6	9.1	1.5	1.7	8.9	10.6	9.2
1954 - 1958	11.4	7.2	2.2	2.8	8.6	11.4	10.6
1959 - 1965	11.4	4.2	9.2	3.9	7.5	11.4	5.4

a Financial bonds.
b 3- to 5-year Treasury notes.
c Differential adjusted for dollar appreciation: value of 100 units invested in U.S. and Mexico in 1945.
Sources: Brothers and Solís, *op. cit.*, p. 74; U.S. *Economic Report of the President;* and Bank of Mexico *Annual Report.*

devaluation. (The 3- to 5-year U.S. Treasury note rate was used, since it has a shorter maturity than the Mexican financial bond rate, but carries a risk of capital loss. In addition, during most of the period under consideration there were few alternatives to placements in the United States as an external hedge against devaluation. Therefore, the U.S. Treasury note rate represents a reasonable foreign-exchange opportunity cost.)

With the reduction of the rate of inflation after 1956, the yields on Mexican financial assets were increasingly attractive in real terms. Furthermore, although nominal interest rates were consistently higher in Mexico than in the United States, devaluation of the peso tended to make U.S. placements more attractive through the mid 1950s. Doubtless owing to the lack of confidence in the continuity of anit-inflationary policy and the stable exchange rate, the public hesitated to increase its holdings of peso-denominated assets significantly through the early 1960s. After that time, however, holdings of domestic financial assets rose sharply. The lag period presumably reflected the wavering confidence of the public in financial policies and the time needed to adjust expectations to new realities. Accordingly, one can conclude that the behavior of Mexican wealth holders is perfectly understandable in terms of a risk-adjusted search for the highest possible real yield on savings. Futhermore, with full convertibility, many speculators would not hold dollar or pesos balances exclusively; instead, they would hold peso-denominated assets for their high nominal yields and shift into dollars when the likelihood of devaluation was great. Thus, the earlier system was highly unstable.

The data suggest that expectations probably play as large a role in the portfolio decisions of wealth holders as does the absolute differential between yields on competing assets. Furthermore, it ought to be stressed that the Bank of Mexico continued to support all fixed-interest peso-denominated securities at par. Therefore, although securities were not nominally liquid, the entire market was in fact almost completely liquid. The increased willingness of the private sector to hold peso-denominated assets allowed the private sector and official agencies such as Nafinsa to finance their expansion through the financial market, especially the market for direct-debt issues, which partly offset the restrictive effects of the authorities' increased control over the total expansion of bank credit.

The magnitude of the increase in demand for private fixed-income securities is visible in Table VII-8, which groups private holders of private fixed-interest securities into three categories: banks, other financial institutions, and the general public consisting of nonfinancial corporations and individuals. The holdings by each of these sectors of the most important fixed-interest securities is shown. Bank-issued securities include financial bonds, which are bonds issued by *financieras,* and bank-issued mortgage bonds. The securities issued by nonbank corporations are various categories of mortgage-related instruments in which the physical plant and equipment of the corporation serve as a guarantee of the face value of the security.[6] As the table indicates, the holdings of financial assets by banks and non-bank financial institutions expanded considerably in the period, growing by 17.4 percent and 12.6 percent per year, respectively, compared to an annual average growth in nominal GNP of 13.0 percent. Far more impressive, however, was the increase in the nonfinancial public's purchase of private securities, which grew by 27 percent per year.[7]

Although several classes of financial institutions benefited from the rise of public willingness to channel savings into domestic financial markets, the performance of private development banks, known as *financeiras,* was most impressive. The *financieras* received funds from the public in the form of time deposits of one year or more and issued bonds with terms of ten years or more, while engaging in long-term lending to domestic industry. *Financieras* tended to be parts of large financial combines that also included a commercial bank, a savings bank, an insurance company and a mortgage bank. The financial combines, in turn, generally had close ties with industrial and commercial enterprises.[8]

The growth of public savings through conventional means thus replaced the earlier system of forced savings through inflation, and a new system of stable finance was established by the mid-1960s. The demand of the Mexican public was sufficiently elastic with respect to yields on financial assets, adjusted for inflation and risk, to provide for alternative sources of finance that could operate in the absence of inflation.

The apparent responsiveness of the private sector to official policies aimed at developing financial markets by providing competitive and stable rates of return on financial assets has far-reaching significance. In the first place, the investment share of national income, which prior to

Table VII - 8

Private Sector Holdings of Private Fixed-Interest Securities, 1954 - 1965

(millions of pesos outstanding at end of period)

	1954	1955	1956	1957	1958	1959	1960	1961	1962	1963	1964	1965
Held by Banks	173	226	284	482	595	501	540	551	592	572	573	912
1. Bank securities	71	66	56	134	100	127	137	170	177	241	242	496
A. Financial bonds[a]	63	49	51	122	92	124	134	166	172	231	231	454
B. Mortgage bonds[a]	8	17	5	12	8	3	3	4	5	10	11	42
C. Other	—	—	—	—	—	—	—	—	—	—	—	—
2. Other securities	102	160	228	348	495	373	403	381	415	331	331	416
A. Mortgage certificates[b]	23	45	40	81	58	50	51	57	93	59	59	91
B. Mortgage obligations[c]	79	115	188	267	437	323	352	324	322	272	272	325
Held by other financial institutions[d]	128	162	213	217	209	225	239	242	246	281	372	468
1. Bank securities	22	20	27	25	18	22	20	33	45	67	125	159
A. Financial bonds	16	15	21	18	12	17	15	28	41	63	120	148
B. Mortgage bonds[a]	5	5	6	7	6	5	5	5	4	4	5	11
C. Other	—	—	—	—	—	—	—	—	—	—	—	—
2. Other securities	105	142	186	192	191	203	219	209	201	214	247	309
A. Mortgage certificates[b]	61	76	88	81	72	78	82	73	68	78	102	117
B. Mortgage obligations[c]	44	66	98	111	119	125	137	136	133	136	145	192
Held by business and individuals	1364	1669	2000	2172	2960	3477	4363	5348	6365	7989	9666	14788
1. Bank securities	214	209	315	228	290	328	682	1453	1992	3195	4833	9575
A. Financial bonds[a]	166	163	206	175	194	221	568	1226	1598	2563	3035	6139
B. Mortgage bonds[a]	47	46	72	29	61	63	73	198	296	603	1796	3434
C. Other	1	—	37	24	35	44	41	29	98	29	2	2

Table VII - 8 (cont.)

	1954	1955	1956	1957	1958	1959	1960	1961	1962	1963	1964	1965
2. Other securities	1150	1460	1685	1944	2670	3149	3681	3895	4374	4794	4833	5213
A. Mortgage certificates[b]	580	770	1064	1292	1166	1284	1448	1547	1716	1986	2093	2161
B. Mortgage obligations[c]	570	690	621	652	1504	1865	2234	2348	2658	2808	2740	3052
Total	1665	2057	2497	2871	3764	4202	5142	6141	7208	8842	10611	15138
1. Bank securities	307	295	398	387	408	477	839	1656	2214	3503	5200	10230
A. Financial bonds	245	227	278	315	298	362	717	1420	1811	2857	3386	6741
B. Mortgage bonds[a]	60	68	83	48	75	71	81	207	305	617	1812	3487
C. Other	1	–	37	24	35	44	41	29	98	29	2	2
2. Other securities	1357	1762	2099	2484	3356	3725	4303	4485	4989	5339	5411	5938
A. Mortgage certificates[b]	664	891	1192	1453	1296	1412	1581	1677	1877	2123	2254	2369
B. Mortgage obligations[c]	693	871	907	1031	2060	2313	2723	2808	3113	3216	3157	3569

a   Bonos hipotecarios.
b   Cédulas hipotecarias.
c   Obligaciones hipotecarias.
d   Finance companies and insurance companies.

Source: Bank of Mexico, *Annual Report.*

163

1954 had been rising due to the process of forced savings through inflation, continued to do so after the price level had been stabilized. This would indicate that, given the proper circumstances, creation of financial incentives and a climate of stability can lead to a rise in the savings rate. Sufficient elasticity of savings with respect to yields on alternative assets apparently exists (at least in the moderately advanced developing countries) to justify a strategy of financial market innovation. A whole range of policy instruments for the development of financial markets can be expanded as an aid to the process of economic development.

The rise in holdings of assets such as time deposits as well as relatively liquid long-term assets suggests that interest-rate policy can play an important role in dampening inflation. The rise in demand for near money and similar assets that accompanied the rise in real interest rates indicated that the demand for money balances (defined as M1 plus time deposits) rises with a reduction of the rate of inflation and the consequent rise in real interest rates (or conversely the removal of the implicit tax on money balances through inflation). The rise in demand for money balances is equivalent to a decline in the income velocity of money. Therefore, higher real interest rates can serve to restrain inflation as the inflationary impact of a given expansion of credit is reduced.

The growth of financial intermediation that accompanied reduced inflation and increased real interest rates led to a change in the pattern of savings and investment. This also has important implications for financial processes of developing countries. According to an analysis developed by McKinnon, there exists a high degreee of complementarity between the demand for money and the demand for physical capital in less-developed countries. A high potential demand exists in developing countries for money and near money as financial assets. This demand arises from money's risk-free character and high liquidity. In view of the imperfections of other financial markets, the public should, other things being equal, have a high preference for money as an investment asset. However, inflation levies an implicit tax on money balances, thus shifting demand away to real goods and foreign assets, which offer a hedge against price increases and devaluation. As a result, considerable efforts have to be made to circumvent the financial markets: wealth holders place funds in real estate or flight capital; businesses accumulate excess inventories and overinvest in plant and equipment; and small farmers and merchants tend to hoard crops and inventories.[9] (Because of the free convertibility of the Mexican peso, foreign assets also tended to be an exceptionally attractive speculative investment in Mexico.) Given this suppressed demand for money and near money, funds are diverted away from lending institutions and smaller borrowers are forced to rely on moneylenders and other informal credit arrangements. On the other hand, a reduction in inflation tends to channel funds into the financial system while lessening reliance by the public upon hedges against inflation. With increased resources, the financial system will be able to direct resources to a broader range of borrowers. Presumably, this will lead to a greater efficiency, both in the financial system and the economy at large.

Although in the Mexican case a wider range of financial assets other than merely money showed substantial growth as a result of the decline in inflation, the experience of Mexico generally supports McKinnon's contention. At the same time, it should be stressed that, owing to the central bank's policy of redeeming fixed-interest securities at par, Mexican financial assets have many of the qualities of money (specifically, of being risk-free and liquid) that, according to McKinnon's hypothesis, would induce the public to want to hold large money balances.

One problem that remains is that no measurable increase in the general level of efficiency occurred as a result of the reduction in inflation and the ensuing growth of financial intermediation. The investment share of income rose, but no increase in the rate of growth took place; thus, the marginal capital/output ratio was rising. It would be hard to attribute a decline in measured efficiency to the emergence of stronger financial markets. Probably the government's allocative policies in succeeding years tended to lower the level of efficiency. In particular the policy of subsidizing the development of protected capital-intensive industries and lessening the emphasis on agriculture probably tended to shift resources into sectors where productivity gains were lower. (This argument will be fully pursued in the next chapter.)

THE ROLE OF THE EXTERNAL SECTOR IN DOMESTIC STABILIZATION

Although most of the measures that resulted in the stabilization of the price level and the development of the financial system were domestic, the authorities assumed that the external sector directly influenced the development of the domestic financial system. The authorities gave serious consideration to the balance of payments impact of domestic monetary measures. Specifically, the Bank of Mexico reacted to international capital flows with adjustments in domestic monetary policy.[10] In addition, the likely effect of monetary measures on the trade balance and international reserves received consideration in the formulation of monetary policies.

Beyond these balance-of-payments considerations, which are similar to those of other countries, in the eyes of Mexican officialdom the public perception of the exchange risk was a critical determinant in its choice of assets, due to the sizable depreciations the peso had undergone. Therefore, it was an important objective of official policy to eliminate the exchange risk from the mind of the public by pursuing policies designed to maintain balance-of-payments equilibrium and to convince the public that the authorities would continue such policies in the future. Rodrigo Gómez spelled this out in his 1957 lecture to CEMLA participants:

> We have a people that thinks in terms of dollars . . . a dollar-minded people. Hence, the commotions caused by devaluation are stronger in Mexico than in other countries. I, therefore, firmly believe that Mexico should not pursue an inflationary growth pattern, and that we must achieve progress with a stable money that improves confidence in savers and avoids sterile speculation.[11]

Because of the exchange-risk factor and a deep lack of confidence in the peso as a result of earlier inflation and financial collapse, the Finance Ministry and the Bank of Mexico gave exceptionally high importance to the role of expectations. In practice and in rhetoric, the authorities constantly referred to the level of reserves and the prospect of exchange-rate stability. For example, in his 1959 speech to the Banker's Convention, Gómez stated that

> . . . measures to maintain the regime of free convertibility and the inalterable exchange rate of our currency have strengthened our faith in stability and the economic progress of Mexico.[12]

Part of the central bank's strategy of lessening the exchange risk in the public mind was an operational policy in the foreign exchange market that sought to eliminate virtually all possibility of flexibility between the dollar and the peso.

The objective of removing the possibility of any divergence between the peso and the dollar was also the dominant consideration in central bank exchange-market policy. Even though the Bretton Woods Agreement allowed for 1 percent fluctuation on either side of the par value, the Bank of Mexico maintained a single rate, 12.49 pesos per U.S. dollar. The possibility of private bank positioning in foreign exchange was reduced to a bare minimum. The banks must liquidate any net change in their foreign position daily. Furthermore, Mexican banks were forbidden to deal in forward transactions in foreign currencies.[13]

THE EVOLUTION OF THE BALANCE OF PAYMENTS

With the achievement of domestic price stability and the increased role of foreign capital in domestic investment, the structure of the balance of payments changed fundamentally. Between the end of World War II and 1954, the country passed through two very similar balance-of-payments cycles. Each was characterized by an underlying situation of excess domestic demand, which caused the current account to move deeply into deficit. With only small net capital inflows, the level of reserves dropped sharply. Recessions in the United States in 1948 and 1953 led to a fall in Mexican exports, which in turn led to balance-of-payments crises that left Mexico with the alternatives of restricting domestic growth or devaluing. In each case, Mexico chose to devalue, and in each case a current account surplus was re-established.

After the 1948 devaluation the cycle began one more, but after the 1954 devaluation the pattern was quite different. The current account deficit indeed persisted, as Table VII-9 shows. The small current account surplus that the country achieved in 1955 disappeared and the current account has been in deficit in every subsequent year. Nevertheless, owing to increased foreign borrowing, capital inflows were large enough to offset the current account deficit and also to increase international reserves. Indeed, the distinctive feature of the Mexican balance of payments in the years following the 1954 devaluation was not any improvement of the current account balance. Rather, it was the country's increasing ability to finance growing current account deficits with capital

Table VII - 9
The Balance of Payments, 1954 - 1965
(millions of dollars)

	1954	1955	1956	1957	1958	1959	1960	1961	1962	1963	1964	1965
I. Current account balance	-45	22	-123	-293	-268	-147	-311	-221	-156	-206	-402	-376
A. Exports of goods & services	1,048	1,208	1,324	1,257	1,268	1,320	1,372	1,463	1,587	1,709	1,848	1,989
1. Exports of goods	616	739	807	706	709	723	739	804	900	936	1,022	1,114
2. Tourism	86	188	134	129	134	145	155	164	179	211	241	275
3. Border transactions	247	262	278	313	316	354	366	393	407	446	463	500
4. Workers remittances	28	25	38	33	36	38	36	34	32	31	29	12
5. Other	24	24	25	24	24	30	28	28	26	35	46	44
B. Imports of goods & services	1,094	1,186	1,447	1,550	1,536	1,447	1,683	1,684	1,743	1,915	2,250	2,365
1. Import of goods	789	884	1,072	1,155	1,129	1,007	1,186	1,139	1,143	1,240	1,493	1,560
2. Border transactions	162	151	172	193	189	221	221	242	245	265	277	295
3. Investment income	75	80	120	117	123	129	142	148	159	186	236	236
4. Debt service	11	14	15	17	22	25	30	35	54	55	55	62
5. Other	42	41	46	45	49	56	63	75	77	66	89	93
II. Capital account	63	222	218	162	129	151	194	288	164	244	575	172
A. Long-term	112	129	150	192	193	142	120	226	261	301	513	172
1. Direct investment	93	105	126	132	100	81	-38	119	127	117	162	214
2. Development credits (net)	41	58	49	90	125	78	189	185	148	155	397	-22
3. Other	-22	-34	-25	-30	-32	-17	-31	-18	-14	29	-46	-20
B. Short-term	-49	93	68	-30	-64	9	74	2	-97	-58	63	-31
III. Errors & omissions	-44	-43	-34	118	62	52	108	-89	9	72	-141	213
IV. Changes in official reserves	-26	202	61	-14	-77	56	- 9	-22	17	110	32	-21
V. Level of official reserves (end of year)	225	427	488	474	397	453	444	423	440	549	581	560

Source: Banco de México, S.A.

Table VII - 10

The Current Account Deficit and Capital Inflows, 1946 - 1965
(millions of pesos)

	1946 - 1949	1950 - 1953	1954 - 1957	1958 - 1961	1962 - 1965
Current account deficit	343	400	439	947	1140
Total capital inflow	141	385	662	762	1125

Source: Banco de México, S.A.

inflows. This appears clearly in Table VII-10, which shows these two items in four-year periods from 1946 to 1965. The effect of the devaluation on the current account balance was visible mainly in the transition period, 1954–1957, and even then the current account merely remained at about the same level as it had been in the earlier four-year period. The critical adjustment in the balance of payments occurred on capital account, where total inflows increased sufficiently to stabilize the balance of payments and thus maintain the exchange rate at 12.50 pesos per dollar.

In effect, the short-term policy response of the authorities to external disequilibrium also changed. Until 1954, the burden of adjustment fell entirely on the current account, and the only policy instruments employed were import controls and devaluation. After the 1954 devaluation, on the other hand, adjustments occurred partly on current account, where the main policy tool was changes in domestic monetary policy which reduced import demand. On capital account, changes in monetary policy reversed financial capital flows, while external borrowing compensated for current account deficits.

On a year-by-year basis, the evolution of individual items of the balance of payments do not appear to present a consistent pattern. A much clearer trend emerges, however, when the data are adjusted by moving averages, as in Table VII-11. Over the period, the current account deficit grew, but in an orderly manner. The growth of the dollar value of

Table VII - 11

Selected Items of the Balance of Payments, 1954 - 1965
(three-year moving averages, millions of dollars)

Year	1954	1955	1956	1957	1958	1959	1960	1961	1962	1963	1964	1965	Annual average rate of growth in percent
Current account	-90	-48	-49	-131	-228	-235	-242	-226	-229	-195	-254	-328	22.0
Exports[a]	999	1073	1193	1263	1283	1282	1320	1385	1474	1586	1715	1849	5.8
Imports[a]	-1089	-1121	-1242	-1394	-1511	-1517	-1562	-1611	-1703	-1781	-1969	-2177	6.6
Capital account	64	113	167	200	169	147	158	211	215	232	327	320	17.5
Long-term	83	98	130	157	178	175	151	183	222	283	358	328	14.3
Direct investment	68	80	108	121	118	104	48	54	69	121	135	164	13.3
Development capital	39	44	49	66	88	98	131	151	174	162	233	177	16.4
Other	-24	-26	-27	-30	-29	-27	-28	-22	-21	—	-10	-13	—
Short-term	-19	15	37	43	-9	-28	7	28	-7	-51	-31	-8	—

a Goods and services.
Source: Banco de México, S.A.

exports averaged some 6 percent between 1954 and 1965, while imports grew slightly faster, leading to a progressive, but controlled, widening of the current account deficit. Long-term trade policies centered on import substitution along with a minor emphasis on export promotion. In response to both pressures from domestic industrialists to promote industrialization and the goal of limiting import payments, policy was generally protectionist.

The current account deficits were more than offset by capital inflows, which grew at about 19 percent per year. Most of the increased capital receipts were in the form of long-term capital flows, as short-term flows remained more or less balanced in response to changing domestic monetary policy, interest-rate differentials and expectations. Inflows of long-term capital were about equally balanced between private direct investment flows and official borrowings, although the share of the latter gained steadily in importance. As the economy continued to grow rapidly, there were ample opportunities for foreign private investment, either through the establishment of subsidiaries or in partnership with Mexican businessmen, resulting in considerable inflows of direct investment. The government wished to encourage direct private investment inflows, but only on its own terms. It was official policy to encourage domestic industry and, therefore, some sectors were reserved exclusively for Mexican businessmen. In others, where foreign expertise was needed, foreign interests were allowed a minority participation; and in still others, where Mexican investors had not established a presence, foreign investors were allowed relatively free entry. Thus, despite the need for capital flows to maintain balance-of-payments equilibrium and improve domestic technology, the government retained a selective attitude toward private foreign investment.[14] An additional source of private capital inflows was credits to the Mexican private sector, especially from private banks and similar financial institutions. This reflected the continued growth and sophistication of Mexican industry, which took advantage of a generally increased international mobility of capital.

Public capital flows became increasingly important in the post-devaluation period. By the late 1950s, they became greater than private flows and had assumed a critical role in stabilizing external accounts. Indeed, as will be explained below, external borrowing had reached the point where it, along with the resulting public capital flows, became necessary for the maintance of the fixed exchange rate.

It was mentioned earlier that part of the stabilization strategy was to remove the incentive to capital flight and to encourage inflows of funds from industrial countries. The authorities were successful in stemming capital flight and indeed were eventually able to attract significant flows of private capital from the developed countries. This can be clearly seen in Table VII-12, which shows the Mexican bilateral position with the United States. The asset side represents Mexican indebtedness to the United States in the form of loans and bond issues, and the liability side represents mostly Mexican deposits in the United States. An increase in the asset position of the United States represents a flow of capital into Mexico. Since the United States was virtually the only alternative market available to Mexicans in most of the period, the data gives a clear idea of what was occurring in the behavior of the Mexican public.

At the beginning of the period, Mexican nationals tended to hold considerable net short-term assets in the United States, mostly in the form of bank deposits but also in the form of money market placements. Meanwhile, Mexicans received small amounts of long-term credits from American financial institutions. This is the classic pattern one would expect of a country with a vulnerability to capital flight and few financial connections. In the pre-1954 period, short-term placements by Mexicans were reduced somewhat as memories of the 1949 devaluation faded. With the 1954 devaluation, however, there was a second capital flight, reflected in a sharp increase in short-term deposits. Another capital flight occurred during 1963-1964, which began in late 1962 with the Cuban missile crisis. The improvement in Mexico's ability to obtain credit from U.S. banks is clear, and as the period progressed, banks were increasingly willing to extend short-term credit.

By 1958, Mexican long-term credits from U.S. banks were large enough to offset the short-term capital outflows. By 1965, the development of Mexican financial markets and the improvement of the short-term borrowing capability had advanced to the point where even the short-term position reflected an inflow into Mexico. As a whole, the bilateral position moved increasingly toward a net asset position for the United States, meaning that Mexico had attained the capability of attracting regular inflows of capital. In other words, the absence of exchange controls was irrelevant. The underlying market incentive was for capital to flow into Mexico.

As the foregoing discussion implies, an international economic policy

Table VII - 12

U.S. Position with Mexico, 1950 - 1965
(millions of dollars, end of period)

	1950	1951	1952	1953	1954	1955	1956	1957	1958	1959	1960	1961	1962	1963	1964	1965
ASSETS	111.7	153.6	135.2	138.1	167.6	207.3	298.8	390.5	468.1	529.7	603.2	721.9	768.3	917.2	1305.0	1291.7
Short-term	94.0	122.2	107.2	117.5	142.4	181.9	242.6	263.8	329.0	318.2	382.3	466.3	464.8	525.4	719.6	750.1
Bank	70.6	90.6	88.6	92.9	115.7	153.7	212.9	231.0	293.0	290.8	343.4	425.0	407.9	465.1	643.9	673.7
Nonbank	23.4	31.6	18.6	24.6	26.7	28.2	29.7	32.8	36.0	27.4	38.9	41.3	56.9	60.3	75.7	76.4
Long-term	17.7	31.4	28.0	20.6	25.2	25.4	56.2	126.7	139.1	211.7	220.9	255.6	303.5	391.8	585.4	541.6
Bank	4.8	20.0	17.2	8.0	17.6	18.8	41.7	107.1	106.5	175.4	182.0	171.2	194.9	322.4	512.0	476.8
Nonbank	12.9	11.4	10.8	12.6	7.6	6.6	14.5	19.6	32.6	36.3	38.9	84.4	108.6	69.4	73.4	64.8
LIABILITIES	-123.2	-165.1	-241.3	-191.0	-332.9	-417.9	-436.9	-393.2	-428.1	-448.2	-404.7	-500.8	-537.7	-677.0	-742.1	-707.5
Short-term	-213.1	-165.0	-241.2	-190.5	-332.9	-417.9	-436.9	-393.2	-428.1	-448.2	-403.9	-500.3	-537.0	-676.6	-741.9	-707.5
Bank	-207.1	-158.2	-231.2	-328.9	-413.7	-413.7	-433.0	-386.3	-418.2	-442.4	-397.3	-494.7	-531.1	-668.8	-734.7	-702.6
Nonbank	- 6.0	- 6.8	- 10.0	- 7.3	- 4.0	- 4.2	- 3.9	- 6.9	- 9.9	- 5.8	- 6.6	- 5.6	- 5.9	- 7.8	- 7.2	- 4.7
Long-term	- 0.1	- 0.1	—	- 0.1	—	—	—	—	—	—	0.8	- 0.5	- 0.7	- 0.4	- 0.2	- 0.2
Bank	- 0.1	- 01.	- 0.1	- 0.1	—	—	—	—	—	—	0.8	- 0.4	- 0.2	—	—	—
Nonbank	—	—	—	- 0.1	—	—	—	—	—	—	—	- 0.1	- 0.5	- 8.4	- 0.2	- 0.2
NET POSITION[a]	-101.5	- 12.5	-106.1	- 52.4	-165.3	-210.6	-138.1	- 2.7	40.0	81.7	189.3	221.1	230.6	240.2	562.9	584.2
Short-term	-119.1	- 43.8	-134.0	- 73.0	-190.5	-236.0	-194.3	-129.4	- 99.1	-139.9	- 21.6	- 34.0	- 72.2	-151.2	- 22.3	- 42.8
Bank	-136.5	- 67.6	-142.6	- 90.3	-213.2	-260.0	-220.1	-155.3	-125.2	-151.6	- 53.9	- 69.7	-123.2	-203.7	- 90.8	- 28.9
Nonbank	7.4	24.8	8.6	17.3	22.7	24.0	25.8	25.9	26.1	21.6	32.3	36.7	51.0	52.5	68.5	71.7
Long-term	17.6	31.3	27.9	20.6	25.2	25.4	56.2	126.7	139.1	211.7	210.9	255.1	302.8	391.4	585.2	541.4
Bank	4.7	19.9	17.1	8.6	17.6	18.8	41.7	107.1	106.5	175.4	181.2	170.8	194.7	322.4	512.0	476.8
Nonbank	12.9	11.4	10.8	12.6	7.6	6.6	14.5	19.6	32.6	36.3	38.9	84.3	108.1	69.0	73.2	64.6

[a] (-) = net liability position.
Source: U.S. Treasury, *Bulletin*.

had evolved that, in combination with domestic financial policies, provided for a high rate of growth, stable prices, a dynamic financial system and balance-of-payments equilibrium. Therefore, the last of the major structuralist arguments—that economic development necessarily leads to balance-of-payments disequilibrium and that developing countries must accept either periodic devaluation or exchange controls—is not supported by the Mexican experience. Indeed, the Mexican experience seems to suggest that, regardless of the validity of any terms-of-trade hypothesis, sufficient resources exist in the international economic system which can be channeled into economic development, provided that the individual country adopts a proper mix of financial policies.

INTERNATIONAL ECONOMIC POLICY AND FOREIGN PUBLIC BORROWING

The Role of External Borrowing

The Mexican strategy in stabilizing the balance of payments required that the public sector achieve access to foreign credit in order to offset growing current account deficits. The strategy had already been spelled out in 1954 when it was decided that further devaluation was unacceptable and that greater and more predictable capital inflows would require establishing a network of international financial relations to increase the sources of capital flows. As has been pointed out in earlier chapters, Mexico had developed good working arrangements with a variety of foreign creditors, based on the relatively high level of skills of Mexican administrators and the country's record of stability and development. Building upon its good relations with the IMF, the Eximbank, the IBRD, and private commercial banks, the Mexican public sector sought to enlarge its network of financial contacts and thus to borrow larger amounts from a wider variety of creditors and on better terms. The enlargement of the circle of creditors and the improvement of terms began under Carillo Flores. However, in the 1950s, foreign debt remained small, and efforts focused mainly on increasing the volume of loans. Under Ortiz Mena, the objective increasingly became to improve the conditions of borrowing by lengthening the maturities of loans and lowering interest rates. The country began to emphasize highly visible prestige operations.

Table VII - 13

Sources of Long-Term Development Borrowing, 1955 - 1965
(percent of total borrowing in period)

	1955	1956	1957	1958	1959	1960	1961	1962	1963	1964	1965
Eximbank	1.9	4.6	17.8	21.3	10.9	12.6	28.0	10.5	2.2	3.1	6.0
IBRD	45.2	22.9	7.8	9.6	3.3	2.2	3.2	5.6	15.9	10.0	10.0
IDB	0	0	0	0	0	0	0	0	2.9	2.0	2.7
AID	0	0	0	0	0	0	0	0	.4	.7	3.8
Private institutions	52.8	72.5	74.4	69.1	85.8	85.3	68.8	83.1	68.3	76.4	70.9
External bonds	—	—	—	—	—	—	—	—	10.3	7.7	6.6
Total borrowing (millions of dollars)	73	102	145	207	198	346	355	392	428	776	417

Source: Nacional Financiera, Annual Report 1965, and Banco de Mexico, S.A.

175

The latter served to reinforce domestic confidence in the exchange rate while also enabling the country to improve its ability to negotiate with foreign lenders.[15] External borrowing served both to help finance the public investment program and to support the balance of payments. In order to coordinate external borrowing with other objectives, the Special Commission on External Financing was established in 1954. This body approved all proposed external borrowing by the public sector, using criteria such as the importance of the proposed project, the terms of loans, and the possibility of internal financing, as well as the impact of external finance on the balance of payments.[16] It was likely, therefore, that the Commission would approve more applications for overseas borrowing at times of balance-of-payments pressure. At the same time, public sector entities will be encouraged to resort to foreign borrowing in times of balance-of-payments pressure.

One of the explicit goals of the country's international economic policy was to diversify its sources of credit, which had been mainly the Eximbank and, to a lesser degree, commercial banks in the United States. As Table VII-13 shows, the country succeeded in broadening its sources of

Table VII - 14

Geographical Distribution of Overseas
Borrowing by Nacional Financiera, 1942 - 1965
(percentage of total borrowed in the period)

	1942-1954	1955-1959	1960	1961	1962	1963	1964	1965
International organizations	18.8	19.3	18.0	49.6	33.4	26.1	8.4	45.2
United States[a]	78.9	66.8	64.7	n.a.	19.6	30.2	54.8	39.4
United Kingdom	—	1.4	—	n.a.	1.9	6.8	15.2	7.0
France	0.9	3.8	2.0	n.a.	11.3	13.3	8.1	4.6
Italy	0.4	6.0	0.3	n.a.	14.6	4.7	0.1	2.9
Canada	0.8	0.6	2.2	n.a.	8.4	10.7	1.6	0.5
Switzerland	—	1.3	—	n.a.	—	—	—	5.3

[a] includes Eximbank, AID, and Private Creditors.
Sources: El Mercado de Valores, and Nacional Financiera, *Annual Reports.*

long-term credit. The earlier dependence upon Eximbank was sharply reduced. Among official lenders, the World Bank gradually replaced the Eximbank as the country's largest single creditor, while the IDB and AID also eventually began operations on a modest scale. Despite the considerable growth of credit from official institutions, the growth of credit from private institutions was much greater by far.

In addition to increasing the number of agencies that the authorities dealt with, another objective of international economic policy was to broaden the geographical base of borrowing and lessen the earlier dependence on the United States. As Table VII-14 shows, the country also had considerable success in this domain. The earlier situation, in which Mexico depended almost exclusively on U.S. financial institutions with some loans from the IBRD, was completely reversed. Another source of external finance developed in 1963, when Mexico began issuing economic development bonds in the New York market, which were generally well received by the investing public. Besides providing an additional source of foreign finance, these operations further improved the prestige of the country and thereby advanced the country's international financial strategy.

Relations with External Creditors

The objective of raising increasingly greater sums on increasingly favorable terms led to a concerted policy of establishing good relations with external lending agencies, both public and private. The most important factors underlying Mexican success in this sphere were the country's record of stability, rate of growth, and history of repayment, but an explicit effort to develop a network of credit relationships was also a significant factor. As Ortiz Mena said in 1961,

> The most important consideration in the solidity of the peso is, on the one hand, the expansion of production and investment. But not less important is the climate of confidence and the international reputation of Mexico, not only in international institutions, but on the part of private investors.[17]

Even though its immediate balance-of-payments problem was overcome right after the 1954 devaluation, Mexico continued to maintain cordial relations with the IMF. Mexico's successful use of relatively orthodox stabilization policies enhanced its standing with the IMF, and hence the Fund wished to use Mexico as an example to other Latin American countries. For example, in 1958 a Fund spokesman wrote an article criticizing the policies of Latin American countries, including deficit financing, excessive credit expansion and multiple exchange-rate practices, while citing the experience of Mexico since the 1954 devaluation as proof that there was no conflict between growth and stability.[18]

The standby credit of $23.5 million from the IMF was repaid in 1955. While Mexico had no ongoing need of IMF credit, the good relations Mexico had with the Fund and the Fund's open approval of Mexican policies clearly improved the country's image as a sound credit risk to both official and private borrowers. In 1965 the Fund started using pesos as a support for other currencies.

The distinctive feature of the capital account was a steady growth of long-term public capital inflows. Since it had acquired international prestige, the Nacional Financiera continued to play the leading role in obtaining external credits.[19] As a result of Nafinsa's policy of creating a diversified network of sources of credit, the list of Mexico's creditors grew longer with the passage of time. The role of Eximbank declined somewhat from earlier years, but it still remained a major supplier of external funds, and in some years it was the largest single lender.[20]

Mexico's rising borrowing from the World Bank reflected that institution's confidence in Mexican financial policies and the ability of Mexico to formulate projects that met approval of the IBRD from the points of view of economic soundness and engineering feasibility. World Bank lending has generally not been geographically dispersed, and a handful of countries, including Mexico, India and Japan, has generally managed to obtain disproportionately high shares of total loans.[21] The IBRD, like other international institutions, publicly praised Mexican performance. In 1958, Eugene R. Black, president of the IBRD, cited Mexican use of World Bank loans as "a clear example to the world" of the possibility that existed for less-developed countries to profitably use the resources of the international financial system in economic development.[22]

Around 1960, two additional public sources of funds came into being. The Inter-American Development Bank (IDB) was established in 1959 as a Latin American regional development bank, modeled on the World Bank. Although Mexico received sizable sums from this institution, its share of total loans was less striking than at the World Bank. The IDB

probably gave more consideration to factors such as an even geographi-
cal distribution of loans and the needs of each country, as opposed to the
IBRD which based its operations on narrowly technical grounds. The
Agency for International Development, a U.S. government agency
founded in 1960 to provide "soft" loans, also extended some credits to
Mexico.

Along with its network of public long-term capital, Mexico gained considerably wider access to private credit. Even before the 1954 devaluation, most capital inflows consisted of private bank loans and suppliers'
credits. However, because of the country's balance-of-payments instability, credits generally tended to be for very short maturities. As will be
seen shortly, in the predevaluation period most capital flows came from
U.S. commercial banks, but most external debt was owed to the Eximbank, indicating that banks were unwilling to make long-term commit-
ments. The great success that Mexico registered with private credit in-
situtions was in obtaining longer-term loans at progressively lower
interest rates and of increasing the number of private credit institutions.
(In 1960 the Prudential Life Insurance Company of America began to
purchase securities of Nacional Financiera and became the country's
single largest private creditor by 1965.) Mexico's private creditors included every large U.S. commercial bank and a great number of
medium and small-sized banks (see Table VII-15). Many small commercial banks wishing to have some international loans in their portfolios,
but without sufficient resources to engage in country evaluations, have
tended to lend to Mexico because the country appeared to offer the least
credit risk in Latin America. Moreover, a large variety of European,
Canadian, and Japanese banks became creditors of Mexico. In addition
to long-term borrowing, Mexico also developed a network of contracts
with private commercial banks in the industrial countries which gave the
authorities access to short-term credits. The availability of short-term
lines of credit from private sources proved to be a valuable asset in maintaining reserves and the stability of the overall balance of payments. For
example, in periods of deficit, foreign short-term borrowings could be
accumulated, which could either be repaid or converted into long-term
debt in successive periods.

The factor that most impressed foreign private creditors was Mexico's
record of political stability, wherein the government changed hands
peacefully each six years while providing for relative continuity of

Table VII - 15

Distribution of Borrowing by National Financiera by Creditors, 1942 - 1965
(thousands of dollars)

Total	3,269,562
Export-Import Bank	667,373
International Bank for Reconstruction and Development	615,800
Interamerican Development Bank	125,586
Agency for International Development	64,000
Private sources	519,787
The Prudential Insurance Co. of America	120,000
Banque Nationale pour le Commerce et l'Industrie	82,820
Chase Manhattan Bank	49,787
Bank of America	57,101
Crédit Lyonnais	31,134
Crédit National	30,608
Kreditanstalt für Wiederaufbau	19,027
Continental Illinois National Bank	22,000
Chemical Bank New York Trust Co.	19,600
Manufacturer's Hanover Trust Co.	13,500
The Meadowbrook National Bank Group	11,500
Others	62,170
Other creditors	22,313
Guarantees, endorsements, etc.[a]	1,049,721

[a] Mostly from private sources.
Source: Nacional Financiera, *Annual Report, 1965.*

economic policy. With the passage of time, the country's record of repaying its debts increasingly became a factor in the banks' willingness to improve terms of credit. In addition, the competence of Mexican officials clearly had a favorable impact on foreign lenders. Finally, the strenuous efforts of the Mexicans themselves to develop a network of financial ties was a major element in their successful creation of a system of international supports for the balance of payments. Once again, the Mexicans emphasized the confidence factor. Mexican spokesmen made extensive efforts to publicize their country's achievements and to improve understanding of Mexican development in the industrial countries.[23] As the network of creditors grew, competition among them increased, thus improving the terms of borrowing. By 1965, Mexico had emerged with the highest credit rating among less-developed countries, measured both by the variety of its private foreign creditors and the favorable commercial terms on which it could borrow. Although the Mexican authorities publish no consistent data series showing the terms of debt, official spokesmen have continually stressed the steady improvement. In fact, the interest that Mexico paid on external bonds was rather high compared to official bonds issued by developed countries. However, hardly any developed country could place bond issues in the world market at all. For example, in 1965 when the prime rate in the United States was 5 percent, Mexican interest rates ranged from less than 1 percent for AID credits to 7.5 percent for external bonds. Of the total amount borrowed, about half was at rates of more than 6 percent, while a quarter of all credit carried rates of 5-6 percent, and a quarter had interest rates below 5 percent.[24] During the mid-1960s, Mexico was the major user of international borrowing facilities among developing countries and virtually the only less developed country that was able to utilize international bond markets.[25] It was not until 1970 that a significant number of developing cities began to use the private credit market for development borrowing.

While Mexico has received substantial funds on increasingly favorable commerical terms, it has had little access to "soft" funds, that is, funds on easier terms than are available on a profit-making basis. Mexico received no loans from the IBRD's soft loan agency (IDA), AID funds were small, and eventually the country's line of credit was canceled owing to Mexico's access to other sources of credit.

External Debt

As a result of rising foreign borrowing, the country sharply increased its public external debt. This appears clearly in Table VII-16 which shows the development of external long-term indebtedness of the Mexican public sector. With public borrowing increasing sharply, public debt rose continuously as a percentage of current account earnings. As a result, official policy had to give increased consideration to the terms of public debt. The Special Commission on External Financing was increasingly obliged to consider the structure of indebtedness in authorizing external

Table VII - 16

The Growth of External Public Debt, 1942 - 1965

(millions of dollars)

Years	Disburse-ments	Debt service			Net transfer	Total debt	Net increase in debt	Exports of goods and services	Debt service as a percent-age of exports
		Amorti-zation	Interest	Total					
1942	10.0	0.7	0.2	0.9	9.1	9.3	9.3	272.5	.3
1943	—	1.1	0.3	1.4	-1.4	8.2	-1.1	410.1	.5
1944	—	1.1	0.3	1.4	-1.4	7.0	-1.2	432.2	.4
1945	8.3	1.2	0.3	1.5	6.8	14.1	7.1	500.7	.3
1946	37.4	4.5	0.9	5.4	32.0	47.0	32.9	570.1	.7
1947	30.2	8.8	2.2	11.0	19.2	68.4	21.4	713.9	1.3
1948	20.2	12.0	2.6	14.6	5.6	76.6	8.2	715.5	1.9
1949	31.8	14.5	3.3	17.8	14.0	94.0	17.4	701.1	2.8
1950	30.7	18.8	4.3	23.1	7.6	105.8	11.8	826.7	3.0
1951	35.8	22.5	5.1	27.6	8.2	119.0	13.2	917.8	2.5
1952	58.3	21.1	5.3	26.4	31.9	156.3	37.3	983.7	2.5
1953	48.4	19.0	6.3	25.3	23.1	185.8	29.5	963.7	2.3
1954	49.6	24.8	6.8	31.6	18.0	225.4	39.6	1,048.2	2.9
1955	208.4	33.1	8.9	42.0	166.4	400.7	175.3	1,208.1	3.6
1956	102.3	60.2	14.4	74.6	27.7	442.8	42.1	1,323.7	5.3
1957	145.9	75.6	15.6	91.2	54.7	513.1	70.3	1,257.2	6.0
1958	207.1	117.4	18.4	135.8	71.3	602.7	89.6	1,267.5	9.0
1959	197.7	151.3	22.7	174.0	23.7	649.1	46.4	1,319.8	12.0
1960	364.5	182.3	29.7	212.0	152.5	813.4	164.3	1,371.8	12.7
1961	354.5	178.3	33.7	212.0	142.5	983.5	170.1	1,463.4	12.8
1962	391.6	248.5	51.2	299.7	91.9	1,126.6	143.1	1,586.8	17.6
1963	427.9	231.6	54.8	286.4	141.5	1,315.4	188.8	1,709.3	15.2
1964	776.2	368.1	53.8	421.9	354.3	1,723.5	408.1	1,847.9	19.2
1965	552.9	452.5	69.8	522.3	0.6	1,808.4	84.9	1,989.1	22.7

Source: Banco de México, S.A.

Table VII - 17

External Indebtedness of the Public Sector by Creditors, 1954 - 1965
(percent of total debt)

	1954	1955	1956	1957	1958	1959	1960	1961	1962	1963	1964	1965
Eximbank	53.4	40.5	30.1	26.8	27.5	23.8	20.3	24.6	22.4	16.7	8.4	8.3
IBRD	28.7	36.1	36.7	31.5	28.5	25.8	18.9	15.7	14.9	17.6	16.6	17.5
AID	0	0	0	0	0	0	0	0	0	0.2	0.4	1.2
IDB	0	0	0	0	0	0	0	0	0.3	1.2	1.9	2.4
Private institutions	17.9	23.5	33.3	41.8	44.0	50.4	60.9	59.7	62.4	61.9	66.9	64.6
Bond-holders	0	0	0	0	0	0	0	0	0	2.4	5.8	6.0
Total debt outstanding (millions of dollars)	225	265	3.8	389	499	556	766	954	1,101	1,125	1,615	1,699

Source: Nacional Financiera, Annual Report, 1965, and Banco de México, S.A.

borrowing in order to prevent excessive foreign indebtedness and to prevent "bunching" in single years. The increase in the level of debt gave the Mexican authorities additional incentive to push harder for an easing of credit terms.[26] As public debts mounted as a percentage of current account earnings, the country eventually had to consider supplementary measures to improve the balance of payments, such as increasing domestic tax efforts to finance economic development and the development of export industries.

The sources of Mexican public indebtedness also changed over the period, as seen in Table VII-17. At the beginning of the period, more than half of the external debt was owed to the Eximbank and more than 80 percent was owed to official agencies. By the end of the period, however, the IBRD was the largest single official creditor, while private financial institutions grew in importance eventually accounting for two thirds of external debt. The rising importance of private financial institutions in Mexican borrowing reflected the willingness of these institutions to advance larger sums for longer periods under increasingly favorable terms. It may also indicate that the private financial sector can play as important a role as public financial entities in the finance of economic development. Private financial institutes are apparently willing to channel credit into general economic development and on terms that are fairly flexible and beneficial to the economic development process.

SUMMARY

In the years after the 1954 devaluation, Mexico was able to develop a system of domestic and international finance that proved capable of mobilizing increasing amounts of resources to support economic development. The system was capable of yielding a high rate of growth, and financing a program of public investment in a context of stability. Internally the system required increased voluntary savings and dynamic financial markets which, in turn, depended upon high real yields and a low exchange risk. On the external side, the system involved growing current account deficits that were financed by increasing capital inflows. The need to increase capital inflows led the authorities to pursue an explicit policy of external borrowing, which resulted in the development of a large network of foreign creditors and an increase in foreign debt.

In effect, Mexico had come full circle. Having used inflationary techniques with good results for twenty years, the country then became the prime example of the use of conventional development policy. Just as Mexico was a classic example of the use of forced savings through inflation, the experience of Mexico between 1954 and the early 1970s suggests that economic development can proceed under conditions of price and balance-of-payments stability, and that international economic policy can play a positive role in the economic development process.

NOTES

1. Speech to 1957 Bankers' Convention, in *Textos de Rodrigo Gómez* (Mexico: Gráficas Panamericanas, 1967), pp. 30–31. A similar statement was made in a speech to participants in CEMLA program August 1957 in *ibid*, pp. 107–108. Also see: Dwight S. Brothers and Leopoldo Solís, *Mexican Financial Development* (Austin: University of Texas Press, 1966), pp. 88–92.

2. Antonio Ortiz Mena, "La Política Financiera en los Ultimos Cinco Años," in *El Mercado de Valores,* Vol. XXIII (November 18, 1963), pp. 599–605. For a full-1er elaboration of the doctrine of· stabilizing development (desarrollo estabilizador), see: Antonio Ortiz Mena, "*Stabilizing Development: A Decade of Economic Strategy in Mexico* (Mexico: Ministry of Finance, 1969), and *Logros y Desarrollos de México en el Campo Económico: El Camino Recorrido por Nacional Financiera* (Mexico: Nacional Financiera, 1964).

3. Brothers and Solis, *op. cit.,* pp. 93–94; and John E. Koehler, "Information and Policy-Making: Mexico," (unpublished Ph.D. dissertation, Economics Department, Yale University, 1967), pp. 25–35.

4. For a discussion of the role of reserve requirements in Mexican stabilization, see: Mario Ramón Beteta, "The Central Bank: Instrument of Economic Development in Mexico," in *Mexico's Recent Economic Growth: The Mexican View,* Tom E. Davis (ed.), (Austin: University of Texas Press, 1967), pp. 75–86, and Arturo Ruiz Equihau and Leopoldo Solís, "Los Instrumentos de Política Monetaria y de Crédito en México," in *Técnicas Financieras,* Vol. VI (January–February 1967), pp. 272–297.

5. Koehler, *op. cit.,* pp. 37–51. Also see: Miguel Mancera, "La Política Monetaria y Crediticia," in *Revista Bancaria,* Vol. XX (January, 1972) pp. 3–11.

6. For a discussion of the various securities, see: Daniel Carl Falkowski, "Nacional Financiera, S.A., de Mexico: A Study of a Development Bank," unpublished Ph.D. dissertation (Department of Economics, New York University, 1972), pp. 66–105.

7. See: Robert Lee Bennett, *The Financial Sector and Economic Development: The*

Mexican Case (Baltimore: Johns Hopkins University Press, 1965). Using a flow of funds model, Bennett found that there was a sharp change in the pattern of finance in Mexico following the devaluation. Direct finance was replaced by a growth of indirect finance through intermediaries. Similarly, the government relied on external borrowing. The research of Raymond Goldsmith indicates a rising share of financial assets as a proportion of national wealth; see: *The Financial Development of Mexico* (Paris: OECD Development Centre, 1966), pp. 240–248.

8. For a full discussion of the development and structure of the capital markets, see: Antonín Basch, *El Mercado de Capitales en México* (Mexico: CEMLA, 1968), especially chapters II and III, pp. 13–90; and O. Ernest Moore, *Evolución de las Instituciones Financieras en México* (Mexico: CEMLA, 1963). For a discussion of the financieras, see: Antonio Campos Andapia, *Las Sociedades Financieras Privadas en México* (Mexico: CEMLA, 1963), pp. 72–79; and Richard S. Eckhaus, "Estructura del Sector de las Financieras en México, 1940–1970," *CEMLA Boletín Mensual*, Vol. XXI (May 1975), pp. 256–287.

9. Ronald J. McKinnon, *Money and Capital in Economic Development* (Washington: The Brookings Institution, 1973), pp. 89–116.

10. Brothers and Solís, *op. cit.*, pp. 117–143. There is some controversy between Brothers and Solís and Griffiths who claims that international flows of funds do not limit the authorities' ability to control money supply. See: B. Griffiths, *Mexican Monetary Policy and Economic Development* (New York: Praeger, 1972), pp. 76–83. In any case, Ernesto Hernández Catá has amassed considerable empirical evidence that in recent years substantial movements of funds have taken place in response to interest-rate changes; see: "International Movements of Private Financial Capital: An Econometric Analysis of the Mexican Case," unpublished Ph.D. dissertation, (Economics Department, Yale University, 1974). For a discussion of the objectives and techniques balancing growth against price and balance of payments stability, see: Carlos Bazdresch, "La Política Monetaria Mexicana: Una Primera Aproximación," in *La Económica Mexicana*, Leopoldo Solís (ed.) Vol. II *Política y Desarrollo* (Mexico: Fondo de Cultura Económica, 1973), pp. 138–156.

11. Gomez, *op. cit.*, pp. 113–114.

12. *Ibid*, p. 46. For more formal statements of the orthodox view of the relationship between internal and external stability, see: Enrique Padilla A., "La Dinámica de la Economía Mexicana y el Equilibrio Monetario," in *El Trimestre Económico*, Vol. XXV (July–September 1958), pp. 349–377; and Leopoldo Solís M. and Sergio Ghigliazza, "Estabilidad Económica y Política Monetaria," in *El Trimestre Económico*, Vol. XXX (April–June, 1963), pp. 256–265.

13. Information about official foreign exchange policy is based on Bank of

Mexico circulars of June 6, 1954 and July 25, 1972. Additional information was obtained in an interview with Luis Chico Pardo, assistant manager, Foreign Department, Bank of Mexico, April 22, 1974.

14. Luis Urrutia, "Política de Inversiones," in *Revista de Economía,* Vol. XXI (June 1958), pp. 143–147.

15. Antonio Ortiz Mena, "El Crédito de Mexico," in *El Mercado de Valores,* Vol. XXV (May 24, 1965), pp. 333–339.

16. "La Comisión Especial de Financiamientos Exteriores," in *El Mercado de Valores,* Vol. XVIII (April 7, 1958), pp. 158–159.

17. Antonio Ortiz Mena, "La Política Hacendaria Mexicana," in *El Mercado de Valores,* Vol. XX (January 30, 1961), pp. 54–55.

18. Jorge del Canto, "América Latina: Desarrollo Económico y Estabilidad Económica," in *El Trimestre Económico,* Vol. XXV (July–September 1958), pp. 395–411.

19. Alfredo Navarrete, "La Experiencia de México en el Uso de los Instrumentos de Política Financiera," in *El Mercado de Valores,* Vol. XXIII (March 11, 1963), pp. 121–123, and "La Administración Financiera en el Desarrollo Económico de México," in *Revista de Economia,* Vol. XXVII (April 1964), pp. 107–115; and Antonio Carrillo Fores, "Las Fuentes Internacionales para el Financiamiento del Desarrollo Económico en Latinoamérica," in *El Mercado de Valores,* Vol. XXII (December 24, 1962), pp. 769–776.

20. Mexican relations with the Eximbank were so close that in 1962 Harold F. Linder, president of the Export-Import Bank, delivered a speech warmly praising Mexico's use of Eximbank resources and referring to the relationship between Mexico and the Eximbank as a "long-standing alliance for progress." "México y el Banco de Exportaciones e Importaciones: Una Antigua Alianza para el Progreso," in *El Mercado de Valores,* Vol. XXII (April 9, 1962), pp. 177–181.

21. In 1971, Mexico was the largest single borrower from the IBRD's "hard" loan facility. India received about the same amount as Mexico in "hard" loans and an equal amount of "soft" financing. Edward S. Mason and Robert E. Asher, *The World Bank Since Bretton Woods* (Washington: The Brookings Institution, 1973), p. 195.

22. *Comercio Exterior,* Vol. VIII (July 1958), p. 369.

23. For example, in an article aimed at a foreign audience, Antonio Carrillo Flores discussed Mexican achievement and prospects for the future in order to generally improve the image of Mexico abroad and particularly to create a favorable climate of opinion among potential investors. See: "Mexico Forges Ahead," in *Foreign Affairs,* Vol. XXXVI (April 1958), pp. 491–503.

24. Alfredo Navarrete, *Finanzas y Desarrollo Económico* (Mexico: Libros SELA, 1968), pp. 113–114.

25. Robert G. Hawkins, Walter L. Ness, Jr., and Il Sakong, "Improving the Access of Developing Countries to the U.S. Capital Market," New York University. Graduate School of Business Administration, Center for the Study of Financial Institutions, *The Bulletin* (1974), especially pp. 23–40.

26. Rosario Green, *El Endeudamiento Público Externo de México: 1940–1973* (Mexico: El Colegio de México, 1976.)

Chapter VIII

The Resurgence of Inflation After 1970 and the Devaluation of 1976

After having successfully developed a technique of noninflationary growth in the mid-1950's and having used this technique throughout the 1960s, Mexico began to experience inflation after 1970. The earlier consensus supporting stable growth was weakened, as the seeming inability of the system to resolve serious problems of resource allocation, income distribution and social equity caused policy-makers up to the highest levels to question the country's capacity to deal with its fundamental problems. The resurgence of inflation occurred at the same time that inflation was accelerating in all countries, but the inflation was more severe in Mexico than in the industrial countries and reflected distinctly Mexican conditions.

During 1972–1974, fiscal discipline was relaxed and once again an inflationary cycle began that left the peso overvalued. Though attempts were subsequently made to restore balance through higher taxes and some real growth was indeed sacrificed, the government was unwilling to take deflationary measures strong enough to reduce inflation to a rate compatible with the fixed exchange rate. With the country experiencing large current account deficits and a persistent capital flight, the peso was finally cut loose from the dollar in September 1976.

189

THE STRUCTURAL PROBLEMS OF MEXICAN ECONOMIC DEVELOPMENT

During the presidency of Gustavo Díaz Ordaz (1964–1970) the government remained committed to the pattern of "stabilizing development." Antonio Ortiz Mena, who had served as finance minister under Lopez Mateos, remained as finance minister, thus emphasizing the government's continued commitment to the stable pattern of development. The pattern of financial development was essentially unchanged. Domestic financial markets continued to develop. New instruments for investment were introduced, such as certificates of deposit and *pagarés,* short-term instruments similar to commercial paper. Externally, Mexico gained access to an ever wider circle of creditors, including the Eurodollar and Eurobond markets.

Despite continued advances in the field of finance, problems on the real side of the economy became obvious. Most seriously it appeared that the unemployment and underemployment were worsening despite the country's rapid economic growth. As made clear in earlier chapters, since World War II Mexico had pursued a policy of import-substituting industrialization in the private sector combined with rising state investment in basic infrastructure. When domestic industrialists could persuade the government that domestic production of a given product was feasible, the full range of official support was extended to domestic industry through protective tariffs, import licenses, quotas and outright import prohibitions. In addition, domestic industrialists received support in the form of government spending and preferential access to credit. In its early phases, import-substitution efforts had centered on the production of consumer goods, especially consumer durables, but as time passed protection was extended to a widening range of capital goods. Regulations were passed requiring that increasing shares of components of manufactured goods be produced domestically.

Foreign investors could become eligible for official protection. A large share of investment in import-substituting projects took the form of direct investment by foreign investors in Mexican subsidiaries, usually by importing techniques from their home countries to Mexico. Although protectionist development pattern was satisfactory in terms of the growth of aggregate income, it tended to produce structural distortions that were socially intolerable.

The weakness of Mexico's policies is simply the general weakness of protectionist import substitution. In the absence of trade restrictions one would expect any country to specialize in production of those goods in which it has a comparative advantage. In the case of Mexico, one would expect a specialization in agriculture, mining, and labor-intensive industry. With restrictions, however, trade would grow slower than income as a whole. (Exports declined from 15 percent of GNP in 1951 to 8 percent in 1974.) A policy that restricts market forces in the consumer goods sector while allowing the import of capital goods is clearly likely to shift production in favor of goods having a high content of imported capital goods.[1] The country will produce goods which it does not have a competitive advantage.

Mexican policy tended to favor industrialization and urbanization at the expense of agriculture. In contrast to earlier phases of growth in which agriculture had been a leading sector, the policy of favoring in-

Table VIII - 1

Growth of Real Gross Domestic Product by Sector
(annual increase in percent)

	1965 - 1970	1971 - 1975
Total	6.7	5.5
Agriculture	2.7	1.8
Mining	3.3	3.5
Petroleum	9.2	7.8
Manufacturing	8.3	5.8
Electricity	13.2	8.2
Commerce	6.8	5.0
Transport	7.5	7.8
Other Services	6.0	6.0

Source: Bank of Mexico, *Annual Report*, 1975.

dustrialization tended to deprive the agricultural sector of funds. A long-term stagnation of agriculture set in. As Table VIII-1 shows, agriculture proved to be the slowest growing sector of the economy. Indeed, agricultural output grew proportionately less than population, which grew at an annual rate of 3.5 percent.

There were important differences among producers in the agricultural sector. A minority of farmers who could obtain credit and gain access to advanced techniques were able to make substantial gains in productivity, but most were unable to obtain credit and improve efficiency. The problem was especially acute in the case of those with small holdings, and those living on the *ejidos,* plots collectively owned by communities but worked by individual farmers. The *ejido* system, which proved to be a workable political solution to the demands of landless peasants, proved to be an unsatisfactory means of increasing earnings for farmers.

The poor performance of Mexican agriculture had far-reaching effects on the course of economic development. Most of the population still depended upon agriculture for their livelihood, but real per capita output in agriculture was falling. The inability of the agricultural sector to provide employment for growing labor force or even to maintain levels of earnings led to migration to the cities, which in turn aggravated the problems of urban overcrowding, pressures on public services, underemployment in the cities, and potential political instability. The inability to produce enough food domestically to maintain 1965 levels of per capita food consumption from domestic sources led to inadequate nutrition, pressure on food prices, and pressures on the trade balance.[2]

The growth of an urban proletariat, living at low standards, created political pressures for subsidies, particularly for a relatively cheap food supply. Political pressure to maintain low food prices worsened the problem of low income in agriculture and generated demand for imported food. As the demand for nonagricultural employment was growing, the economy's capacity to satisfy such demand was stagnating.

Import substitution represented an indirect subsidy to high-cost domestic producers that tended to utilize capital-intensive techniques of production that were more suited to the needs of the industrial countries than to those of Mexico.[3] Such techniques led to high wages for the small number of workers who could find employment in advanced industries,

Table VIII - 2

Sectorial Distribution of the Labor Force, 1950 - 1970

Sectors	Labor force (thousands of persons)			Percent of total labor force			Annual average growth rate		
	1950	1960	1970	1950	1960	1970	1950 - 1970	1950 - 1960	1960 - 1970
Primary	4,935.8	6,235.3	5,388.5	59.50	55.30	40.88	0.44	2.36	-1.45
Agriculture	4,836.3	6,088.7	5,206.6	58.30	54.00	39.50	0.37	2.33	-1.55
Mining	99.5	146.6	181.9	1.20	1.30	1.38	3.06	3.95	2.18
Secondary	1,227.8	2,007.0	2,839.3	14.80	17.80	21.54	4.28	5.04	3.53
Manufacturing	978.9	1,556.0	2,205.3	11.80	13.80	16.73	4.14	4.74	3.55
Construction	224.0	405.9	580.0	2.70	3.60	4.40	4.87	6.12	3.63
Electricity	24.9	45.1	54.0	0.30	0.40	0.41	3.95	6.12	1.82
Tertiary	1,774.2	2,954.2	4,192.9	21.39	26.20	31.81	4.39	5.23	3.56
Services	1,774.2	2,954.2	4,192.9	21.30	26.20	31.81	4.39	5.23	3.56
Other	356.8	78.9	760.6	4.30	0.70	5.77	—	—	—
Total	8,295.6	11,275.4	13,181.3	100.00	100.00	100.00	2.34	3.12	1.57

Source: Trejo, *El Desempleo en México*, pp. 688 - 689.

but to a shrinking capacity of industry as a whole to generate employment. In the face of a rapidly growing population, workers were being divided into a minority of well-paid, well-organized workers, and an underemployed majority.[4] Workers were being forced to leave land by the agricultural sector's inability to generate enough income. As Table VIII-2 shows, employment in agriculture rose through the 1950s but declined through the 1960s.[5]

The secondary sector (manufacturing, construction and electricity) could provide adequate living conditions, but it possessed only a limited capacity to absorb the workers released by agriculture. Of the 5 million increase in the labor force, only 1.8 million went into the secondary sector. Most of the increase in the work force occurred in the tertiary (service) sector, a sector in which there exists considerable underemployment or concealed unemployment.

The problem of its underemployment is serious enough and poorly defined enough to warrant some extended discussion. In Mexico, as in most developing countries, there is only a rudimentary system of social insurance, and hence there is little incentive for workers to declare themselves unemployed. The inability of the economy to generate employment is reflected in large numbers of workers being engaged in work of low marginal productivity which provides a minimum income; with sufficient complementary resources, these workers would be capable of doing more productive work. Some obvious examples that are commonly seen in developing countries are the large number of street vendors and bootblacks.

Measuring underemployment is a difficult task. Some of the common measures for classifying a worker as underemployed include those 1) working less than full time; 2) earning less than the minimum wage; 3) working at less than one's capacity; and 4) working at a job with zero or near zero productivity. One analyst claimed that the test of working for less than the minimum wage showed that about 45 percent of the work force was underemployed.[6] (See Table VIII-3.) Some one third of the labor force in trade and services and two thirds in agriculture were categorized as unemployed. Such data are of course difficult to interpret, for they provide no comparison with other countries or with other periods of Mexican history. Nevertheless, since almost half of the Mexican labor force was apparently unable to find satisfactory employment, the problem was clearly serious.

Table VIII - 3

Underemployment by Sectors
(thousands of workers)

Sectors	Total labor force	Underemployed	Underemployed as percentage of labor force
Total	12,995	5,761	44.5
Agriculture	5,145	3,514	68.3
Mining and petroleum	170	23	13.5
Construction	571	133	23.2
Electricity	53	4	6.6
Commerce	951	297	31.2
Transport	391	52	14.1
Services	2,158	842	39.0
Other	747	259	34.6

Source: Rosenzweig, *op. cit.*, p. 839.

The heavy reliance on foreign borrowing as an integral part of the development pattern was criticized on at least two grounds. The country was obliged to commit increasing amounts of resources to debt service. While it is difficult to specify at what point foreign debt becomes an unbearable problem, clearly there are limits beyond which the ability to easily contract foreign debt is merely a means of postponing difficult decisions about needed measures to restructure the underlying balance of payments.

In addition, the ease of access to foreign credit undoubtedly weakened efforts to raise domestice savings. It is often assumed that increases in official capital flows allow the country to use the entire proceeds of foreign loans to increase domestic investment beyond the capabilities of domestic savings. However, this approach has recently been challenged. [7] In all likelihood, foreign borrowing probably has some positive effects on the total level of investment, but also tends to diminish efforts to increase domestic savings. In particular, the availability of foreign loans in Mexico probably slowed the authorities' efforts to develop new exports and contributed to the general reluctance of the authorities to raise taxes. It is uncertain to what degree this represents a distortion of the intended purpose of foreign borrowing. It is surely a worthy objective to maintain standards of consumption in developing countries. Moreover, there may be strong political constraints on the reduction of consumption. Nevertheless, to the degree that foreign resources lessen efforts to increase domestic savings, it tends to undermine one of the objectives of the process of economic development.

In the eyes of its critics, Mexican economic development was benefiting a few privileged sectors of the economy while the situation of the majority was worsening. Moreover, critics believed the system, which implied low rates of taxation and widening current account deficits would only be sustained by increasingly large amounts of foreign borrowing.

THE IMPACT OF CRITICISM OF THE POLICY-MAKING PROCESS: THE RELAXATION OF FISCAL DISCIPLINE

In the early 1970s, the dissatisfaction with the results of economic development that began to surface critically undermined the consensus on policy that had existed since the mid-1950s. The entire system of price stability, financial markets, and a fixed exchange rate became the focal point in a growing debate over the direction of that economic development. The underlying issue was not price stability or the exchange rate, but whether the entire economic policy since 1954 was really effective in changing the lot of the vast majority of Mexicans. The critics contended that by making a financial stability and particularly the fixed exchange-rate the cornerstone of economic policy, the authorities subordinated domestic goals to the balance of payments and thereby rendered the country incapable of dealing with the fundamental problems of under-employment and economic dualism.[8] Defenders of stable growth countered by pointing to the great increase in domestic and foreign resources for development that resulted from stability, also arguing that the system was flexible enough to accommodate any needed changes in economic policy.[9]

It is of course true that the issue of the allocation of resources among sectors and activities in entirely separate from the issue of stable or inflationary growth. Nevertheless, as the commitment to stability weakened the issue of inflationary versus stable growth again surfaced. Moreover, with a generation's experience of stability, the public perhaps took the benefits of stability for granted. Those urging inflationary policies again argued in favor of a "trade-off" between inflation and growth, with those advocating inflationary growth using the argument of pressing social needs while attempting to cast advocates of stability as lacking social concern. Moreover, critics of the existing arrangements apparently believed that the government would change its behavior only if forced to do so by circumstances, and inflation and devaluation would force the government to change its policy. Finally, the same system that had produced growth with stability had also produced the distortions of the country's import-substituting growth pattern, and the system as a whole thus appeared less worth defending.

It was argued in earlier chapters that the key to stable development was the acceptance by the entire decision-making structure of the public sector (the president, the Finance Ministry and the central bank) of constraints on public spending and credit expansion. In the early 1970s, this consensus was seriously eroded in the entire public sector, save the Bank of Mexico. Once again, the debate on stability that had proceeded through the early 1950s was opened again. The Bank of Mexico remained a staunch defender of stability. However, the Finance Ministry, which had traditionally supported the central bank, became indecisive and was unable to resist pressures for spending from other public agencies, which either openly advocated inflationary growth or pressed for increase of public spending.

A series of articles by prominent economists, including many from official institutions, challenged the system of stable development and particularly the fixed-exchange rate. In 1974, Gerardo Bueno of Nacional Financiera, published an article in a well-known economic journal exposing the debate to public view and argued that the peso has been overvalued for several years.[10] Clearly the bureaucracy was losing its commitment to stable development. (In conversations with Mexican officials at the time, one had the distinct impression that the advocates of stability were on the defensive.)

The balance of political forces that was capable of influencing the government had changed over time. The trade unions, which had earlier been mere tools of government policy, became increasingly able to pry concessions from the government. The government became committed to defending a rising real wage particularly for the well-organized workers. The unions of course favored greater social benefits and sustained growth in order to stimulate employment. Furthermore, the government was apparently willing to listen to other constituencies that were less formally organized, such as the opinion elite and the urban and rural underemployed. In summary, a variety of factors was pushing the authorities toward a more inflationary spending policy, as the government was recognizing more claims on resources than it could possibly deliver.

THE ECHEVERRIA ADMINISTRATION 1970—1976

Domestic Inflation

When Luis Echeverría assumed the presidency in December 1970, the pattern of "stabilizing development" was nearly two decades old. The new president inherited both its successes and its limitations. Furthermore, his mandate in economic policy was unclear. He was at once expected to maintain the country's record of price stability and also make progress in favor of less privileged classes and redistributing income. The latter objective required both a high rate of growth and an increase in social expenditure. At first, Echeverría gave first priority to stabilization. Heavy spending at the end of his predecessor's presidential term had led to a sharp deterioration of the current account balance. Therefore, in 1971 the government pursued a contractionary policy. Starting in 1972, however, the emphasis shifted to expansion in order to raise levels of income and increased social spending to improve the fate of the masses.

The pressures to accelerate growth and social spending were reflected in a burst of inflationary finance.[11] Expenditure outran revenue, as an insufficient support was available for higher taxes or a reduction of old programs.

The president and his closest advisers apparently began to accept the arguments that basic changes were needed in the pattern of development and that inflation could advance development. However, rather than attempt to make a deliberate decision to redirect spending toward more efficient and socially desirable channels, while cutting back on others and raising taxes, the de facto pattern of behavior that was adopted was to simply allow additional spending. The institutional procedure under which finance ministers had been able to resist pressures for spending and to enforce discipline over public expenditure was relaxed considerably. President Echeverría in many instances reportedly personally intervened in public spending decisions and overruled subordinates favoring fiscal restraint. The level of public expenditure and the size of the budget deficit began to accelerate and surpassed all previous levels in 1974. (See Table VIII-4.) The financial system was incapable of supporting an expansion of government spending of this magnitude without inflation. (See Table VIII-5.) The rapid increase of the budget deficit was financed in large part by an expansion of central bank credit to the government, which in turn resulted in considerable increases in domestic credit. The growth of the money supply began to accelerate swiftly, and by the end of 1973, consumer prices were rising at more than a 20 percent annual rate. The control over public spending and domestic liquidity which had characterized Mexican economic development since the mid-1950s was faltering, thus weakening the foundation of Mexico's financial system and the basis for its earlier high rates of growth.

With the surge of inflation in the industrial countries in 1970 inflation in Mexico worsened. The rise in import prices put pressures on domestic costs, while the acceleration of price increases in the outside world further contributed to a relaxation of monetary and fiscal discipline. However, it ought to be stressed that, Mexican official statements to the contrary, the worldwide burst of inflation in 1973 did not cause the Mexican inflation, which had already gotten under way a full year earlier. Furthermore, other countries that simultaneously experienced the world inflation were able to reduce their domestric inflation to rates compatible with world levels, whereas Mexico was not.

Although holdings of financial assets at first kept pace with the growth of national income, Mexican financial markets no longer offered the safe and competitive returns they earlier had. Moreover, as it became impossible to contain dissent over exchange-rate policy, it became clear that the currency might eventually have to be devalued and capital flight began. Thus the financial markets were losing their characteristics of safety and dependability.

Table VIII - 4

Federal Government Budget, 1965 - 1975
(millions of pesos)

	1965	1966	1967	1968	1969	1970	1971	1972	1973	1974	1975
Expenditure	28,263	26,361	28,018	32,594	39,516	40,202	41,314	59,062	75,813	104,130	145,126
Revenue	20,093	21,755	22,745	27,348	30,212	33,868	36,530	42,336	53,822	72,043	103,078
Deficit	8,170	4,606	5,273	5,246	9,304	6,334	4,787	16,726	21,991	31,237	42,048
Expenditure as percentage of Gross domestic product	11.5	9.5	9.1	9.6	10.5	9.6	9.1	11.5	12.2	12.8	14.6
Deficit as percentage of Gross domestic product	3.3	1.7	1.7	1.5	2.4	1.5	1.0	3.3	3.5	3.8	4.2

Sources: Bank of Mexico, Indicadores Económicos, and International Monetary Fund, International Financial Statistics.

Table VIII - 5

Domestic Monetary Expansion and Inflation, 1967 - 1975

(percent change over previous year)

	1965	1966	1967	1968	1969	1970	1971	1972	1973	1974	1975
Central Bank											
Claims on government	217.8	13.3	-62.0	7.5	361.2	3.4	17.7	162.9	58.6	57.1	33.1
Credit to government	89.2	10.2	-27.7	8.7	107.7	1.3	-4.7	68.1	55.6	62.7	29.7
Net domestic credit	15.6	10.6	-3.4	7.2	41.3	9.7	3.4	30.2	34.2	42.5	27.1
Money supply	5.7	12.2	9.3	14.1	15.0	10.7	7.6	17.9	22.4	20.7	21.4
Wholesale prices	1.9	1.3	2.8	1.9	2.6	5.9	3.7	2.9	15.7	23.0	10.5
Consumer prices	3.6	4.2	3.0	2.3	3.7	5.2	5.8	4.2	12.1	22.5	16.8

Sources: Bank of Mexico, *Indicadores Económicos*, and International Monetary Fund, *International Financial Statistics.*

The Balance of Payments

Between 1970 and 1974, the Mexican balance of payments was characterized by an impressive growth of exports, and by a sharp simultaneous growth of the current account deficit. Continued Mexican growth in the face of the post-1973 world recession and the increased incentive to import stemming from the resurgence of domestic inflation all caused import demand to grow extremely rapidly.

In the early 1970s the authorities began to modify the earlier pattern of growth, which had given only limited attention to the export sector. A massive attempt was made to promote the export of manufactured goods, which resulted in a quadrupling of the export of manufactured goods between 1970 and 1973. Enormous efforts were made to subsidize the expansion of manufactured exports, through tax rebates and special credit facilities. Many categories of manufactured goods, such as textiles, processed food, and machinery, grew at impressive rates. (See Table VIII-6.) By 1973, almost half of Mexican exports consisted of manufactured goods. Even as manufactured exports were expanding, however, agricultural exports leveled off and fell in 1974, reflecting the long-term neglect of agriculture and excess domestic demand for food.

Exports received an additional stimulus from the commodity boom of 1973–1974. Although the stagnating agricultural performance limited gains in agricultural exports, exports of metals and minerals (excluding petroleum) rose 50 percent between 1973 and 1974. Beginning in 1974, Mexico also made substantial gains in exporting petroleum, shifting from a small net import position in 1973 to a $500 million export surplus in 1975. Despite this remarkable expansion of exports, the current account deficit widened considerably in 1973 and 1974, as excess demand in Mexico led to a continuing rise in imports.

In late 1974, the world economic slowdown was reflected in declining demand for Mexican exports. Despite a quadrupling of oil export earnings and continued efforts to promote manufactured exports, export revenue was virtually unchanged between 1974 and 1975. (See Table VIII-7.) Imports, meanwhile, continued to rise, reflecting real domestic growth, an increasingly overvalued exchange rate, and rising import prices. Even increasingly tighter direct controls after 1974 failed to halt the growth of imports. At the same time, net invisible earnings virtually

Table VIII - 6

The Growth of Main Export Commodities, 1965 - 1975
(annual percentage change)

		1965 - 1970	1971	1972	1973	1974	1975
I.	Agriculture, livestock and fishing	-0.1	1.5	24.7	14.9	-7.2	-4.0
II.	Mineral products	-0.4	-12.1	15.3	1.0	102.1	58.4
III.	Manufactured goods	11.2	22.7	24.2	40.7	52.3	-19.4
	Processed foods	7.2	12.0	11.0	22.8	52.8	-31.3
	Textiles and clothing	5.9	32.7	52.8	15.9	58.0	-75.0
	Chemicals	13.3	11.0	14.0	50.0	52.3	-26.9
	Machinery and equipment	70.0	40.7	59.8	86.0	27.2	8.4
	Total	2.8	6.0	18.6	27.5	27.1	0.3

Source: Bank of Mexico, Indicadores Económicos.

Table VIII - 7

The Balance of Payments, 1966 - 1975

(U.S. $ millions)

	1966	1967	1968	1969	1970	1971	1972	1973	1974	1975
I. Current account	- 296	- 514	- 632	- 589	- 946	- 726	- 762	-1,223	-2,613	-3,770
Trade	- 442	- 645	- 779	- 693	-1,046	- 891	-1,053	-1,750	-3,191	-3,720
Export	1,163	1,104	1,181	1,385	1,281	1,363	1,665	2,063	2,755	2,860
Imports	-1,605	-1,749	-1,960	-2,078	-2,327	-2,254	-2,718	-3,813	-5,946	-6,580
Invisibles	146	131	147	104	100	165	291	527	578	- 50
II. Capital account	275	520	681	637	1,003	886	988	1,415	2,652	3,908
Long-term	213	315	379	694	504	669	753	1,685	2,525	4,340
Direct investment (net)	109	4	117	197	201	196	190	287	273	362
Borrowing[1] (net)	102	212	148	449	324	451	546	1,378	2,378	3,478
Other	2	99	114	48	- 21	22	17	20	- 126	500
Short-term[2]	62	205	302	- 57	499	217	235	- 270	127	- 432
III. SDRs allocations	–	–	–	–	45	40	39	–	–	–
IV. Official balance[3]	21	- 6	- 49	- 48	- 102	- 200	- 265	- 192	- 39	- 138

1   Public and private sector.
2   Includes errors and omissions.
3   Increase in assets or decrease in liabilities is (-).
Sources: Bank of Mexico, *Annual Report,* and *Indicadores Económicos.*

disappeared in 1975. As a result the current account deficit reached almost $4 billion in 1975.

Some improvement in export performance occurred with the U.S. recovery in 1976. However, by this time, the current account deficit became so large and confidence had weakened to such an extent that a balance of payments crisis appeared inevitable.

In order to maintain a stable exchange rate with respect to the dollar, the authorities increasingly had to seek an ever greater amount of foreign credits in order to offset the growing current account deficit. Borrowing from international organizations, especially overseas bond markets and from foreign commercial banks had to be sharply accelerated. Clearly the country's access to foreign credit was simply a means of postponing fundamental decisions about the economy.

The massive increase in foreign debt that occurred during 1973–1975 reopened the issue of the role of foreign borrowing in economic development. Many Mexicans became uneasy about a system in which too many decisions depend upon the ability to increase foreign debt, in which foreign debt accounts for a large fraction of national wealth, and in which debt service ties down a large share of export receipts. By the same token, foreign creditors began to view the country in a somewhat less favorable light due to the deteriorating domestic economy and mounting external debt.

THE 1974–1975 ANTI-INFLATION EFFORT

By 1974 it was clear that continued inflationary finance would provoke a balance of payments crisis, which the government wanted to avoid. Thus the Echeverría administration pursued policies designed to postpone devaluation until the 1976 election. During 1974–1975, the thrust of policy was to introduce mildly deflationary measures to reduce inflation and avoid devaluation without compromising earlier advances toward increased social spending and without provoking a recession. Simultaneously, the president thought to pacify left-wing forces by taking an increasingly bold "Third World" posture.

Measures taken in 1974 included both a restrictive demand-management policy and measures to preserve the purchasing power of lower-income groups. Public agencies raised their charges, thus increasing revenue and lessening dependence upon budget transfers. The annual rate of growth of public expenditue was reduced to 27 percent from 40 percent a year earlier. Further reductions in the deficit were achieved by tax increases later in 1974. With this tightening of fiscal policy, the need for central bank financing of the deficit eased somewhat. Consequently, the central bank was able to reduce the rate of growth of the money supply to about 20 percent per year.

The measures had a considerable impact in the course of 1974. The annual rate of inflation declined from 25 percent to less than 15 percent. Nevertheless, further progress against inflation was limited, since it was unacceptable to endure an outright recession. The underlying rate of inflation was reduced only to about 15 percent annually—a rate that still left the peso increasingly overvalued.

THE 1976 DEVALUATION

The government continued to fight a holding action in 1975. Real GDP growth declined to 4 percent in 1975 and 2 percent in 1976. However, further progress against was unlikely without an intensified stabilization program, which the government was unwilling to undertake. Thus in 1975 the government borrowed heavily overseas, while waiting for 1976 which would bring a recovery of demand in the industrial countries to spur export demand and a new president to deal with the economic crisis. However, results in 1976 were disappointing. Despite a substantial increase in real growth in the industrial countries and continued expansion of oil exports, export revenue grew only 10 percent in the first three quarters of 1976 from a year earlier. Although import growth was held to less than 5 percent in the same period, the current account balance remained virtually unchanged. Thus, it appeared that an exchange-rate adjustment was needed to correct the current account imbalance.

The problem of capital flight intensified. Some estimates place the capital flight as high as $4 billion. Thus, foreign borrowing had to be accelerated, not only to finance a large current account deficit but also to offset a huge capital outflow. Probably, borrowing was in the neighborhood of $6-7 billion.

By mid-1976, Mexican lines of credit with the private banks were exhausted. In effect, the country had run out of resources. In July 1976, conversations with the IMF were begun. The Fund agreed that an exchange rate adjustment was necessary. It is unclear whether alternative solutions were considered but, given the small amount of resources available to Mexico and the impracticality of exchange control, floating was probably inevitable. Thus, on September 1, 1976, the peso was again cut loose from the dollar and allowed to find its own level in the market.

Over the next six months, the peso depreciated from 12.5 per dollar to 22.8. As it had 22 years earlier, devaluation unleashed a panic in Mexico. A flight from domestic financial assets took place, with large numbers of Mexicans exchanging demand deposits for peso notes and, where possible, changing pesos for dollars. Merchants demanded payment in dollars, prices were raised immediately, and hoarding began.

In his last months in office, President Echeverría reportedly fell victim to a siege mentality and served out his term in isolation. He accepted the inevitability of devaluation, but refused to take any needed actions to complement the devaluation. Indeed, he allowed for wage settlement with gains in excess of 20 per cent and refused to act when landless agricultural workers began seizing land. In the waning days of the Echeverría Administration, rumors were rife that exchange controls, a freezing of bank deposits, or even a military coup were imminent.

NOTES

1. Saúl Trejo Reyes, "El Sector Externo en la Economía Mexicana: Crecimiento Óptimo y Política de Exportaciones," in *El Trimestre Económico,* Vol. XLII (April–June 1975), pp. 399–427. For more general discussions of the problems of the relations between industrialization and the capacity of the economy to create employment, see: Werner Baer and Micheal E. A. Herve, "Employment and Industrialization in Developing Countries," in *Quarterly Journal of Economics,* Vol. LXXX (February 1966), pp. 88–107; "Comment" by Benjamin I. Cohen and Nathaniel H. Leff, in *Quarterly Journal of Economics,* Vol. LXXXI (February 1967), pp. 162–164; Gustav Ranis, "Industrial Sector Labor Absorption," in *Economic Development and Cultural Change,* Vol. XXI (April 1973), pp. 387–408; and D. Morawetz, "Employment Implications of Industrialization in Developing Countries," in *The Economic Journal,* Vol. LXXXIV (September 1974), pp. 491–542. For an intelligent and passionately argued presentation of the case against unbalanced industrialization, see Jonathan Powers, "The Alternative to Starvation," in *Encounter,* Vol. XLV (November 1975), pp. 11–35.

2. Saúl Trejo Reyes, "El Desempleo en México: Características Generales," in *El Trimestre Económico,* Vol. XLII (July–September 1975), pp. 671–694. Fernando Rosenzweig, "Política Agrícola y Generación de Empleo en México,"

in *El Trimestre Económico*. Vol. XLII (October–December 1975), pp. 837–856. Guadalupe Rivera Marín, "Los Mercados Internos: Uno de los Grandes Problemas del Desarrollo Económico de México," in *El Trimestre Económico*, Vol. XXXIX (January–March 1972), pp. 111–124. Vladimir Brailovsky, "Comentarios Sobre la Tenencia la Tierra en México," in *Investigación Económica*, Vol. XXIX (April–June 1969), pp. 307–318.

3. Saúl Trejo Reyes, "El Desempleo en México: Caracteristicas Generales," pp. 680–682; James H. Street, "The Technological Frontier in Latin America: Creativity and Productivity," in *Journal of Economic Issues*, Vol. X (September, 1976), pp. 538–559; Stephen H. Hellinger and Douglas A. Hellinger, *Unemployment and the Multinationals: A Strategy for Technological Change in Latin America* (Port Washington, N.Y.: Kennikat Press, 1976).

4. Saúl Trejo Reyes, "Expansión Industrial y Empleo en México," in *El Trimestre Económico*, Vol. XLIII (January–March, 1976), pp. 33–57.

5. Trejo Reyes, "El Desempleo en México: Caracteristicas Generales," pp. 684–685.

6. Rosenzweig, *op. cit.,* pp. 839–845.

7. For example see: Kaj Areskoug, *External Public Borrowing: Its Role in Economic Development* (New York: Praeger, 1969), especially conclusions, pp. 93–103. For a review of the literature on this topic see: Raymond F. Mikesell and James E. Zinser, "The Nature of the Savings Function in Developing Countries: A Survey of the Theoretical and Empirical Literature," in *Journal of Economic Literature*, Vol. XI (March 1973), pp. 12–15. Also see: H. B. Chenery and P. Eckstein, "Development Alternatives for Latin America," in *Journal of Political Economy*, Vol. LXXVIII (supplement to July–August 1970), pp. 966–1006; and R. B. Griffiths and J. L. Enos, "Foreign Assistance; Objectives and Consequences," in *Economic Development and Cultural Change*, Vol. XIX (April 1970), pp. 313–337.

8. Gerardo Bueno Z., "La Paridad del Poder Adquisitivo y las Elasticidades de Importación y Exportación en México," in *El Trimestre Económico*, Vol. XVI (April–June 1974), pp. 313–323. Eduardo Navarrete, "Desequilibrio y Dependecia: Las Relaciones Económicas Internacionales de México," in *La Sociedad Mexicana Presente y Futuro*, Miguel S. Wionczek (ed.), Mexico: Fondo de Cultura Económica, 1974, pp. 98–134.

9. Manuel Uribe Castañeda, "Estrategia de Infraestructura para el Desarrollo del Sector Externo," in *Pensamiento Político*, Vol. XIV (December 1973), pp. 473–486, and "El Significado Económico del Gasto Social," in *Pensamiento Político*, Vol. XV (April 1974), pp. 497–508.

10. Bueno, *loc. cit.* See René Patricio Villareal, "El Desequilibrio Externo en el Crecimiento Económico de México: Su Naturaleza y Mecanismo de Ajuste Optimo: Devaluación, Estabilización y Liberación," in *El Trimestre Económico*, Vol.

XLI (October–December 1974), pp. 775–810; Carlos Bazdresch, "La Política Económica," in *Plural,* Vol. II (August 1973), pp. 18–20.

11. For a well-argued and humorous attack on excessive government spending and interference in the market as a cause of devaluation, see Luis Pazos, *Devaluación y Estatismo en México* (Mexico: Editorial Diana, 1976).

Chapter IX

Conclusion

After having reviewed the Mexican experience, the tasks that remain at the end of this inquiry are to review the roles of inflation and stability in Mexican development, to evaluate the contribution that financial policy has made to Mexican economic development, to assess the meaning of the Mexican experience for other developing countries, and finally to comment upon the likely development of the financial system now that inflation and exchange-rate instability are again serious problems.

THE PAST EXPERIENCE OF MEXICO

Inflation and Economic Development

Since the rate of growth was virtually identical in the inflationary period 1945–1954 and the stable period 1954–1970, the obvious conclusion is that growth and stability were unrelated, at least in the sense that one did not directly cause the other. The source of Mexican growth in all periods has been the rapid increases in productivity brought about by the increases in investment. Public sector investment spending was both a source of growth in itself and a stimulus to the growth of other sectors of the economy, as massive infrastructure outlays unified the country into a single market and created external economies for the private sector. Private sector investment in import-substitution industry, in agriculture, and to a lesser degree in export-related activities responded to the opportunities for profit that official policy provided, and similarly raised the overall level of productivity.

In the first inflationary period, 1936–1945, investment increased beyond the amount that would have been spontaneously undertaken by the private sector, using voluntary private savings, and the government sector, using only tax revenues. The adjustment to a higher level of investment took place through a fall in real consumption and a resulting redistribution of income toward the government and private investment arising from inflation. In the 1930s, when the world was suffering from depressed conditions, the inflationary process clearly acted as a spur to investment by increasing the resources available to those sectors of the economy that were capable of undertaking new investments. The aggressive public spending policies of the Cárdenas period plainly increased domestic investment beyond the level that would have been possible with purely voluntary domestic savings. The near collapse of the domestic economy in the revolution, the virtual disappearance of the domestic financial system and the severe contraction of world trade and capital flows in the Depression all suggest that the country had only deficit spending and inflationary finance as an alternative to stagnation. The fact that other free market economies under more favorable circumstances could not achieve a spontaneous recovery and had to wait for the stimulus of war further suggests that Mexican policy-makers properly perceived their options as stagnation or an increasingly activist role for public investment.

In all likelihood, this proposition was still valid through the immediate postwar years. Although a policy of price stability might have been viable at that time, the continually rising share of investment in national income apparently indicated that inflation, accompanied by devaluation, still was efficient in redirecting resources from domestic consumption to capital formation.

By the early 1950s, this policy was encountering diminishing returns as the costs of inflation began to mount. The reduction of real consumption through inflation met resistance as the sectors of the economy that saw their consumption decline attempted to protect their standards of living; thus, inflationary financing of development encountered political barriers. Inflation was also extremely wasteful. Considerable amounts of savings were diverted into highly unproductive assets, such as real estate or flight capital, whose main function was to hedge against inflation. Thus, it should be recognized that in general one of the costs associated with inflationary growth is the channeling of scarce savings into unproductive assets and a net loss of efficiency. Inflation undermined the development of voluntary savings by making productive savings uncompetitive with speculation.

In all periods Mexico had to finance a volume of investment greater than the volume of savings that was immediately available from voluntary sources. At first, the problem was overcome under inflation by transfers of income to the high-investment sectors. Under stability, by contrast, the solution involved creating mechanisms to stimulate voluntary savings transfer funds from savers to investors, and by external borrowing.

The inflationary policy of 1936–1954 represented a direct means of facilitating the structural transformation of the economy; this, in turn, was directly linked to the emergence of a new class of domestic capitalists following the Mexican revolution, and with the rise of a state committed to undertaking productive investment. The inflationary policies from Cárdenas to Alemán thus represented a further transfer of power and resources to new and modernizing centers of economic power that the regime wished to create, namely, a centralized innovating state and a class of domestic capitalists.

The achievement of stable finance coincided with the emergence of a sizable middle class that wished to accumulate savings and channel its excess funds into conventional financial markets. Attitudes appropriate to the growth of such a class, including the expectation that thrift and sound investment will produce predictable rewards, are clearly those of a broad middle class which is capable of undertaking significant savings and which seeks outlets to protect its savings and accumulate wealth.

The Contribution of the External
Sector to Economic Development

In both the inflationary and the stable periods, the external sector played a significant and beneficial role in the development of the Mexican economy. From the end of World War II until the early 1950s, exports of goods and services were growing at the same rate as GNP while capital inflows were generally small. After the 1954 devaluation, the growth of exports was slower, but capital inflows were significantly larger and thus a sizable international transfer of resources occurred that allowed the country to import needed capital goods and technology from the outside world. The well-developed network of international borrowing eased the problem of foreign-exchange scarcity that has dogged other less-developed countries, at least to the degree that the external constraint on growth was operative at a higher rate of growth than in most other less-developed countries.

The exchange-rate policy of each period was an integral part of financial policy. The de facto policy of devaluation allowed the country to proceed with its policy of growth through inflation. Despite all controversies about inelasticity of imports and exports with respect to exchange-rate adjustments, the only three postwar years in which Mexico was able to achieve current account surpluses were the years following devaluations, and this despite the acceleration of growth in those years. Indeed, two of the three highest rates of GNP growth were registered in 1950 and 1955, years immediately following devaluations. The rapid increase in exports and domestic growth following devaluations suggests that exchange-rate adjustments can be efficient means to foster export-led growth.

The policy of maintaining a stable exchange rate was successful inasmuch as it complemented the domestic objective of price stability and allowed the country to pursue a balance-of-payments policy based upon extensive foreign borrowing. The objective of domestic policy was to favor domestic industry while importing large amounts of capital goods. This policy of borrowing heavily from overseas institutions provided for a large flow of real resources to complement domestic savings and provide needed foreign exchange. This sizable current account deficits that the country financed represented large domestic investment in excess of domestic savings.

The other essential element of exchange-rate policy has been the absence of exchange controls with the passage of time. The argument that exchange controls would not have worked in Mexico appears increasingly persuasive. While in the strictest sense exchange controls were not necessary under stability since there was no tendency toward capital flight, one can still hypothetically ask whether controls would have been desirable. For instance, it may be argued that the absence of controls forced the country to adopt policies that were less favorable to economic development than would have been possible with controls, such as higher taxes on capital or more inflationary policies. This line of reasoning appears implausible. An essential element in Mexican economic development between 1954 and 1970 was the high returns on financial investment based in part upon confidence in the financial system. The incentive to place funds in the financial system will exist whether or not controls exist. If the incentives to financial investment are absent, wealth holders will find ways of avoiding any exchange control, whether by capital flight through a black market in currency or by an increase in nonfinancial investment. Thus, free convertibility functioned as part of the official financial strategy the essence of which was to create suitable conditions for the development of private voluntary savings.

THE MEANING OF THE MEXICAN EXPERIENCE FOR THE DEVELOPING COUNTRIES

The choice between inflationary and stable growth patterns that Mexico faced remains a dilemma for developing countries. The Mexican experience suggests that inflationary growth can be an effective pattern of promoting forced savings and of transferring resources between sectors of the economy. There are, however, clear limits to the effectiveness of inflationary growth. Inflation produces growth only when it raises investment by effectively lowering real consumption. Inflationary growth based on forced savings has highly regressive effects on the distribution of income and is, therefore, objectional on social grounds. It is important to stress that inflation will more often than not reduce real growth, since few governments can pursue policies of forced savings through inflation for a prolonged time. Therefore, it is understandable why most South American countries that experienced inflation had rather poor rates of growth. In most cases, the budget deficits that produced inflation resulted not from increased spending on capital equipment but from subsidies to consumption. While an inflationary transfer of income may have occurred in those countries, they basically took the form of an implicit tax on traditional exporting sectors with an indirect transfer to urban workers and some emphasis on import-substituting industries. Yet, one is hard pressed to find examples, other than Mexico, where inflation was used as a means of increasing savings. On the other hand, it is probably no accident that the group of Latin American countries that consistently had the highest rates of growth were the countries of Central America, which were politically conservative, economically stable, and not overly committed to the structural transformation of society. Therefore, it is essential to recognize the critical political prerequisites for countries contemplating inflationary growth. Unless governments are willing to use price changes to reduce consumption, the net effect of inflation will be to reduce and distort savings and hence to reduce growth. The Mexicans could successfully pursue inflation as a growth strategy only because the government was strong enough to allow a considerable drop in the living standards of the majority of the population. Even in the Mexican case, though, the process reached the point where the authorities perceived a significant threat to political stability and had to reverse the process.

The transfers of real income through inflation is destabilizing politically because it lowers the living standards of most while creating new wealth and power in other areas of society. Therefore, the options of other developing countries where political stability is more precarious are undoubtedly far more limited.

The stable period in Mexican economic development is meaningful to other countries inasmuch as it suggests that even countries without a history of sophisticated financial markets, and indeed even with a record of instability, can greatly increase domestic savings within a reasonable amount of time. The key to success in this area is the development of financial investments with competitive rates of return. The importance of competitive yields in financial markets in the foundation of the model of financial reform was stressed by McKinnon, who, using examples of financial reform in Japan and Germany and the case of South Korea from 1964 to 1970, found that following an increase in real interest rates, sharp rises in savings and visible changes in the asset preferences of the public occurred. The evidence seems to indicate that a wide variety of countries under varying circumstances exhibit considerable elasticities of savings with respect to yields on financial assets.[1] Accordingly, a growth strategy of increasing savings through raising the yields on financial investment seems to be viable.

With respect to international economic policy, Mexico clearly evolved a policy mix that allowed the country to mobilize considerable resources for economic development. The use of stable exchange rates and high domestic yields to stimulate favorable capital flows and the creation of a network of external credit is indicative of the potential that exists in the international financial system to obtain resources for economic development.

FINANCIAL POLICY, STABILITY, AND THE FUTURE OF ECONOMIC DEVELOPMENT IN MEXICO

Stability, the cornerstone of Mexican economic growth in the past generation, has now become a thing of the past. Rapid inflation has been present since 1972, and in September 1976 the fixed exchange rate had to be abandoned. However, while the shortcomings of the system of growth through stability and import substitution have become plain, the country has not yet evolved an alternative system. The future financial and economic system will only evolve with time; but it is nevertheless worthwhile to specify the problems that Mexico will face in coming years and to suggest what now appears the best way to deal with these problems.

In the first place, Mexico must now change its basic pattern of economic development. The pattern of import substitution has proven to cause structural disequilibria, misallocations of resources and intolerable social problems. Import-substituting industrialization has led to the impoverishment of the countryside and the creation of an urban proletariat with an enormous potential for political instability. It has to be a central objective of national policy to correct this structural imbalance through investments in activities that utilize the country's most abundant resource, labor. In recent years there has been a tendency to identify the policy of "stabilizing development" with policies of import substitution and to attribute the failures of the latter to the former. However, as has been argued throughout this work, the issue of export-led growth versus import-substituting growth is completely distinct from the issue of inflationary versus stable growth. To return to stability in no way implies a restoration of import substitution.

It should come as no surprise to those who have read this far that a principal policy conclusion of this inquiry is that Mexico should continue to seek growth with price stability. One of the underlying assumptions of this inquiry has been that there is no sustainable trade-off between real growth and inflation. The detailed examination of Mexican economic history throughout this work seems to bear this argument out. The postwar experience of other Latin American countries gives no indication of such a trade-off. Moreover, since 1970, Mexico and the industrial countries' real growth has declined as inflation has risen. While the inflation of recent years is by no means the only cause of the recent decline in real gowth, it is a major contributor.

It may be politically tempting to pursue inflationary policies in order to obtain slightly increased income and employment in the short run. However, experience demonstrates that the problems resulting from inflation, both the distortions of inflation and the deflation that is inevitably needed after a bout of inflation far outweigh the short-run benefits of inflation. Mexico could increase its growth rate to 8 percent in 1972 and maintain a respectable growth rate in 1973. However, the average annual growth rate for the period 1971–1975 was only slightly more than 5 percent, compared to the postwar average of 6.5 percent; and, Mexico's problems are far from over.

One reason that many commentators believe that inflation can produce growth in developing countries is that the concept of demand management, which may be applicable to the industrial countries, has been mistakenly transplanted into the context of a labor-surplus economy. In an industrialized economy with a potentially high level of income, it is possible that a deficiency of aggregate demand can cause a fall in income, an underutilization of plant and equipment, and unemployment. In developing economies, on the other hand, low income and unemployment are likely to be serious problems, regardless of whether supply and demand are properly matched. The problem is not to achieve full utilization of capacity, but to increase capacity, and to increase it in a way that makes best use of the country's most abundant resources.

Mexico's problem has arisen because too many resources have been devoted to capital-intensive industrialization, thus creating an underutilization of the labor force. The solution can only be found by removing the incentives to inefficiency that have been created and developing conditions in which a more satisfactory use of resources occurs. The post-1970 effort to correct structural distortions by expanding demand, was thus bound to fail. Although the discipline necessary to maintain stable growth is difficult, inflationary growth has even more serious disadvantages.

For inflation to yield growth, it must produce forced savings, and such a policy is both socially objectionable and unlikely to succeed. While there have been some cases of growth with forced savings through inflation, few governments in Latin America have been able to pursue such policies for any appreciable time. Such a policy was possible in Mexico a generation ago, but with the new strength of the urban proletariat and the trade unions it is clearly now impossible. In current conditions inflation in Mexico is likely to result in a South American-style structural inflation, in which the urban working classes can obtain often continued subsidies while distortions grow in the economy and the rate of growth declines.

Nor does a system of inflation-indexing offer any answer. It is true that since 1968 Brazil has used indexing as a means of overcoming the distortions of inflation and still managed to increase its rate of growth. However, while a technical means of offsetting inflation may be available, it does not in itself represent a means of achieving growth. The Brazilians used indexing as a means of protecting investment rather than consumption, and the increases in investment and in efficiency resulting from this policy were sources of Brazilian growth. The Brazilian government was denounced for allowing real wages to drop for a prolonged period, and the Brazilians established a harsh authoritarian government to enforce its policy decisions.[2] Thus, the idea of adopting indexing to achieve growth with inflation becomes less attractive as the full implications of such a policy became clear.

The issue at the end of this work is the same as it was in the beginning. The problem of development is to increase savings and to raise the level of productivity. At this point in its history, Mexico has encountered some problems involving the allocation of resources, a problem that can only be solved by dismantling the system of protection and subsidies, and a problem which inflation does nothing to solve. Mexico has developed a distinctive and highly effective means of generating savings, an achievement which is in grave danger from inflation and an unstable currency. The evidence from Mexico's own history suggests that a strategy of increasing savings through higher yields on financial investment is viable, and no alternative system is. It would be a tragedy to see the financial achievements of the past generation destroyed.

Since Mexico has no workable alternative to stable growth, it is essential to return to a pattern of growth which does not involve isolation from major international financial markets but which, reflecting the scarcity of savings, offers attractive rates of real return on capital. The new system of finance would have to be adapted to the contemporary world of relatively high world inflation and floating exchanges. It may involve a floating peso and developing a forward market. However, there should be no illusion that a return to inflationary growth is sustainable for any period of time.

For the past two generations, Mexican accomplishments in economics and finance have been well in advance of those in most developing countries. The country is now passing through a crisis, in which its entire pattern of developmen is being tested. The mere fact that Mexico is passing through a difficult phase in its histroy is not, in itself, grounds for pessimism. It is only by passing through periods of trial that nations, like individuals, learn from their mistakes.

NOTES

1. Ronald I. McKinnon, *Money and Capital in Economic Development* (Washington: The Brookings Institution, 1973), pp. 89–116.

2. Walter L. Ness, Jr., "Financial Market Innovation as a Development Strategy: Initial Results from the Brazilian Experience," in *Economic Development and Cultural Change,* Vol. XXII (April 1974), pp. 453–474.

Bibliography

Official Documents and Data Sources
Mexico

Bank of Mexico, *Annual Report,* various issues.

————, *Disposiciones Sobre Divisas, Oro, Plata, Pagos al Ampara de Convenios, Financiamiento del Extranjero y Comercio Exterior.*

————, Economic Research Department. Unpublished statistical data. Comisión Nacional Bancaria. *Memoria Estadística, 1952–1961.*

————, *Memoria Estadística, 1962–1966.*

Comisión Nacional de Valores. *Los Bancos y el Mercado de Valores,* various issues.

————, *Memoria Anual,* various issues.

Dirección General de Estadística. *Anuario Estadístico Compendiado,* various issues.

Ministry of Finance, *Discursos Pronunciados por los cc. Secretarios de Hacienda y Crédito Público en las Convenciones Bancarias Celebradas del Año 1934 a 1958.* (Mexico: 1958)

Nacional Financiera S.A., *Informe Anual,* various issues.

————, *Statistics on the Mexican Economy,* 1966.

International Organizations

Combined Mexican Working Party (group composed of economists from IBRD and Nacional Financiera), *The Economic Development of Mexico* (published for IBRD) (Baltimore: Johns Hopkins University Press, 1953).

Interamerican Development Bank, *Annual Report,* various issues.

International Bank for Reconstruction and Development, *Annual Report,* various issues.

————, *The International Bank for Reconstruction and Development, 1946–1953* (Baltimore: Johns Hopkins University Press, 1953).

220

————, *The World Bank, IFC and IDA: Policies and Operations* (Washington: IBRD, 1962).

————, *Policies and Operations: The World Bank, IDA and IFC* (Washington: IBRD, 1971).

International Monetary Fund, *Annual Report on Exchange Restrictions,* various issues.

————, *Annual Report of the Executive Directors,* various issues.

————, *Financial Policy and Economic Development in Mexico: Report of a Mission of International Monetary Fund* (Washington: June 24, 1955).

————, *International Financial Statistics,* various issues.

United Nations, Commission on Trade and Development (UNCTAD), *The International Monetary Situation: Impact on World Trade and Development* (TD/ 140/Rev. 1) (New York, 1972).

————, *Trade Prospects and Capital Needs of Developing Countries* (TD/34/Rev. 1) (New York, 1968).

United Nations, Economic Commission for Latin America (ECLA).

————, *El Desequilibrio Externo en el Desarrollo Económico Latinoamericano: El Caso de México,* (E/CN/12/48) (La Paz, Bolivia, 1957), 2 volumes.

————, *The Economic Development of Latin America in the Postwar Period,* (E/CN/12/ 659/Rev. 1) (New York, 1961).

————, *Economic Bulletin for Latin America* (quarterly), various issues.

————, *Economic Survey of Latin America* (annual), various issues.

————, *External Financing in Latin America* (E/CN/12/649/Rev. 1, 1965) (New York, 1965).

————, *Statistical Bulletin for Latin America* (annual), various issues.

United States

Economic Report of the President (annual), various issues.

Department of the Treasury, *Bulletin* (monthly), various issues.

Books

Adelman, Irma, and Cynthia Taft Morris, *Economic Growth and Social Equity in Developing Countries.* Stanford, Calif., Stanford University Press, 1973.

Alba, Victor, *Politics and the Labor Movement in Latin America.* Stanford, Calif., Stanford University Press, 1968.

Arce Cano, Gustavo, *Nueva Política Monetaria y Banca Central para el Desarrollo.* Mexico, Ediciones Botas, 1971.

Areskoug, Kaj, *External Public Borrowing: Its Role in Economic Development.* New York, Praeger, 1969.

Baer, Werner, and Isaac Kerstenetzky (eds.), *Inflation and Growth in Latin America.* Homewood, Ill., Richard D. Irwin Inc., 1964.

Baklanoff, Erik N., *Expropriation of U.S. Investments in Cuba, Mexico and Chile*. New York, Praeger, 1975.

Basch, Antonín, *El Mercado de Capitales en México*. Mexico, CEMLA, 1968.

Beltran, Enrique, *et al.*, *México: Cincuenta Años de Revolución* (4 vols.). Mexico, Fondo de Cultura Económica, 1960.

Bennett, Robert Lee, *The Financial Sector and Economic Development: The Mexican Case*. Baltimore, Johns Hopkins University Press, 1965.

Beteta, Ramón, *Tres Años de Política Hacendaria*. Mexico, Ministry of Finance, 1951.

Bett, Virgil M., *Central Banking in Mexico: Monetary Policy and Financial Crises, 1864–1949*. Ann Arbor, University of Michigan Press, 1957.

Brandenburg, Frank R., *The Making of Modern Mexico*. Englewood Cliffs, N.J., Prentice-Hall, 1964.

Brothers, Dwight S., and Leopoldo Solís, *Mexican Financial Development*. Austin, University of Texas Press, 1966.

Call, Tomme Clark, *The Mexican Venture*. New York, Oxford University Press, 1953.

Campos Andapia, Antonio, *Las Sociedades Financieras Privadas en México*. Mexico, CEMLA, 1967.

Carrillo Flores, Antonio. *Homenajes y Testimonios*. Mexico, by the Author, 1967.

Cooper, Richard N., *Currency Devaluation in Developing Countries*. (Princeton: Essays in International Finance, No. 86), June 1971.

Costanzo, G. A., *Programas de Estabilización en América Latina*. Mexico, CEMLA, 1961.

de Oteya, José Andrés., *Políticas de Fomento de los Mercados de Capitales*. Mexico, CEMLA, 1971.

Derossi, Flavia, *The Mexican Entrepreneur*. Paris, OECD Development Centre, 1971.

Diaz Alejandro, Carlos F., *Exchange-Rate Devaluation in a Semi-Industrialized Country: The Experience of Argentina, 1958–61*. Cambridge, Mass.: MIT Press, 1965.

Dimarco, Eugenio Luis (ed.), *International Economics and Development: Essays in Honor of Raul Prebisch*. New York, Academic Press, 1972.

Donges, Juergen, *Brazil's Trotting Peg: A New Approach to Greater Exchange Flexibility in Less Developed Countries*. Washington: American Enterprise Institute for Policy Research, 1971.

Fei, John C. H., and Gustav Ranis, *Development of the Labor Surplus Economy*. Homewood, Ill.: Richard D. Irwin, Inc., 1964.

Freithaler, William O., *Mexico's Foreign Trade and Economic Development*. New York: Praeger, 1968.

Friedman, Irving S., *Foreign Exchange Control and the Evolution of the International Payments System*. Washington: International Monetary Fund, 1958.

Friedman, Milton, *Money and Economic Development.* New York: Praeger, 1973.

Glade, William P., and Charles W. Anderson, *The Political Economy of Mexico.* Madison: University of Wisconsin Press, 1963.

Goldsmith, Raymond N., *The Financial Development of Mexico.* Paris: OECD Development Centre, 1966.

Gómez, Rodrigo, *Economic Growth and Monetary Stability: Lectures Delivered by Maurice Frere and Rodrigo Gómez.* Washington, The Per Jacobsen Foundation, 1964.

———, *Textos de Rodrigo Gómez, 1953–1967.* Mexico, Gráficas Panamericanas, 1967.

Green, Rosario, *El Endeudamiento Público Externo de México: 1940–1973.* Mexico: El Colegio de México, 1976.

Griffin, Keither, *Financing Development in Latin America,* (ed.), (London: Macmillan, 1970).

Griffiths, Brian, *Mexican Monetary Policy and Economic Development.* New York, Praeger, 1972.

Gurley, John G., and Edward S. Shaw, *Money in a Theory of Finance.* Washington: The Brookings Institution, 1960.

Haberler, Gottfried, *Theory of International Trade.* London, William Hodge and Co., 1950.

Hansen, Roger D., *The Politics of Mexican Development,* Baltimore, Johns Hopkins University Press, 1971.

Hellinger, Stephen H., and Douglas A. Hellinger, *Unemployment and the Multinationals: A Strategy for Technological Change in Latin America.* Port Washington, N.Y., Kennikat Press, 1976.

Johnson, Harry G., *Economic Policies Toward Less Developed Countries.* Washington, The Brookings Institution, 1967.

———, *Essays in Monetary Economics.* London, Allen and Unwin, 1967. pp. 281–292.

Johnson, John T., *Political Change in Latin America: The Emergence of the Middle Sectors.* Stanford, Calif., Stanford University Press, 1965.

Jones, Ronald W., and Richard E. Caves, *World Trade and Payments.* Boston: Little, Brown & Co., 1973.

Kahlil, Raouf, *Inflation and Economic Development in Brazil, 1946–63.* Oxford, Clarendon Press, 1973.

Kemmerer, Edwin W., *Inflation and Revolution: Mexico's Experience of 1912–1917.* Princeton, N.J., Princeton University Press, 1940.

Kindleberger, Charles P., *Economic Development.* New York, McGraw-Hill, 1965.

———, *International Economics,* Homewood, Ill., Richard D. Irwin, 1973.

———, *Money and Power: The Economics of International Politics and the Politics of International Economics.* New York, Basic Books, 1970.

King, John A., Jr., *Economic Development Projects and their Appraisals: Cases and Principles from the Experience of the World Bank*. (Published for the Economic Development Institute, International Bank for Reconstruction and Development) Baltimore, Johns Hopkins University Press, 1967.

King, Timothy, *Mexico: Industrialization & Trade Policies Since 1940*. Published for OECD Development Centre, London, Oxford University Press, 1970.

La Cascia, Joseph S., *Capital Formation and Economic Development in Mexico*. New York, Praeger, 1969.

McKinnon, Ronald I., *Money and Capital in Economic Development*. Washington, The Brookings Institution, 1973.

Maizels, Alfred, *Exports and Economic Growth of Developing Countries*. Cambridge, England, Cambridge University Press, 1968.

Manero, Antonio, *La Revolución Bancaria en México, 1865–1955*. Mexico, Talleres Gráficos de la Nación, 1957.

Mason, Edward S., and Robert E. Asher, *The World Bank Since Bretton Woods*. Washington, The Brookings Institution, 1973.

Maynard, Geoffrey, *Economic Development and the Price Level*. London, Macmillan, 1962.

Meade, J. E., *A Neo-Classical Theory of Economic Growth*. London, Allen and Unwin, 1962.

———, *The Theory of International Economic Policy, Vol. I: The Balance of Payments*. London, Oxford University Press, 1963.

Meier, Gerald M., *The International Economics of Development*. New York, Harper and Row, 1968.

Mikesell, Raymond F., *Foreign Exchange in the Postwar World*. New York, The Twentieth Century Fund, 1954.

Moore, O. Ernest, *Evolución de las Instituciones Financieras en México*. Mexico, CEMLA, 1963.

Moreno Castañeda, Gilberto, *El Nuevo Orden Monetario de México*. Guadalajara, Gráficos, 1944.

Mosk, Sandford, *Industrial Revolution in Mexico*. Berkeley, University of California Press, 1950.

Nassef, El Sayed Mohamed Abdel Mabood, *Monetary Policy in Developing Countries: The Mexican Case*. Rotterdam: University of Rotterdam Press, 1972.

Navarrete, Alfredo, *Finanzas y Desarrollo Económico*. Mexico, Libros SELA, 1968.

Navarrete, Ifigenia M. de, *La Distribución del Ingreso y el Desarrollo Económico de México*. Mexico, Escuela Nacional de Economía, 1960.

Nurkse, Ragnar, *Problems of Capital Formation in Underdeveloped Countries and Patterns of Trade and Development*. New York, Oxford University Press, 1967.

Ortiz Mena, Antonio, *Logros y Desarrollos de México en el Campo Económico: El Camino Recorrido por Nacional Financiera*. Mexico, Nacional Financiera, 1964.

————, *Stabilizing Development: A Decade of Economic Strategy in Mexico.* Mexico, Ministry of Finance, 1969.

Paauw, Douglas S., *Development Strategies in Open Dualistic Economies.* Washington, National Planning Association, 1970.

Pani, Alberto J., *El Problema Supremo de México.* Mexico, Imp. de Manuel Casas, 1955.

Pazos, Luis, *Devaluación y Estatismo en México.* Mexico, Editorial Diana, 1976.

Pérez Galliano, Arturo, *et al., América Latina y la Liquidez Internacional.* Mexico, CEMLA, 1970.

Reynolds, Clark, *The Mexican Economy.* New Haven, Conn., Yale University Press, 1970.

Scammell, W. M., *International Monetary Policy* (second edition). New York, St. Martin's Press, 1967.

Schlesinger, Eugene R., *Multiple Exchange Rates & Economic Development.* Princeton, N.J., Studies in International Finance, No. 2, 1952.

Schott, Francis H., *The Evolution of Latin American Exchange-Rate Policies Since World War II.* Princeton, Essays in International Finance, No. 32, January 1959.

Siegel, Barry N., *Inflación y Desarrollo: La Experiencia de México.* Mexico, CEMLA, 1958.

Stern, Robert M., *The Balance of Payments.* Chicago: Aldine, 1973.

Tamagna, Frank, *La Banca Central en América Latina.* Mexico, CEMLA, 1963.

Thorbecke, Erik (ed.), *The Role of Agriculture in Economic Development.* New York, Columbia University Press, 1969.

Thorbecke, E., and I. Adelman, *The Theory & Design of Economic Development.* Baltimore, Johns Hopkins University Press, 1966.

Vanek, J., *Estimating Foreign Resource Needs for Economic Development.* New York, McGraw-Hill, 1967.

Vernon, Raymond, *The Dilemma of Mexico's Development.* Cambridge, Mass., Harvard University Press, 1963.

———— (ed.), *Public Policy and Private Enterprise in Mexico.* Cambridge, Mass., Harvard University Press, 1964.

Wilkie, James W., *The Mexican Revolution: Federal Expenditures and Social Change Since 1910.* Berkeley, University of California Press, 1967.

Wionczek, Miguel S. (ed.), *La Sociedad Mexicana: Presente y Futuro.* Mexico, Fondo de Cultura Económica, 1973.

Articles

Adelman, I., and H. B. Chenery, "Foreign Aid and Economic Development: The Case of Greece," in *Review of Economics and Statistics,* Vol. XLVIII (February 1966), pp. 1–19.

Alemann, Roberto T., "Argentina," in *Economic Development Issues: Latin America.* New York, Committee for Economic Development (Supplementary paper No. 21, 1967), pp. 1–58.

Alexander, Sidney, "Devaluation Versus Import Restriction as an Instrument for Improving Foreign Trade Balance," in *IMF Staff Papers,* Vol. I (April 1951), pp. 379–391.

Alvarado, José, "El Extraño Caso de la Secretaría de Hacienda," in *Problemas Agrícolas e Industriales de México,* Vol. V (January–March 1955), pp. 163–168.

Areskoug, Kaj, "Foreign Capital Utilization and Economic Policies in Developing Countries," in *Review of Economics and Statistics.* Vol. LV (May 1973), pp. 182–189.

Baer, Werner, and Michel E. A. Herve, "Employment and Industrialization in Developing Countries," in *Quarterly Journal of Economics,* Vol. LXXX (February 1966), pp. 88–107.

Banco Nacional de México, "La Experiencia Monetaria y de Crédito en México" in *Revista Bancaria,* Vol. I (November–December 1953), pp. 583–592.

Bazdresch, Carlos, "La Política Económica," in *Plural,* Vol. II (August 1973), pp. 18–20.

———, "La Política Monetaria Mexicana (Una Primera Aproximación)," in *La Economía Mexicana,* Leopoldo Solís (ed.), Vol. II *Política y Desarrollo.* Mexico, Fondo de Cultura Económica, 1973, pp. 138–156.

Bennett, Robert L., "Financial Innovation and Structural Change in the Early Stage of Industrialization: Mexico, 1945–59," in *Journal of Finance,* Vol. XVIII (December 1963), pp. 666–683.

Bernstein, E. M., "Some Economic Aspects of Multiple Exchange Rates," in *IMF Staff Papers,* Vol. I (September 1950), pp. 224–237.

Beteta, Mario Ramón, "The Central Bank: Instrument of Economic Development in Mexico," in *Mexico's Recent Economic Growth,* Tom E. Davis (ed.), Austin, University of Texas Press, 1967, pp. 45–70.

Blair, Calvin P., "Nacional Financiera: Entrepreneurship in a Mixed Economy," in *Public Policy and Private Enterprise in Mexico,* Raymond Vernon (ed.), Cambridge, Mass., Harvard University Press, 1964, pp. 191–240.

Brailovsky, Vladimir, "Comentarios Sobre la Tenencia de la Tierra en México," *Investigación Económica,* Vol. XXIX (April–June 1969), pp. 307–318.

Brandenburg, Frank R., "Organized Business in Mexico," in *Inter-American Economic Affairs,* Vol. XII (Winter 1958), pp. 26–50.

Brimmer, Andrew F., "Central Banking and Economic Development," in *Journal of Money Credit and Banking,* Vol. I (November 1971), pp. 780–792.

Bronfenbrenner, Martin, and F. D. Holzman, "Survey of Inflation Theory," in *American Economic Review,* Vol. LIII (September 1963), pp. 593–661.

Brothers, Dwight S., "Private Foreign Investment," in *Constructive Change in Latin America*. Pittsburgh, University of Pittsburgh Press, 1968, pp. 87–116.

———, "El Financiamiento de la Formación de Capital en México, 1950–61," in *Comercio Exterior*, Vol. XIII (December 1963), pp. 901–910.

Bueno Z., Gerardo, "La Paridad del Poder Adquisitivo y las Elasticidades de Importación y Exportación en México," in *El Trimestre Económico*, Vol. XVI (April–June 1974), pp. 313–323.

———, "The Structure of Protection in Mexico," in *The Structure of Protection in Developing Countries*, Bela Balassa (ed.). Baltimore, Johns Hopkins University Press, 1971, pp. 169–202.

Calderón, Guillermo, "Las Inversiones Extranjeras y el Ahorro Interno," in *Revista de Economía*, Vol. XXI (June 1958), pp. 148–153.

Campos Salas, Octaviano, "Una Política de Relaciones Económicas Internacionales," in *Comercio Exterior*, Vol. IV (June 1954), pp. 219–224.

Cárdenas, Felipe, "Comisión Nacional Bancaria," in *Revista de Administración Pública*, No. 6 (April–May 1957), pp. 17–23.

Carrillo Flores, Antonio, "Las Fuentes Internacionales para el Financiamiento del Desarrollo Económico en Latinoamérica," in *El Mercado de Valores*, Vol. XXII (December 24, 1962), pp. 769–776.

———, "Mexico Forges Ahead," in *Foreign Affairs*, Vol. XXXVI (April 1958) pp. 491–503.

———, "La Orientación Fundamental de Nuestra Política Económica," in *Revista Fiscal y Financiera*, Vol. XVI (April 1956), pp. 13´–24.

Chenery, H. B., and M. Bruno, "Development Alternatives in an Open Economy: The Case of Israel," in *Economic Journal*, Vol. LXXII (March 1962), pp. 79–103.

Chenery, H. B., and P. Eckstein, "Development Alternatives for Latin America," in *Journal of Political Econony*, Vol. LXXVIII (supplement to July–August, 1970), pp. 966–1006.

Chenery, H. B., and A. MacEwan, "Optimal Patterns of Growth and Aid: The Case Of Pakistan," in I. Adelman & E. Thorbecke, (eds.), *The Theory and Design of Economic Development*, Baltimore, Johns Hopkins University Press, 1966.

Chenery, H. B., and A. M. Strout, "Foreign Assistance and Economic Development," in *American Economic Review*, Vol. LVI (September 1966), pp. 679–733.

"La Comisión Especial de Financiamientos Exteriores," in *El Mercado de Valores*, Vol. XVIII (April 7, 1958), pp. 158–159.

Corden, W. M., "International Monetary Reform and the Developing Countries: A Mainly Theoretical Paper," in *Monetary Problems of the International*

Economy, Robert A. Mundell and Alexander K. Swoboda (eds.), Chicago, University of Chicago Press, 1969, pp. 283–304.

Davis, Horace B., "Labor and the State in a Semi-Colonial Country: Mexico," in *Weltwirtschaftliches Archiv*, Band 74 (1955), pp. 283–306.

Davis, Tom W., "Eight Decades of Inflation in Chile, 1879–1959: A Political Interpretation," in *Journal of Political Economy*, Vol. LXXI (August 1963), pp. 389–397.

De Beers, John S., "El Peso Mexicano, 1941–1949," in *Problemas Agricolas e Industriales de México*, Vol. V (January–March 1953), pp. 7–135.

de Iturbide, Aníbal, "La Devaluación del Peso Mexicano: Cuatro Conferencias," in *El Trimestre Económico*, Vol. XI (August 1948).

de Vries, Margaret C., "Multiple Exchange Rates: Expectations and Experience," in *IMF Staff Papers*, Vol. XII (July 1965), pp. 282–313.

del Canto, Jorge, "América Latina: Desarrollo Económico y Estabilidad Económica," in *El Trimestre Economico*, Vol. XXV (July–September 1958), pp. 395–411.

"Devaluación," editorial in *Revista de Economia*, Vol. XVII (May 1954) pp. 133–134.

Domar, Evsey D., "Expansion and Employment," in *American Economic Review*, Vol. XXXVII (March 1947), pp. 34–55.

Donnelly, John T., "External Financing and Short-Term Consequences of External Debt Servicing for Brazilian Economic Development, 1947–1968," in *Journal of Developing Areas*, Vol. VII (April 1973), pp. 411–430.

Dorrance, G. S., "The Effect of Inflation on Economic Development," in *IMF Staff Papers*, Vol. X (March 1963), pp. 1–47.

Dovring F., "Papel de la Agricultura dentro de las Poblaciones en Crecimiento, México: Un Caso de Desarrollo Reciente," in *El Trimestre Económico*, Vol. XXXV (January–March 1968), pp. 25–50.

Eckhaus, Richard S., "Estructura del Sector de las Financieras en México, 1940–1970," in *CEMLA, Boletín Mensual*, Vol. XXI (May 1975), pp. 256–287.

Emery, Robert F., "Mexican Monetary Policy Since the 1954 Devaluation," in *Inter-American Economic Affairs*, Vol. XII (Spring 1959), pp. 72–84.

———, "The Use of Interest-Rate Policies as a Stimulus to Economic Growth," Washington, Board of Governors of the Federal Reserve System, *Staff Economic Studies*, No. 65 (September 1974).

Escobedo, Gilberto, "The Response of the Mexican Economy to Policy Actions," in *Federal Reserve Bank of St. Louis Review*, Vol. LV (June 1973), pp. 15–23.

———, "Formulating a Model of the Mexican Economy," in *Federal Reserve Bank of St. Louis Review*, Vol. LV (July 1973), pp. 8–19.

———, "Los Indicadores para Medir el Resultado de la Política Monetaria en México," in *Comercio Exterior,* Vol. XXIII (October 1973), pp. 1007–1025.

———, "Formulación de un Modelo para la Economía Mexicana," in *CEMLA; Boletín Mensual,* Vol. XXI (February–March 1975), pp. 58–70.

Espinosa de los Reyes, Jorge, "La Distribución del Ingreso Nacional," in *La Economía Mexicana,* Leopoldo Solis (ed.), Vol. I, *Análisis por Sectores y Distribución.* Mexico, Fondo de Cultura Económica, 1973, pp. 324–342.

Ferreirro, Elena P., "Devaluación y Consumo," in *Revista de Economía,* Vol. XVIII (July 1955), pp. 174–179.

Flanders, M. J., "Prebisch on Protectionism: An Evaluation," in *Economic Journal,* Vol. LXXIV (June 1964), pp. 305–326.

Flores de la Pena, Horacio, "La Mecánica del Desarrollo Económico," in *Revista de Economía,* Vol. XXV (August 1962), pp. 300–305.

———. "La Elasticidad de la Oferta y el Desarrollo Económico," in *El Trimestre Económico,* Vol. XXII (January–March 1955), pp. 1–12.

Fraustro, Oscar, "Nacional Financiera, S.A." in *Revista de Administractión Pública,* No. 5 (January–March 1957), pp. 19–28.

Gasser, Micha. "Los Paises Subdesarrollados y el Tipo de Cambio Flexible," in *El Trimestre Económico,* Vol. XLIX (October–December 1973), pp. 893–903.

Gleason, Rubén Galicia, "Papel de los Créditos del Exterior en el Financiamiento del Desarrollo Económico," in *Investigación Económica,* Vol. XV (Fourth Quarter 1955), pp. 497–558.

Griffiths, K. B., and J. L. Enos, "Foreign Assistance: Objectives and Consequences," in *Economic Development and Cultural Change,* Vol. XIX (April 1970), pp. 313–337.

Gudin, E., "Multiple Exchange Rates: The Brazilian Experience," in *Economia Internazionale,* Vol. IX (August 1956), pp. 501–509.

Harrod, R. F., "An Essay in Dynamic Theory," in *Economic Journal,* Vol. XLIX (March 1939), pp. 14–37.

———, "Domar and Dynamic Economics," in *Economic Journal,* Vol. LXIX (September 1959) pp. 451–464.

Hanson, James S., and Robert C. Vogel, "Inflation and Monetary Velocity in Latin America," in *Review of Economics and Statistics,* Vol. XV (August 1973), pp. 365–371.

Hause, John C., "The Welfare Costs of Disequilibrium Exchange Rates," in *Journal of Political Economy,* Vol. LXXIV (August 1966), pp. 333–352.

Hawkins, Robert, G., Walter L. Ness, and Il Sakong, "Improving the Access of Developing Countries to the U.S. Capital Market," New York University, Graduate School of Business Administration Center for the Study of Financial Institutions, *The Bulletin* (1974).

Hirschman, Albert O., "The Political Economy of Import-Substituting Industrialization in Latin America," in *Quarterly Journal of Economics*, Vol. LXXXII
(February 1968), pp. 1–32.

Huergo, Ernesto H., "Causes, Fines y Efectos de la Devaluación," in *Revista de
Economía*, Vol. XVII (June 1954), pp. 177–179.

Irvine, Reed J., and Robert F. Emery, "Interest Rates as an Anti-Inflationary
Instrument in Taiwan," in *National Banking Review*, Vol. IV (1966), pp.
29–39.

Johnson, Harry G., "Political Economy Aspects of International Monetary Reform" in *Journal of International Economics*, Vol. II (September 1972), pp.
401–424.

Johnston, Roger D., "Should the Mexican Government Promote the Country's
Stock Exchange," in *Inter-American Economic Affairs*, Vol. XXVI (Winter
1972), pp. 45–60.

Kafka, Alexandre, "Indexing for Inflation in Brazil," in *Essays on Indexation and
Inflation*, Washington, American Enterprise Association for Policy, 1974, pp.
87–98.

———, "Some Aspects of Latin America's Financial Relations with the International Monetary Fund," in *Socio-Economic Change in Latin America*, Alberto
Martinez Piedras (ed.), Washington, Catholic University of America Press,
1970, pp. 87–103.

Kaldor, Nicholas, "Economic Growth and the Problem of Inflation," parts I and
II in *Económica*, Vol. XXVI (August 1959 and September 1959), pp. 212–
226 and 287–298.

———, "Alternative Theories of Distribution," in *Review of Economic Studies*, Vol.
XXIII (1955–1956), pp. 83–100.

Khatkhate, Deena R., "Analystic Basis of the Workings of Monetary Policy in
Developing Countries," in *IMF Staff Papers*, Vol. XIX (November 1972), pp.
533–559.

Konig, Wolfgang, "International Financial Institutions and Latin American Development," in *Latin America in the International Economy*, Victor L. Urquidi
and Rosemary Thorp (eds.), New York, John Wiley & Sons, 1973, pp. 116–
169.

Krasner, Stephen D., "The International Monetary Fund and the Third World,"
in *International Organization*, Vol. XXII (Summer 1968), pp. 670–688.

Kravis, Irving B., "Trade as a Handmaiden of Growth: Similarities Between the
Nineteenth and Twentieth Century," in *Economic Journal*, Vol. LXXX (December 1970), pp. 850–872.

———, and N. A. Adams, "Trade as a Handmaiden of Growth: An Inter-
change," in *Economic Journal*, Vol. LXXXIII (March 1973), pp. 203–209.

Krueger, Anne O., "Some Economic Costs of Exchange Controls: The Turkish

Case," in *Journal of Political Economy,* Vol. LXXIV (October 1966), pp. 466–480.

Lagunilla Inarritu, Alfredo, "Un Desequilibrio Fundamental de Desarrollo," in *Comercio Exterior,* Vol. V (December 1955), pp. 495–498.

——, "La Tasa Natural en el Mercado de Capitales de México," in *El Trimestre Económico,* Vol. XV (July–September 1948), pp. 229–242.

Laidler, and J. M. W. Parkin, "Inflation—A Survey," in *Economic Journal,* Vol. LXXXV (December 1975), pp. 741–810.

Lewis, W. Arthur, "Economic Development with Unlimited Supplies of Labor," in *Manchester School of Economic and Social Studies,* Vol. XXII (May 1954), pp. 139–191.

Lewis, Oscar, "Mexico Since Cárdenas," in *Social Change in Latin America Today,* New York, Vintage Books, 1960, pp. 285–345 (published for Council on Foreign Relations).

Linder, Harold K., "México y el Banco de Exportaciones e Importaciones: Una Antigua Alianza para el Progreso," in *El Mercado de Valores,* Vol. XXII (April 9, 1962), pp. 177–181.

López Romero, Adolfo, "Desarrollo Económico de México" in *El Trimestre Economico,* Vol. XXIX (January–March, 1962), pp. 30–69.

López Rosado, Diego, and Juan F. Noyola Vásquez, "Los Salarios Reales en México, 1939–1950," in *El Trimestre Económico,* Vol. XVIII (April–June 1951), pp. 201–209.

McKinnon, Ronald I., "Foreign Exchange Constraints in Economic Development and Efficient Aid Allocation," in *Economic Journal.* Vol. LXXVII (June 1964), pp. 388–409.

——, "The Monetary Approach to Exchange-Rate Policy in Less Developed Countries," in *Exchange-Rate Policy in Southeast Asia,* Herbert G. Grubel and Theodore Morgan (eds.), Lexington, Mass., D. C. Heath & Co. 1973, pp. 67–102.

Mancera, Miguel, "La Política Monetaria y Crediticia de México," in *Revista Bancaria,* Vol. XX (January 1972), pp. 3–11.

Manne, Alan S., "Key Sectors of the Mexican Economy, 1960–1970," in *Studies in Process Analysis,* A. S. Manne and H. M. Markowitz (eds.), New York, John Wiley & Sons, Inc., 1963, pp. 379–415.

Marshall, Jorge, "Efectos Económicos de Ciertas Prácticas de Cambio Múltiple," in *El Trimestre Económico,* Vol. XX (July–September 1953), pp. 375–394.

——, "Exchange Controls and Economic Development," in *Economic Development for Latin America: Proceedings of a Conference Held by The International Economic Association,* Howard S. Ellis and Harvey C. Wallich (eds.), London, Macmillan, 1961, pp. 430–469.

Martínez Escamilla, Ramón, "La Fuerza de Trabajo Mexicana: Algunos Cambios

Fundamentales, 1940–1970," in *Investigación Económica,* Vol. XXXIII (April–June 1974), pp. 257–274.

Martínez Ostos, Raúl, "El Banco de México," in *Banca Central,* N. H. de Kock (ed.), Mexico, Fondo de Cultura Económica, 1946, pp. 395–457.

Maynard, G., and W. Van Rijckeghem, "Argentina 1967–70: A Stabilization Attempt That Failed," in *Banca Nacionale del Lavoro Quarterly Review,* No. 103, (December 1972), pp. 396–412.

Messuti Domingo, Jorge, "El Sistema Financiero y el Crecimiento Económico," in *El Trimestre Económico,* Vol. XXXV (July–September 1968), pp. 517–537.

Michaels, Michael, "Devaluation, Cost Inflation and the Supply of Exports," in *Economia Internazionale,* Vol. IX (February 1956), pp. 34–61.

Mikesell, Raymond F., and James E. Zinser, "The Nature of the Savings Function in Developing Countries: A Survey of the Theoretical and Empirical Literature," in *Journal of Economic Literature,* Vol. XI (March 1973), pp. 1–26.

Morawetz, D., "Employment Implications of Industrialization in Developing Countries," in *The Economic Journal,* Vol. LXXXIV (September 1974), pp. 491–542.

Moyo, Edmundo, *et al.,* "Análisis Sobre Salarios Minimos Elaborado por la CTM," in *Revista de Economia.* Vol. XVI (December 1953), pp. 359–367.

Moyo Porras, Edmundo, "Efectos de la Devaluación en la Industria de Transformación," in *Revista de Economia,* Vol. XVII (May 1954), p. 142.

Mujica, Emilio, "Los Salarios en la Industria," in *Revista de Economia,* Vol. XV (September 1952), pp. 270–284.

Mundell, Robert A., "The Monetary Dynamics of International Adjustment Under Fixed and Flexible Exchange Rates," in *Quarterly Journal of Economics,* Vol. LXXIV (May 1960), pp. 227–257.

Nash, Manning, "Economic Nationalism in Mexico," in *Economic Nationalism in Old and New States,* Harry G. Johnson (ed.), Chicago, University of Chicago Press, 1967, pp. 71–84.

Navarrete, Alfredo, "La Experiencia de México en el Uso de los Instrumentos de Política Financiera" in *El Mercado de Valores,* Vol. XXIII (March 11, 1963), pp. 121–123.

———, "La Administración Financiera en el Desarrollo Económico de México," in *Revista de Economia,* Vol. XXVII (April 1964), pp. 107–115.

———, "Algunos Efectos de la Situación Económica Internacional en La Economía Mexicana," in *Investigación Económica,* Vol. XIII (Fourth Quarter 1953), pp. 247–257.

———, "Una Hipótesis Sobre el Sistema Económico de México," in *El Trimestre Económico,* Vol. XVIII (January–March 1951), pp. 21–55.

————, "Mexico's Balance of Payments and External Financing," in *Weltwirtschaftliches Archiv,* Band 101 (1968), pp. 70–86.

————, "Nacional Financiera Como Mobilizadora de Recursos del Exterior," in *El Mercado de Valores,* Vol. XXV (November 22, 1965), pp. 823 and 834–838.

————, "Las Relaciones Financieras Internacionales de México," in *Investigación Económica,* Vol. XV (Second Quarter 1955), pp. 179–190.

————, "El Sector Público en el Desarrollo Económico" in *Investigación Económica,* Vol. XVII (First Quarter 1957), pp. 40–55.

Navarrete, Eduardo, "Desequilibrio y Depedencia: Los Relaciones Económicas Internacionales de México," in *La Sociedad Mexicana Presente y Futuro,* Miguel S. Wionczek (ed.), Mexico, Fondo de Cultura Económica, 1974, pp. 98–134.

Navarrete, Ifigenia M. de, "Desequilibrio Externo y Desarrollo Económico," in *Comercio Exterior,* Vol. VII (November 1957), pp. 592–595.

Needleman, Carolyn, and Needleman, Martin, "Who Rules Mexico: A Critique of Some Current Views of the Mexican Political Process," in *The Journal of Politics,* Vol. XXXI, (November 1969), pp. 1011–1034.

Ness, Walter L., "Financial Markets Innovation as a Development Strategy: Initial Results from the Brazilian Experience," in *Economic Development and Cultural Change,* Vol. XXII (April 1974), pp. 453–472.

————, "Some Effects of Inflation on Financing Investment in Argentina and Brazil," in *Financial Development and Economic Growth: The Economic Consequences of Underdeveloped Capital Markets,* Arnold W. Sametz (ed.), New York, New York University Press, 1972., pp. 228–254.

Noyola Vásquez, Juan F., "La Evolución del Pensamiento Económico en el UItimo Cuarto de Siglo y su Influencia en América Latina," in *Investigación Económica,* Vol. XVI (Third Quarter 1956), pp. 407–426.

Noriega Herrera, Alberto, "Las Devaluaciones Monetarias de México, 1938–54," in *Investigación Económica,* Vol. XV (January–March 1965), pp. 150–169.

Ortiz Mena, Antonio, "El Crédito de México," in *El Mercado de Valores,* Vol. XXV (May 24, 1965), pp. 333–339.

————, "Los Créditos Exteriores y el Desarrollo Industrial," in *El Mercado de Valores,* Vol. XXV (November 27, 1965), pp. 823–829.

————, "La Política Financiera en los Ultimos Cinco Anos," in *El Mercado de Valores,* Vol. XXIII (November 18, 1963), pp. 599–605.

————, "La Política Hacendaria Mexicana," in *El Mercado de Valores,* Vol. XX (January 30, 1961), pp. 54–55.

Padgett, L. Vincent, "Mexico's One-Party System: A Re-evaluation," in *American Political Science Review,* Vol. LI (December 1957), pp. 995–1008.

Padilla, Enrique, "La Devaluación del Peso Mexicano: Cuatro Conferencias," in *El Trimestre Económico,* Vol. XV (October–December 1948), pp. 396–412.

————. "La Dinámica de la Economía Mexicana y el Equilibrio Monetario," in *El Trimestre Económico*, Vol. XXV (July–September 1958), pp. 349–377.

Papanek, G. F., "The Effect of Aid and Other Resource Transfers on Savings," in *Economic Journal*, Vol. LXXXII (September 1972).

Parks, Richard W., "The Role of Agriculture in Mexican Economic Development," in *Inter-American Economic Affairs* (Autumn 1964), pp. 3–27.

Powers, Jonathan, "The Alternative to Starvation," in *Encounter*, Vol. XLV (November 1975), pp. 11–35.

Prebish, Raul, "Economic Development or Monetary Stability: The False Dilemma," in *UN, Economic Bulletin for Latin America*, Vol. VI (March 1961), pp. 1–25.

Purcell, Susan Kaufman, "Decision-Making in an Authoritarian Regime: Theoretical Implications from a Mexican Case Study," in *World Politics*, Vol. XXVI (October 1973), pp. 28–55.

Ramos, Guillermo Uriarte, "La Devaluación y el Comercio Exterior," in *Revista de Economía*, Vol. XVIII (July, 1955).

Ramos, Gustav, "Industrial Sector Labor Absorption," in *Economic Development and Cultural Change*, Vol. XXI (April 1973), pp. 387–408.

————, and J. C. Fei, "Foreign Assistance and Economic Development: Comment," in *American Economic Review*, Vol. LVIII (September 1968), pp. 897–912; "Reply," by H. B. Chenery and A. M. Strout, pp. 912–916.

Redding, David C., "The Economic Decline of Uruguay," in *Inter-American Economic Affairs*, Vol. XX (Spring 1967), pp. 55–72.

Rivera Marın, Guadalupe, "Los Mercados Internos: Uno de los Grandes Problemas del Desarrollo Económico de México," in *El Trimestre Económico*, Vol. XXXIV (January–March 1972), pp. 111–124.

Romero Kolbeck, Gustavo, "The Economic Development of Mexico: Financing the Infrastructure," in *Economic Development Issues: Latin America*. New York, Committee for Economic Development, Supplementary Paper No. 21, 1967, pp. 173–209.

————, "La Devaluación Monetaria," in *Revista de Economía*, Vol. XVII (May 1954), pp. 135–137.

Rosenzweig Hernandez, Fernando, "El Proceso Politico y el Desarrollo Económico de México, in *El Trimestre Económico*, Vol. XXIX (October–December 1962), pp. 513–530.

————, "Política Agrícola y Generación de Empleo en México," *El Trimestre Económico*, Vol. XLII (October–December 1975), pp. 671–694.

Ruiz Equihau, Arturo, and Leopoldo Solís, "Los Instrumentos de Política Monetaria y de Crédito en Mexico," in *Técnicas Financieras*, Vol. VI (January–February 1967), pp. 285–295.

Ruiz, Rosa María Tirado de, "La Hacienda Pública y sus Funciones Económicas," in *Revista de Administración Pública,* No. 11 (January–March 1959), pp. 69–82.

Sabas Robledo, "Causas de las Devaluaciones en México Desde 1938" in *Revista de Económica,* Vol. XVIII (July 1955), pp. 167–173.

———. "Comercio Exterior, Desequilibrio de Fomento y Devaluación," in *Revista de Economía,* Vol. XVII (June 1954), pp. 181–185.

———. "Effectos de la Devaluación en el Desarrollo Económico," in *Revista de Economía,* Vol. XVII (May 1954), pp. 137–141.

Saenz, Josué, "Problemas Monetarios," in *Comercio Exterior,* Vol. VII (October 1957), pp. 535–538.

Salera, Virgil, "The Depreciation of the Mexican Peso," in *Inter-American Economic Affairs,* Vol. III (Autumn 1949), pp. 65–69.

Scott, Robert E., "Budget Making in Mexico," in *Inter-American Economic Affairs,* Vol. IX (Autumn 1955), pp. 3–20.

Sedwitz, Walter J., "Mexico's 1954 Devaluation in Retrospect," in *Inter-American Economic Affairs,* Vol. X (Autumn 1956), pp. 22–44.

Seers, Dudley, "A Theory of Inflation and Growth in Underdeveloped Economies Based on the Experience of Latin America," in *Oxford Economic Papers* (New Series), Vol. XIV (June 1962), pp. 173–195.

Solís, Leopoldo, "The Financial System in the Economic Development of Mexico," in *Weltwirtschaftliches Archiv,* Band 101 (1968), pp. 36–48.

———. "Hacia Un Análisis General a Largo Plazo del Desarrollo Económico de México," in *Demografía y Economía,* Vol. I (1967), pp. 40–91.

———, "Inflación, Estabilidad y Desarrollo: El Caso de México,"in *El Trimestre Económico,* Vol. XXV (July–September 1968), pp. 483–516.

———, "Mexican Economic Policy in the Post-War Period: The Views of Mexican Economists," in *The American Economic Review,* Vol. LXI (June 1971), Part II, *Supplement Surveys of National Policy Issues and Policy Research,* pp. 3–67.

———, and Sergio Ghigliazza, "Estabilidad Económica y Política Monetaria," in *El Trimestre Económico,* Vol. XXX (April–June 1963), pp. 256–265.

Street, James H. "The Technological Frontier in Latin America: Creativity and Productivity," *Journal of Economic Issues,* Vol. X (September, 1976), pp. 538–559.

Sturmthal, Adolf, "Economic Development, Income Distribution and Capital Formation in Mexico," in *Journal of Political Economy,* Vol. LXII (June 1955), pp. 181–197.

Sweeney, Timothy D., "The Mexican Balance of Payments, 1947–50," in *IMF Staff Papers,* Vol. III (April 1953), pp. 132–154.

Tanner, Elaine. "The Devaluation of the Mexican Peso," in *Inter-American Economic Affairs,* Vol. III (Summer 1949), pp. 3–31.

Tello, Carlos, "Agricultural Development and Land Tenure in Mexico," in *Weltwirtschaftliches Archiv*, Band 101 (1968), pp. 21–35.

————, "El Sector Agrícola y el Desarrollo Económico de los Paises Latinoamericanos," in *El Trimestre Económico*, Vol. XXXII (January–March 1965), pp. 89–116.

Thompson, John, "Argentine Economic Policy under the Ongania Regime," in *Inter-American Economic Affairs*, Vol. XXIV (Summer 1970), pp. 51–75.

Trejo Reyes, Saúl, "Los Patrones del Crecimiento Industrial y la sustitución de Importaciones en México," in *La Economía Mexicana*, Leopoldo Solís (ed.), Vol. I, *Análisis por Sectores y Distribución (Mexico: Fondo de Cultura Económica)*, 1973, pp. 153–161.

————, "El Sector Externo en la Economía Mexicana: Crecimiento Optimo y Política de Exportaciones," in *El Trimestre Económico*, Vol. XLII (April–June 1975), pp. 399–427.

————, "El Desempleo en México: Características Generales," in *El Trimestre Económico*, Vol. XIII (July–September 1975), pp. 671–694.

————, "Expansión Industrial y Empleo en México," in *El Trimestre Económico*, Vol. XLIII (January–March 1976), pp. 33–57.

Tyler, William G., "Exchange-Rate Flexibility Under Conditions of Endemic Inflation: A Case Study of Recent Brazilian Experience," in *Leading Issues in International Economic Policy;* C. Fred Bergsten and William G. Tyler (eds.), Lexington, Mass.: D. C. Heath and Co., 1973.

Uribe Castaneda, Manuel, "Estrategia de Infraestructura para el Desarrollo del Sector Externo," in *Pensamiento Político*, Vol. XIV (December 1973), pp. 473–486.

————. "El Significado Económico del Gasto Social," in *Pensamiento Político*, Vol. XV (April 1974), pp. 497–508.

Uriquidi, Víctor L., "Obstáculos al Desarrollo Económico," in *Revista de Economía*, Vol. XIV (February, 1951), pp. 18–25.

————, "Problemas Fundamentales de la Economía Mexicana," in *Cuadernos Americanos*, Vol. LXIV (January–February 1961), pp. 69–106.

Urrutia, Luis, "Política de Inversiones," in *Revista de Economía*, Vol. XXI (June 1958), pp. 143–147.

Villareal, René Patricio, "El Desequilibrio Externo en el Crecimiento Económico de México;Su Naturaleza y Mecanismo, de Ajuste Optimo: Devaluación, Estabilización y Liberación," in *El Trimestre Económico*, Vol. XLI (October–December 1974), pp. 775–810.

Walters, Robert S., "UNCTAD: Intervener Between Poor and Rich States," in *Journal of World Trade Law*, Vol. VII (September–October 1973), pp. 527–554.

Weisskopf, Thomas E., "The Impact of Capital Inflow on Domestic Savings in Undeveloped Countries," in *Journal of International Economics,* Vol. II (February 1972), pp. 25–32.

Wilford, D. Sykes. *Monetary Policy and the Open Economy: Mexico's Experience.* New York: Praeger, 1977.

Wionczek, Miguel S. "Diez Años del Banco Internacional y del Fondo Monetario," in *Comercio Exterior,* Vol. VI (October 1956), pp. 471–474.

———. "Financiamiento Internacional del Desarrollo Económico," in *Comercio Exterior,* Vol. IV (November 1954), pp. 442–445.

———. "Incomplete Formal Planning: Mexico," in Planning Economic Development, Everette E. Hagen (ed.), Richard D. Irwin, Inc., 1963, pp. 150–183.

Wionczek, Miguel S., "Las Opiniones Extranjeras Sobre La Devaluación," in *Revista de Economía,* Vol. XVII (May 1954), pp. 148–152.

Woodley, John R. "The Use of Special Exchange Rates for Transactions with Foreign Companies," in *IMF Staff Papers,* Vol. III (October 1953), pp. 254–269.

Unpublished Material

Ambach, Mado R., "Multiple Exchange Rates: An Instrument for Improving Foreign Trade Balance, with Special Reference to the Latin American Countries," unpublished Ph.D.issertation, Economics Department, Yale University, 1952.

Bazdresch, Carlos, "La Deuda Externa y Desarrollo Estabilizador," Mimeographed discussion paper for Mexican Economy Semirtar: Stanford University (March 1974).

Carranza Edwards, Carlos, "La Devaluación Monetaria de 1954: Análisis de sus Causas y Consecuencias," thesis: Escuela Nacional de Economía, Universidad Nacional Autónoma de México, 1967.

Falkowski, Daniel Carl, "Nacional Financiera, S.A. de México: A Study of a Development Bank," unpublished Ph.D. disseration, Department of Economics, New York University, 1972.

Garduño García, Raúl, "Ensayo Sobre El Crecimiento Económico y la Inversión Extranjera," thesis: Escuela Nacional de Economía, Universidad Nacional Autónoma de México, 1966.

Hernández Catá, Ernesto, "International Movements of Private Financial Capital: An Econometric Analysis of the Mexican Case," unpublished Ph.D. dissertation, Economics Department, Yale University, 1974.

Hernandez Lara, Leopoldo, "Las Devaluaciones Monetarias y la Política del

Banco de México," thesis: Escuela Nacional de Economía, Universidad Nacional Autónoma de México, 1966.

Koehler, John E., "Information and Policy-Making: Mexico," unpublished Ph.D. dissertation, Economics Department, Yale University, 1967.

Martinez Ostos, Raúl, Letters dated September 4, 1974, October 1, 1974.

Noriega Herrera, Alberto. "Posibilidad de Establecer Controles de Cambio en México," thesis: Escuela Nacional de Economía, Universidad Nacional Autónoma de México, 1965).

Noyola Vásquez, Juan F., "Desequilibrio Fundamental y Fomento Económico en México," thesis: Escuela Nacional de Economía, Universidad Nacional Autónoma de México, 1949.

Solano Moctezuma, Martha, "Financiamiento Externo del Sector Público de México," thesis: Escuela Nacional de Economía, Universidad Nacional Autónoma de México, 1965.

Váldez Martínez, Gustavo Adolfo, "México Ante el Dólar," thesis: Escuela Nacional de Economía, Universidad Nacional Autónoma de México, 1970.

Interviews

Sergio Ghigliazza G., Assistant Director of Research, Bank of Mexico—March 22, 1974.

Rafael Izquierdo González, Adviser, Bank of Mexico—April 7, 1974.

Carlos Bazdresch, Economist, Nacional Financiera—April 18, 1974.

Leopoldo Solís M., Director, Office of Economic & Social Programs, Secretariat of the Presidency—April 19, 1974.

Javier Márquez, Adviser, Bank of Mexico, Director of CEMLA, 1953–72—April 19, 1974.

Manuel Uribe Castañeda, Manager, Economic Research Department, Bank of Mexico—April 22, 1974.

Luis Chico Pardo, Assistant Director, Foreign Department, Bank of Mexico—April 22, 1974.

Carlos Tello, Assistant Director of Credit, Finance Ministry—April 22, 1974.

Saúl Trejo Reyes, Technical Director, National Minimum Wage Commission—April 24, 1974.

David Ibarra Muñoz, Director of Programs, Nacional Financiera—April 25, 1974.

Alfredo Navarrete Romero, Assistant Director of Finance, Petróleos Mexicanos—April 25, 1974.

Rafael Galván, Secretary General, Union of Mexican Electrical Workers—April 25, 1974.

Jorge Heyser, Former Chairman, National Chamber of Manufacturing Industries—April 30, 1974.

Raúl Martínez Ostos, Former Assistant Director General, Nacional Financiera—April 30, 1975.

Antonio Carrillo Flores, Finance Minister, 1952–58—July 15, 1974.

Walter J. Sedwitz, Executive Secretary for Economic and Social Affairs, Organization of American States—August 20, 1974.

E. Walter Robichek, Deputy Director, Western Hemisphere Division, International Monetary Fund—August 21, 1974.